EMPIRE

MW01068468

The memory of the Roman Republic exercised a powerful influence on several generations of Romans who lived under its political and cultural successor, the Principate or Empire. *Empire and Memory* explores how (and why) that memory manifested itself over the course of the early Principate. Making use of the close relationship between *memoria* and *historia* in Roman thought and drawing on modern studies of historical memory, this book offers case-studies of major imperial authors from the reign of Tiberius to that of Trajan (AD 14–117). The memory evident in literature is linked to that imprinted on Rome's urban landscape, with special attention paid to the Forum of Augustus and the Forum of Trajan, both of which are particularly suggestive reminders of the transition from a time when the memory of the Republic was highly valued and celebrated to one when its grip had begun to loosen.

ROMAN LITERATURE AND ITS CONTEXTS

Empire and Memory

ROMAN LITERATURE AND ITS CONTEXTS

Series editors:
Denis Feeney and Stephen Hinds

This series promotes approaches to Roman literature which are open to dialogue with current work in other areas of the classics, and in the humanities at large. The pursuit of contacts with cognate fields such as social history, anthropology, history of thought, linguistics and literary theory is in the best traditions of classical scholarship: the study of Roman literature, no less than Greek, has much to gain from engaging with these other contexts and intellectual traditions. The series offers a forum in which readers of Latin texts can sharpen their readings by placing them in broader and better-defined contexts, and in which other classicists and humanists can explore the general or particular implications of their work for readers of Latin texts. The books all constitute original and innovative research and are envisaged as suggestive essays whose aim is to stimulate debate.

Other books in the series

Joseph Farrell, *Latin language and Latin culture: from ancient to modern times*

A. M. Keith, *Engendering Rome: women in Latin epic*

William Fitzgerald, *Slavery and the Roman literary imagination*

Stephen Hinds, *Allusion and intertext: dynamics of appropriation in Roman poetry*

Denis Feeney, *Literature and religion at Rome: cultures, contexts, and beliefs*

Catharine Edwards, *Writing Rome: textual approaches to the city*

Duncan F. Kennedy, *The arts of love: five studies in the discourse of Roman love elegy*

Charles Martindale, *Redeeming the text: Latin poetry and the hermeneutics of reception*

Philip Hardie, *The epic successors of Virgil: a study in the dynamics of a tradition*

Empire and Memory

The Representation of the Roman Republic in Imperial Culture

Alain M. Gowing

Professor of Classics
University of Washington

CAMBRIDGE
UNIVERSITY PRESS

CAMBRIDGE UNIVERSITY PRESS
Cambridge, New York, Melbourne, Madrid, Cape Town, Singapore, São Paulo

CAMBRIDGE UNIVERSITY PRESS
The Edinburgh Building, Cambridge CB2 2RU, UK
Published in the United States of America by Cambridge University Press, New York

www.cambridge.org
Information on this title: www.cambridge.org/9780521544801

First published 2005

Printed in the United Kingdom at the University Press, Cambridge

A catalogue record for this book is available from the British Library

ISBN-13 978-0-521-83622-7 hardback
ISBN-10 0-521-83622-0 hardback
ISBN-13 978-0-521-54480-1 paperback
ISBN-10 0-521-54480-1 paperback

Como me duele el olvido ...
– Fher Olvera

Contents

Illustrations

Acknowledgments

I remember quite clearly the moment I decided to write this book. On a damp evening in the early June of 1998 I had the pleasure of walking through Rome's Campus Martius with Alessandro Barchiesi. For a classicist, perhaps no other quarter in Rome is so rich in history and memory, and as our discussion turned to precisely that topic and my own growing interest in it, Alessandro asked, "Have you read Halbwachs?" I had not, I replied ... but I would. Appropriately, somewhere between the Mausoleum of Augustus and the Theater of Pompey, I became persuaded that a study of how the Roman Republic was memorialized in early imperial literature and culture would be useful, especially in light of recent interest in the intersections of history and memory. The topic, however, is a large one, and it has not been my aim to discuss in this book all of the many ways in which the Roman Republic is represented in or affects imperial culture. Much has by necessity been omitted. In keeping with the aim of books in this series, I have focused on a few representative texts and sites in order to describe what I see to be fundamental tendencies and changes as well as to propose a constructive way to think about early imperial culture. Profound thanks are due to the many individuals who contributed to the ideas in this book. I must first and foremost express my deep gratitude to the series editors, Stephen Hinds and Denis Feeney. Both have been indefatigable in their support for this project, and indefatigably patient. I have recorded specific debts to them here and there throughout the text, but their assistance has been more substantial than those notes will suggest. Sandra Joshel, my colleague in the University of Washington Department of History, gave generously of her time and considerable expertise; readings and discussions with her over the course of more than one summer were indispensable toward helping me refine my thoughts on how and why memory mattered to the Romans. Alessandro Barchiesi and my colleague Catherine Connors kindly read and astutely commented on a draft of the manuscript. Parts of the book were presented, in various stages of completion, at several institutions (New York University, the University of Washington, the University of Calgary, Harvard, Princeton, and Stanford). I am grateful for those opportunities and for the helpful discussions they generated. I have benefited as well from numerous conversations with a variety of individuals, in particular Joy Connolly, Larry Bliquez, Ruby Blondell, Jim Clauss, Dan Harmon, John Webster, and John Chesley. I owe special thanks to the participants of my inter-disciplinary graduate seminar on this subject, sponsored by the University of Washington's Center for the Humanities in 1997; to the members of the Center's 2003–4 Society of Scholars, especially my colleagues Sarah Stroup and Robert Stacey, who both read and provided wise advice on a draft of the first chapter; and to the students of several Classical Seminars in Rome, who invariably help me see Rome and its monuments with fresh eyes. And finally, heartfelt thanks go to my wife Anne and son Benjamin for teaching me, in ways books can never do, the value of memory.

CHAPTER

I

Historia/memoria

"optanda erat oblivio"

The emperor Tiberius was once approached by a man who addressed to him a question beginning with the word *meministi* – "do you remember ...?" (Sen. *Ben.* 5.25.2). Scarcely had he uttered that one word when the emperor brusquely interrupted, *non memini ... quid fuerim*, "I do not remember what I was." Tiberius was merely feigning a memory lapse; he doubtless remembered perfectly well what the man was inquiring about – evidently, a previous encounter between the two – but chose to consign it to oblivion. As Seneca puts it, *optanda erat oblivio* (ibid.). Loosely rendered, "it was the emperor's wish to forget."[1]

If, to borrow Millar's succinct definition, the emperor was what the emperor did, he was equally what he remembered.[2] As this small episode

---

[1] *Ti. Caesar inter initia dicenti cuidam: "meministi" – antequam plures notas familiaritatis veteris proferret: "non memini," inquit, "quid fuerim." ad hoc quidni non esset repetendum beneficium? optanda erat oblivio; aversabatur omnium amicorum et aequalium notitiam et illam solam praesentem fortunam suam adspici, illam solam cogitari ac narrari volebat. inquisitorem habebat veterem amicum!* "When someone started to say, 'Do you remember ...?', Tiberius interrupted before he could present more evidence of old acquaintance: 'I do not remember what I was.' Why should this man not have sought a reciprocal benefit? It was the emperor's wish to forget; he was renouncing his relationship with all his friends and companions, wishing only that his current good fortune be considered, that only this should be pondered and talked about. He looked upon an old acquaintance as an investigator!'" On the passage, Roller (2001a), 208–9.

[2] Millar (1977), xi. For the latter notion (generally construed), Roth (1994).

illustrates, however, his memory could be entirely selective, with decisions large and small hinging on what the emperor chose to remember ... and forget. Indeed, memory lay at the very heart of power under the Principate;[3] the phenomenon of *damnatio memoriae* – the (usually) posthumous 'erasing' of someone's memory by having all references to their names removed from inscriptions, portraits defaced, and the like – provides one familiar illustration of how such control might be exerted and, as importantly, why it needed to be exerted.[4] Memories, Romans knew, can be dangerous. For that reason the ability to control and even suppress memory became a crucial component of political authority. Jacques Le Goff's observation applies especially to the Roman aristocracy: "[t]o make themselves the master of memory and forgetfulness is one of the great preoccupations of the classes, groups, and individuals who have dominated ... historical societies."[5] Such an attitude capitalizes on the fact that for members of most societies remembering the past is both a social and political imperative.[6] Romans attached a heightened importance to memory, which manifests itself in almost every aspect of their existence, from celebrations of the dead to oratory to law, suffusing and animating their art, their buildings, and their literature. For Romans the past wholly defined the present, and to forget – to disconnect with – the past, at either the level of the individual or of the state, risked the loss of identity and even extinction.[7] Hence the danger – and sometimes the appeal – of oblivion.

---

[3] Le Goff (1992), 68, 98–100 (citing Veyne). For the link between power and memory see further Terdiman (1993), 19–20.

[4] For discussion of the term and the practice, Flower (1998), Hedrick (2000), 89–94; Varner (2001) provides a very useful case study. The classic study, since much questioned, remains Vittinghoff (1936). See also Le Goff (1992), 67–8.

[5] Le Goff (1992), 54; cf. Connerton (1989), 1; Hampl (1985), 208–9; Sturken (1997); 7–8; Alcock (1994a), 249.

[6] In our era this has become a global concern, as evidenced by UNESCO's "Memory of the World" project (http://www.unesco.org/webworld/mdm/en/index_mdm.html). Cf. the American Memory project (http://memory.loc.gov/ammem/ammemhome.html).

[7] As Carruthers (1990), 13 puts it: "A person without a memory ... would be a person without moral character and, in a basic sense, without humanity. *Memoria* refers not to how something is communicated, but to what happens once one has received it, to the interactive process of familiarizing – or textualizing – which occurs between oneself and others' words in memory." Cf. Roth (1995), 16; Gillis (1994), 3–5, on

The threatened demise of the Republic was a constant concern for Cicero, who was acutely aware that the political system to which he had devoted his life was living on borrowed time. As he put it, *his* Republic was a faded picture of its former self (*picturam ... evanescentem vetustate*) whose moral fiber had become buried in oblivion (*oblivione obsoletos*, *Rep.* 5.1.2). Cicero's anxiety over the loss of memory, evident here and elsewhere and a precursor to the situation under the early Empire, underscores just how grave this threat had become in the second half of the first century BC, when the very political identity of the *res publica* was at stake.[8]

This identity was fundamentally aristocratic in nature; although the Roman political system featured some democratic elements (the tribunate being the most important) and the *populus* was not without influence, real power lay in the Senate, membership in which was determined by both wealth and lineage, and its accompanying magistracies.[9] In design and function, the Republic was deliberately anti-monarchical. While it may be historically practical and neat to mark the end of the Republic and the beginning of the Principate with the assassination of Julius Caesar in 44 BC or the battle of Actium in 31 BC, it took well over a century for the idea and the ideals of the Republic to be purged from the Roman imagination and memory (though they would never be purged entirely). The degree to which the early Principate may have perpetuated certain aspects of the Republic's political character has often come under discussion, and yet the Republic's demise is to be measured not merely in terms of political change, but of gradual shifts in individual and collective psychology as

memory and identity; Isid. *Orig.* 11.1.13 (people without memory are *amentes*, "mindless"). On the importance of memory in Roman culture, Farrell (1997); and Small and Tatum (1995), essentially a survey of recent work on memory and how it may be applied to the study of antiquity, containing much that is useful about the importance of memory in the classical period.

[8] For historical details and analysis of the crisis of the late Republic, Meier (1997³), esp. 207–300. On Cicero's growing concern for the threat to Roman memory, Gowing (2000); and with respect to the *De re publica* specifically, Zetzel (1994), 31–2. Cf., e.g., *de Orat.* 1.38.

[9] On the aristocratic nature of the Republic (a view complicated, to be sure, by Millar [1998]), Hölkeskamp (2000), 205, 222–3 (now more fully explored in Hölkeskamp [2004]), and the work cited therein; Syme (1939), 10–27; Rowe (2002), 42–3.

well.[10] The Republic and its memory came to be used and exploited by many different groups of people: not only by those who, like the early emperors, found it expedient to perpetuate the myth of a *res publica restituta*, a "restored Republic," but also by those who used it to discredit such people or at least underscore their hypocrisy; by those with a nostalgia for the Republic; and by those who sought to sow dissent. However the Republic and its history might be deployed, a deep-seated reverence for the past (or "Republicanism," the term often used to describe this trend) sat awkwardly with the need, at some level and in some quarters, to forget that past or at least certain aspects of it.[11]

The term *res publica* warrants some discussion.[12] It is clear that in many contexts this phrase simply refers to "the state." Yet it is equally clear that *res publica* denoted one thing to Cicero and something quite different to, say, Pliny the Younger. Thus when we find in the *Fasti Praenestini* for January 13, 27 BC, the assertion that the *res publica* had been "restored" (by Augustus) – *res publica restituta* – are we to understand the restoration of the traditional Republic or simply of the state, i.e. "government?" I believe it must be the former. Arguments for the latter – for understanding *res publica* here as meaning little more than "government" – rather reduce the stakes, and seem to be more the product of hindsight than a reflection of a contemporary, early Augustan perspective; such arguments also imply that Augustus was a little less disingenuous about what he had done than seems likely. At this juncture, the *res publica* could be nothing other than the Republic. Surely the truly significant word is *restituta*; the message Augustus sought to convey was that he had *restored* the Republic, not created a new and distinct state. And yet with the passage of time, over the course of the first century, the phrase *res publica* ceased to refer, as it typically must have in the Augustan and perhaps even the Tiberian periods, to what we

[10] On the "continuation" of the Republic, Eder (1990); Sion-Jenkis (2000), 11 (survey of earlier work), 20; Strothmann (2000), 13–14. Sion-Jenkis' discussion (2000), 19–53, of the relationship between *res publica* and *principatus* as political terms is especially enlightening; cf. Eder (1990), 83–4.

[11] Cf. Citroni (2003), x–xi. MacMullen (1966), esp. 13–45, remains the best general exploration of the "Republicanism" of the imperial period.

[12] For full discussion of this and related terms (e.g., *libertas, princeps*), see Lind (1986); see also Flower (2004a), 2–3.

term the "Republic," coming instead to refer to a different sort of *res publica* – the Principate. Thus, to anticipate a text I adduce in the final chapter, when Septimius Severus erects his triumphal arch in AD 203 *ob rem publicam restitutam*, "on behalf of the restoration of the *res publica*," it is simply inconceivable that he imagined he had brought back the pre-Augustan Republic.[13]

This goes to the heart of the phenomenon surveyed in this book, the process of remembering the Republic in the early imperial period and the various transitions that memory undergoes. A crucial step in this process lay in starting to conceive of the "Republic" as an entity to be remembered, independent of the current "state," yet using language that originally drew no such distinction. In much the same way as the traditional language of politics came to acquire new meanings and nuances as time progressed, so too does the established "language" or discourse of Roman culture, at least as manifested in *exempla* and the larger historical tradition, evolve in significant ways from Republic to Principate. Yet for quite some time that language remains the same – literally, as in the case of a word such as *libertas*, and figuratively, as in what a reference to "Cato" might denote.[14] Both become in early imperial culture quintessential *lieux de mémoire*, "places" or focal points where we may glimpse memory being contested and remade. But the tenacity of a term such as *libertas* or an *exemplum* such as Cato points to a striking characteristic of the phenomenon examined here: the recurrent inability of Roman writers to disengage from the pre-imperial past. They repeatedly come back

---

[13] For the *Fasti Praenestini* for Jan. 13, 27 BC, Ehrenberg and Jones (1955²), 45; cf. Suet. *Aug.* 28.1; Appian *BC* 5.132.548, describing Octavian's intent in 36 BC: τὴν ἐντελῆ πολιτείαν ... ἀποδώσειν; Augustus himself claims to have "returned control of the state back to the Senate and the Roman people" in 28 BC (*rem publicam ex mea potestate in senatus populique Romani arbitrium transtuli*, *RG* 34). Yet precisely what is meant by *res publica restituta* has been a matter for debate: see, e.g., Gurval (1995), 5 with n. 1 – citing Judge (1974), who argues that in this phrase *res publica* simply means "the state" – contra Zanker (1990), 89, and passim. But in these texts the "state" he would be "returning" was by definition the Republic. See Syme (1939), 323–4 and passim; Mackie (1986); Galinsky (1996), 42–79; Strothmann (2000) fully explores *restitutio* as one of the conceptual cornerstones of Augustan ideology and propaganda.

[14] As MacMullen (1966), 33, puts it (with particular reference to the shifting meanings of *libertas*), "They still proclaimed the old slogans of their heroes, but the words had changed meaning."

to many of the same events and characters, most associated with the late Republic (e.g., Cicero, Cato the Younger, the civil war between Caesar and Pompey), some with earlier periods (e.g., Camillus, Scipio Africanus, or Cato the Elder). The repetitiveness of topoi will therefore be apparent; it is in isolating the moments of change in attitude toward and deployment of those topoi that we observe shifts in Roman memory.

In the chapters that follow I examine some of the ways the Roman Republic – or to be more precise, several crucial events and characters from the Republican period – were memorialized in post-Augustan Rome, from the reign of Tiberius through that of Trajan (essentially AD 14–117), by which point the Republic for the most part had ceased to serve any serious ideological purpose. I use the term "Republic" chiefly as a chronological as well as cultural marker, to denote the period between the end of the Roman monarchy in 509 BC and the beginning of the Augustan principate in 31 BC; this book is not, in other words, necessarily about institutional politics. In keeping with the aim of books in the series, it does not pretend to be a comprehensive survey of imperial attitudes toward the Republic. Rather, it offers a series of case studies, focusing on certain key texts and monuments in order to formulate a general impression of how the memory of the Republic evolved over time and in particular from one regime to the next.

Thus I focus in Chapter 2 on the Tiberian period (AD 14–37), represented by Valerius Maximus and Velleius Paterculus, the two chief literary lights of a regime that insistently sought to present itself as a seamless continuation of the *res publica restituta* of the Augustan period. I locate the next significant shift in the memory of the Republic in the Neronian period (AD 51–68) and in Chapter 3 argue that this was in fact the era in which any serious hopes of restoring the Republic were laid to rest. I suggest that Lucan's interest in the memory of the civil war between Pompey and Caesar that destroyed the Republic (an interpretation about which he is in no doubt) lies not in the conflict's significance as a beneficial moment of transition but as a point of maximal disorder that leads only to further disorder. By contrast, Seneca's own views of memory and Republican history, as illustrated in his *Epistulae*, supply something of an antidote to Lucan's "Republicanism" and call into question the very relevance of the Republican past to the imperial (and particularly Neronian) present. Chapter 4 focuses on the Flavian and early Trajanic periods, positing Tacitus' *Dialogus* as a watershed moment in imperial memory of the Republic. Cicero receives special attention here; as one of the last great political and literary figures of the late Republic, he inspires Tacitus' own reflections on the current state of the *res publica*. I examine the apparent tension between this text and Pliny's *Panegyricus* (a specimen of the oratorical expertise the *Dialogus* claims to be dead): delivered in AD 100, perhaps a year or so before the publication of the *Dialogus*, this speech celebrating the accession of Trajan proclaims the return of *libertas* (see p. 25). Yet as Pliny's own words make clear, this is a far cry from the *libertas* so often associated with the Republic.

Roman memory, however, particularly of the Republic, hardly resides in texts alone. By way of epilogue, and in order to exploit the powerful associations of place and memory in Roman thought, Chapter 5 considers aspects of the physical transformation of the city of Rome from Augustus through Trajan, during which period the memory of the Republic, once imprinted on the urban landscape, begins to be gradually erased or simply abandoned. The contrast between the Forum of Augustus (dedicated in 2 BC) and the Forum of Trajan (AD 112) exemplifies the transition from a time when the memory of Republic was highly valued and celebrated to one when, a century later, it was becoming little more than a dim memory. In this initial chapter I lay out the premises on which the subsequent discussions are based, none more important than the connection Romans made between *historia* and *memoria*.

Historia and *memoria*

I approach this exercise in mnemohistory fully aware of the limitations imposed by the evidence. By "mnemohistory" I mean an historical or rather historicizing account of the memory of the Republic in the early imperial period.[15] The memory that interests me is itself historical (rather than strictly social) in nature, the evidence for it primarily literary texts and, to some degree, physical remains. It is, therefore, evidence of a highly selective and particularized kind; and the literary evidence naturally presents its own set of interpretive challenges. Nonetheless, it *does* allow us to document the ways some imperial Romans remembered the Republic over time. From their perspective, given the connection

---

[15] For the term and its methodology, Assmann (1997), 6–22; Oexle (1995), 30–2.

between *historia* and *memoria* I discuss below, the texts I will examine certainly may be said to transmit memory.[16]

This evidence is of course bound up in personal and individual memories. Writing under Tiberius (AD 14–37), Velleius Paterculus takes pride in declaring that his great-great-great-grandfather had fought in the Social War of 91 BC (2.16.2, *multum ... atavi mei ... tribuendum memoriae*). Another Tiberian author, Seneca the Elder, insists that his own memory is the source for all the information (much of it historical) and extensive quotations in his *Controversiae* and *Suasoriae* (*Con.* 1. *praef.* 2–5). In Tacitus' *Dialogus*, written several decades after Velleius' *History*, Aper comments that the span of time from Cicero's death in 43 BC to his own time (the dramatic date of the dialogue being ca. AD 75) is really only the length of a single lifetime (*Dial.* 17)[17] – a crucial point, for it suggests that oral memory of the transition from Republic to Principate was still operative for several decades after Actium.[18] Similarly, we often find references to the Republic entirely personalized: Seneca's veneration of Scipio during a visit to the famous general's villa over two centuries after his death (*Ep.* 86), discussed in Chapter 3, is but one example of the reverence accorded to the houses of Republican icons. These attempts to keep alive a connection to the Republican past in some personal way pepper most of the texts I examine in this book, and serve as a useful reminder that elite imperial Romans rarely talked about the Republic in dispassionate, coldly objective terms. At some level that history is inevitably a personal history.[19] What they have *in common* as memory is what matters. Any attempt to categorize the particular *kind* of memory I seek to uncover therefore seems ultimately unsatisfactory and unhelpful (modern scholars of the subject being generally insistent on distinguishing between various modes of memory).[20] It is at once cultural, historical, collective, individual memory, all driven

---

[16] For the capacity of texts (literary and otherwise) to transmit memory, Fentress and Wickham (1992), 5–6, 8–11, and passim.

[17] See Chap. 4 with n. 29.

[18] Le Goff (1992), 98, observes the importance of this: "It is societies whose social memory is primarily oral or which are in the process of establishing a written collective memory that offer us the best chance of understanding this struggle for domination over remembrance and tradition, this manipulation of memory."

[19] Fentress and Wickham (1992), 7.

[20] E.g., Holtorf's (2001) chapter on "Cultural Memory."

by a deep conviction that the Republican past, or certain aspects of it, bears remembering.

What we lack, of course, is the sort of extensive evidence available to someone investigating, say, the memory of the holocaust, one modern event that has generated a multitude of mnemohistories, or the American Civil War.[21] We do not have, that is, eyewitness accounts or interviews, film footage, newspapers, recordings, government documents, etc. – in short, the wide-ranging, detailed evidence that allows the historian to document the development and evolution of memory from a variety of perspectives. What confronts us in examining the evidence from early imperial Rome can only be a slice of Roman cultural and collective memory, and we should not make the mistake of making the part stand for the whole.[22] Nonetheless, such as it is, the evidence embodies and communicates memory.

The situation in Rome comes into sharper focus when we recognize the explicit connection Romans themselves made between *memoria* and *historia*. It is not without reason that the Oxford Latin Dictionary offers "history" as one definition of *memoria* (OLD s.v. 7). *Romans* would have regarded the historian Velleius Paterculus, the epic poet Lucan, and the epistolographer Pliny as all engaged at some level in preserving and handing down memory when they narrate the past, which they obviously do to greater and lesser degrees. And certainly, as we shall see, the authors themselves saw remembrance as an important if not the central aim of their respective projects. This is a phenomenon that therefore cuts across traditional distinctions of genre in a way that will make some modern students of history and memory uneasy.[23] In contrast to the Romans, for example, we would not typically class together as equally

---

[21] Holocaust memory has been extensively explored in a number of media, e.g., film (most notably Lanzmann's 1985 *Shoah*), numerous exhibitions and museums (the United States Holocaust Memorial Museum, for example), and scholarly studies (I would single out, only because of its relevance to my subsequent discussions of the role of monuments, Young [1993]; for other, representative studies, Kenan [2003], LaCapra [1998]). Civil War memory is increasingly the subject of study, e.g., Blight (2001).

[22] Terdiman (1993), 18.

[23] As Sion-Jenkis (2000), 13, observes, no account of the idea of the Republic in the imperial imagination can restrict itself exclusively to the evidence from historiography, even an account as "historical" as hers. Freudenburg (2001), for instance,

reliable documentations of the Vietnam era Coppola's 1979 *Apocalypse Now* or Boublil's and Schönberg's 1989 *Miss Saigon* with Marilyn Young's *The Vietnam Wars 1945–1990* (New York 1991), a standard, well-respected historical study of the era. We have devised separate categories to distinguish between such things: "fiction" (or, euphemistically, "historical fiction") and "non-fiction."

Their "historicity" aside, however, I doubt that anyone would dispute the idea that all three have the capacity to create in the mind of the viewer or reader a "surrogate" memory that will have something in common with that of an individual who lived through the Vietnam era or participated in the war; nor do I deny that the opposite may happen, that the memory they create may have little in common with an actual participant's memory.[24] But that is to question whether the memory is "true" or "false", "transmitted" or "lived," not whether it is in fact a memory at all.[25] Regardless of their origins, such memories become part of the individual's experience and understanding of the past, and, to the extent that such memories are shared, part of the culture's "collective memory."

It is this capacity of texts to *create* or establish memory[26] – or, if you prefer, to fictionalize – that renders them somewhat problematic as sources of historical information. But the Roman view of *historia* and *memoria* inevitably leads to a refashioning of the meaning of the past, requiring authors to give it meaning in the present and decide not only *what* to remember but *how* it should be remembered. This is why from one regime to the next the use of Republican history varies significantly.

---

is a fine example of a genre-specific (Roman satire) study that ably explores "an inherited, 'free-speaking,' old-Republican enterprise that gets remade radically over time precisely because these authors feel and respond to the increasing pressures of totalitarian oversight" ([2001], 4).

[24] For such "created" memories, Burke (1989), 98. Texts are especially capable of this: we might think of the common remark "I remember reading ...," an idiom that really equates the "reading" of the text with the knowledge acquired from reading, linking both with memory.

[25] It is useful in this respect to recall that in his well-known exposition of memory in Book 10 of the *Confessions*, Augustine posits two types of memories, those that are *experta* ("experienced") and those that are *credita* ("believed" or "received") (*Conf.* 10.14).

[26] Miles (1995), 73–4; Farrell (1997), 375. Thus Toni Morrison (1984), 213, defines memory as "willed creation."

In further contrast to the Romans, modern scholars have tended to reject the connection between *memoria* and *historia*, preferring to draw fairly sharp distinctions between the two.[27] Such distinctions, however, are made in light of modern (though not universally accepted) notions of what "history" is or ought to be, namely, a set of "facts" or "truths" arrived at not through or exclusively through recollection and remembrance, which are notoriously fallible, but through rigorous inquiry and research.[28]

In the Roman conception *historia* was a generalizing term that applied not merely to "historiography" or "historical writing" – what we might today consider to be the most legitimate medium of historical inquiry – but to *any* attempt to transmit the past. For the Romans *historia* is less a genre than a definition of subject matter. Poetry is therefore not excluded, nor monuments and inscriptions. Cicero, for example, is perfectly content to cite Ennius' *Annales* as a source of legitimate historical information (*Brut.* 57, 60); indeed, epic poetry is the medium Cicero finds most congenial for his own attempts at history, having composed the *De consulatu suo*, *De temporibus suis*, and a *Marius*. Similarly, Tacitus regards the *carmina* of the Germans as a source of *memoria* and as a form of history, specifically, *annales* (*Ger.* 2.2). And if the form of *historia* was not exclusively prose or historiography proper, its aim was likewise not so much the accurate or "truthful" recording of the past as the preservation and even the *creation* of memory.[29] In this sense, to borrow Hutton's observation about "traditional societies," Romans

---

[27] Most notably, Nora (1984), xix, one of the pioneers in memory studies. Cf. Hobsbawm (1997), 8: "Make no mistake about it. History is not ancestral memory or collective tradition." Lowenthal (1985), 187, admits that "[memory and history] each involves components of the other, and their boundaries are shadowy" but in the end concludes that they are "justifiably distinguished." The issue is usefully explored – coming down in favor of the "interdependence" of memory and history – by Davis and Starn (1989), 1–6, esp. p. 5. See also Hutton (1993), 160–8; Yoneyama (1999), 26–33; Oexle (1995), 18–21.

[28] As Hutton (1993), 155, notes, the "complementary relationship" of history and memory persisted into the nineteenth century.

[29] Thus in *Fam.* 5.12 Cicero views the *historia* (2) planned by his friend Lucceius as establishing a *memoria* (7) of Cicero himself and yet (famously) urges him to fabricate and "embroider" the details (esp. 2–3). The fictive quality of ancient historiography – or rather its different perspective on what constitutes "truth" – has been sufficiently discussed in recent scholarship so as not to require elaboration here. Woodman (1988) remains the seminal study; he discusses the letter to

---

believed imagination and memory to be interchangeable.[30] *Historia* is simply a vehicle for *memoria*,[31] and as such may be subject (as the letter to Lucceius cited in n. 29 suggests) to the same sort of imaginative process that influences *memoria*.

Cicero configures this relationship most succinctly: *historia*, he says in the *de Oratore*, is the *vita memoriae*.[32] History is the "lifeblood of memory," that which gives life to memory and renders it deathless. Without history – or more properly the recording of history – memory will die. "History as memory" is of course a fairly common notion in ancient thought.[33] But I would suggest that in the Roman mind, at least, the connection is rooted in the link between death and life. We know that Cicero believed memory and history enjoyed a close, symbiotic relationship. History enacts memory, and memory, in turn, enlivens history; or to put this yet another way, *historia* stands in the same relation to *memoria* as *corpus* ("body") to *spiritus* or *animus* ("breath"). This is why the Oxford Latin Dictionary offers as one definition of *vivo* "to live on in the memory of men" (s.v. 5c).

In other words, behind the link between *historia* and *memoria*, as the terminology Cicero uses to describe it suggests, lie some related notions

Lucceius in some detail (70–3 and *passim*). In addition to refining our notion of what *historia* meant to both Greeks and Romans (and elaborating how very much it differs from our own), he frequently discusses the similarities between poetry and historiography (esp. in connection with Herodotus and Thucydides).

[30] Hutton (1993), 156. Further on memory and imagination Hampl (1985).

[31] Cicero characterizes Atticus' universal history as comprising *omnem rerum memoriam* (*Brut.* 14). It is worth noting (surprising as it may seem) that Roman historians themselves seldom refer to their product as *historia*. In Tacitus, for example, the word *historia* appears only once, in an entirely generic reference to "histories" written by his predecessors (*Dial.* 3.4). The verb Tacitus most often uses to denote what he is doing is *memorare*, precisely the word used by Silius Italicus to describe his poetic task (*Pun.* 1.1–3); his work is *memoria* (e.g., the *Agricola* is explicitly termed a *memoria*, 3.3, despite the fact that a considerable portion of the narrative derives not from Tacitus' personal recollection but from historical inquiry).

[32] *de Orat.* 2.36: *Historia ... vita memoriae ... qua voce alia, nisi oratoris, immortalitati commendatur?*, "By whose voice other than the orator's is history, the lifeblood of memory, entrusted to immortality?"

[33] Cf., e.g., Cic. *Orat.* 120 (linking *res gestae* and *memoria*); Livy *Praef.* 3; Sal. *Jug.* 4.1, 6 (quoted below) and *Cat.* 1.3; Sen. *Suas.* 6.4, 15; Tac. *Agr.* 1.2; Gel. 1.3.1; Quint. *Inst.* 10.1.31. Further for this sense of *memoria* as *historia* see TLL *s. memoria* 8.675.56–676.36. On the "deathlessness" of memory, Cic. *Leg.* 3.21; Pliny *Ep.* 10.76.

about the connection between the living and the dead in Roman thought. This is an important nuance to grasp, for it explains much about the anxiety imperial Romans felt over the "demise" of the Republic and its memory. One means of appreciating this connection is to consider the experience of traveling along the Appian Way from Bovillae to Rome, an experience that captures a fundamental distinction between Roman culture and our own. The Romans – wealthy ones, anyway, and beginning from the fourth century BC on – were not inclined to hide their dead, to relegate them to some isolated, walled enclosure where concourse with the deceased takes place only when and if you want it. For those who could afford it, the dead took up residence in full view of the living, in well-wrought tombs that often bore their images or were inscribed with brief summaries of their genealogy or careers.[34] A traveler approaching Rome on the Appian Way in the late first century AD would pass by dozens of tombs in close succession, monuments to the families and individuals who over the course of several centuries had lived in and in some cases helped build the great city to which the road led. It was – and is – quite literally a walk through Roman history; here were buried the Horatii and the Curiatii, members of the Metelli, the Scipios, Messala, Seneca, to name only some of the road's more famous inhabitants. In a symbolic sense, then, in order to arrive in Rome's present – in the city of the living – one was first required to travel through Rome's past, through a virtual community of the dead which was at once sacred, immutable, and unmoveable.[35]

In the *De senectute*, Cicero identifies the chief value of tombs, and specifically of inscriptions placed on tombs, as the means by which he can retreat into or refresh the memory of the dead.[36] But there were

---

[34] Purcell (1987), 27–8. On the "public" nature of such tombs, Koortbojian (1996), 210–11.

[35] By law, that is, Roman tombs could not be moved or destroyed (Cic. *Leg.* 2.61; cf. *Cod.* 9.19.5: *lapidem hunc movere ... proximum sacrilegio maiores habuerunt*). *Domus aeternae*, they served as the permanent residence for the deceased, whose memory was to be celebrated and nourished in perpetuity. Halbwachs (1992), 63.

[36] *nec sepulcra legens vereor, quod aiunt, ne memoriam perdam; his enim ipsis legendis in memoriam redeo mortuorum* (*Sen.* 7.21); cf. Varro *LL* 6.49. Funeral inscriptions occasionally refer to themselves (and the place they mark) as a *memoria* (e.g., *CIL* 12.1036). Koortbojian (1996), 233 discusses the "exercise of *memoria*" effected by Roman tombs. Cf. Susini (1988), 121–2.

many other ways in which this could be achieved as well. We need think only of Roman funeral rites, the *laudatio funebris*,[37] or the wax portrait masks, the *imagines*, of the ancestors that adorned the atria of Rome's political elite.[38] The explicit purpose of such masks was, again according to Cicero, to preserve the *memoria* of the deceased.[39] In the course of a year, in fact, Romans celebrated no fewer than four festivals of the dead. These included the Parentalia, celebrated in mid-February (Ovid *F.* 2.537ff.), when family members visited their ancestral tombs, bringing food and offerings for their inhabitants.[40] Needless to say, one does not need sustenance if one does not have life. But if it was the explicit responsibility of the living to care for the memory of the dead – a responsibility Romans took with great seriousness[41] – they did so not merely out of honor or respect. In a very real sense Romans conceived of the dead as continuing to enjoy an existence and even of influencing events in the present.[42]

To put this more concretely, a failure to commemorate, say, Camillus' capture of Veii in 396 would be to consign Camillus to oblivion; it would be a failure to do in the public arena what any family would be expected to do for one of its ancestors. Such commemoration was crucial to the continuation of Roman society (cf., e.g., Cic. *Rep.* 6.23–4.1).[43] That commemoration needed to be repeated, and regularly. Just as festivals

---

[37] Polybius (6.53–4) best describes the Roman funeral and the *laudatio*.

[38] See esp. Flower (1996).

[39] He is alleging that as a magistrate, he has the right to an *imago* that will preserve his memory for future generations, *ius imaginis ad memoriam posteritatemque prodendae* (Cic. 2 *Verr.* 5.36, cf. *pro Rab. Post.* 16; Sal. *Jug.* 4; Ulpian *Dig.* 11.7.2.6; Isid. *Orig.* 15.11.1; Walbank (1957) on Polyb. 6.53.7–8). Further the useful discussion of Shumka (2000), 150–88.

[40] Two other festivals for the dead related to the Parentalia and also celebrated in February were the Feralia and the Caristia; the fourth was the Lemuria, held in May. Scullard (1981), 74–6, 188–9. For graveside feasts, Lindsay (1998), esp. 74–6; Dunbabin (2004).

[41] So Cicero: *vita ... mortuorum in memoria est posita vivorum* (*Phil.* 9.10). Ovid notes one occasion when the Parentalia was not celebrated: Romans were too busy engaged in war and they suffered for the failure to observe the festival (*F.* 2.547–54).

[42] Cumont (1949), 52–4. I naturally simplify a very complex issue (Roman attitudes toward the deceased): further Feldherr (2000), 211–13, with refs.

[43] As Meier stresses (1997[3]), 302–3, this connection with the past was intrinsic to the Roman conception of the Republic. See also Oexle (1995), 32–3.

such as the Parentalia were celebrated annually, historical memory too needed to be "fed." Following Maurice Halbwachs (1992), we might well see in Camillus a character who inhabits Rome's "collective memory", a Republican *exemplum* who had become so much a part of the Roman psyche that it would be virtually unthinkable to contemplate *forgetting* him. While the validity of the term "collective memory," first coined by Halbwachs in 1941 in *Etude de mémoire collective*, has been questioned,[44] the Romans appear to have recognized the concept of a shared memory; this, at least, is implied in the phrase *memoria publica*.[45] Cicero predictably connects this with *historia*, which he posits as the sole means of preserving *memoria publica* or "collective memory" (*memoriae publicae retinendae causa*, Cic. *de Orat.* 2.52). The term, by the way, may be used both in an abstract sense, as in the passage just cited, and in a concrete sense, as in the *Pro Caelio* when Cicero charges Clodius with having burned *memoria publica*, evidently in reference to the public archives.[46] In Cicero's mind, memory is not solely the prerogative of individuals; society at large – the *civitas*, the *res publica* – may also possess memory, and has the same obligation as the individual to preserve its history.[47] It was this drive to remember that kept characters such as Camillus alive in Roman memory for so long.

[44] The full title is *La topographie légendaire des évangiles en terre sainte. Etude de mémoire collective*. For challenges to Halbwachs' ideas see, e.g., Gedi and Elam (1996); cf. Oexle (1995), 23–4. Shrimpton (1997), 15, rightly observes that "[h]istory in the hands of ancient writers ... resembles what Halbwachs has called 'the collective memory.'"

[45] The OLD in fact proposes "collective memory" as one definition of *memoria* (OLD s.v. 7).

[46] *Cael.* 78, with Austin (1960³) ad loc.; cf. similarly *Mil.* 73; see *TLL s. memoria* 8.684.13 for this sense. A related sense seems to be operative at *Leg.* 3.26, where Cicero laments the lack of any mechanism to record in writing *memoria publica* (i.e. in this instance, of law). One might compare the temple of Juno Moneta, which, as has been recently demonstrated, was itself associated through the *libri lintei* that were housed there with the preservation of memory (hence the epithet Moneta): see Meadows and Williams (2001).

[47] It is important to stress, however, that group memory is in fact composed of or determined by individual memories (Halbwachs [1992], 53). Thus (to take one example) Lucan's memory of the civil war between Caesar and Pompey as constituted in the *Pharsalia* reflects the memories both of individuals and of the group (i.e. Romans, the *civitas*, the *res publica*) to which those individuals belong.

Orators and the *ars memorativa*

The preservation of *memoria publica* could be achieved in a variety of ways. Under the Republic, archives certainly served that purpose, as did commemorative practices such as those mentioned above (funeral processions, *laudationes*, festivals, etc.), tombs, inscriptions, and monuments. But surely the greatest repository of *memoria publica* would have been Rome's orators.

As is well known, orators underwent extensive training in memory, identified as one of the five components of rhetoric[48] – the *custos ceterarum ingeni partium* (*Brut.* 219).[49] Building on systems devised by Simonides and Aristotle, Romans developed elaborate mnemotechniques designed to ensure that the well-trained orator could remember with ease what he needed to.[50] What that was could be quite varied – simply the words of the speech to be delivered, bits and pieces of well-known speeches to dress up one's own compositions, but more importantly a large store of precedent and historical information or what Cicero calls the *memoria rerum Romanarum*, a "memory for Roman history." The chief benefit of such knowledge is that it permits the orator to summon, as if from the dead, a host of "invaluable witnesses" (*memoriam rerum Romanarum . . . ex qua, si quando opus esset, ab inferis locupletissimos testis excitaret, Brut.* 322).[51] He means, of course, *exempla*, characters from the past whose deeds have been invested with certain moral authority, the use of which lay at the center of Roman thinking about ethics and morality.[52]

---

[48] *Brut.* 215; cf. *Inv.* 1.7.9, *de Orat.* 1.142–3, *Rhet. Her.* 1.3.

[49] Memory is similarly defined at *Rhet. Her.* 3.28 as the *thesaurum inventorum atque . . . omnium partium rhetoricae custodem*, "the repository of topics and keeper of all the parts of rhetoric" (cf. *de Orat.* 1.18, *Part.* 3; Quint. *Inst.* 11.2.1).

[50] The author of the *Rhetorica ad Herennium* analyzes in detail how an orator might train and deploy his memory at 3.33ff. These techniques and their successors have been fully explored in, e.g., Yates (1966), 1–26 and passim; Carruthers (1990), chaps. 1–4. For classical practices in particular see also Small (1997) and Blum (1969).

[51] Michel (1960), 432–3. Thus the author of the *ad Herennium* stresses the need to acquire a memory of words (*verba*) as well as events and precedents (*res*) (3.33). See Yates (1966), 12–13. On the sorts of things an orator was expected to "remember," further Gowing (2000), 42–51.

[52] I shall have more to say about the phenomenon of exemplarity and its role in the texts to be examined. The bibliography on the subject is extensive: Roller (2001b), n. 2; esp. Litchfield (1914); Chaplin (2000).

Vernant rightly connects the development of mnemotechniques in Greek but especially Roman society with a broader preoccupation with memory. As he construes it, "In different periods and cultures, there is a connection between the techniques of remembering that are practiced, the internal organization of that function, its place in the system of the self, and the image that people have of memory."[53] To put this another way, the memory techniques outlined in texts such as the *ad Herennium* or by Quintilian, or which underlie the praise of memory in texts such as Cicero's *Brutus*, provide clues as to how Romans organized and viewed their cultural and historical memory. Carruthers coins the term "architectural mnemonic" to describe this system (the "house of memory"), and not coincidentally it is a term that applies equally well to a structure such as the Forum of Augustus.[54] This is a point I shall return to in the final chapter, but it is worth bearing in mind, as a further reflection of the degree to which memory permeated Roman culture, that Roman memory is mapped onto the urban landscape in much the same way as it was arranged mentally.

It is precisely because of their memory training that Cicero regards orators as the ones best suited to write *historia*, to render it "deathless" (see n. 32). Quite naturally, then, he identifies the serious threat posed in the last couple of decades of the Republic to the free practice of oratory as a threat to Roman memory. As I have argued elsewhere (see n. 51), the *Brutus* directly addresses this threat. On the surface a survey of Rome's greatest orators, the *Brutus* is clearly a response to the curtailing of "free speech" brought on by the conflict between Caesar and Pompey. With Caesar's victory assured, Cicero swiftly moved to assert – by writing, the only means left to him – the primacy of oratory and orators in the pre-Caesarian Republic, intimating that the suppression of oratory in Caesar's Republic would be counterproductive if not fatal.

The memory of the Republic under Augustus

The assassination of Caesar notwithstanding, this was not an argument that the elder statesman won. With the beheading of Cicero and the severing of his hands in December of 43, the triumvirs permanently

---

[53] Vernant (1965), 51, as cited in Le Goff (1992), 64.
[54] Carruthers (1990), 221 and passim.

silenced the mouth that spoke, and stilled the hands that wrote, the speeches that had been uttered in opposition to Caesarianism. The ensuing civil war brought to a climax more than a century of internal conflict and discord, inflicting on the Roman people a trauma and sense of loss that would take more than a century to heal. As Cicero had certainly foreseen, the triumph of Caesarianism meant the demise of the Republic. It also dealt a serious blow to oratory, and with it one avenue for the continuity of memory and tradition.

Octavian, the future Augustus, quickly sought to assert control over memory. It was no accident that one of his first independent and official acts in 36 BC, with Lepidus out of the way and Antony in the East, was the destruction of documents pertaining to the actions of the triumvirs (Appian *BC*. 5.132.548). He simultaneously announced his intention to restore the Republic (ibid.; cf. pp. 4–5 with n. 13), thus coupling this great political promise with an unambiguous indication that controlling memory would be high on his agenda. Not long thereafter, he eliminated publication of the *acta senatus* (Suet. *Aug*. 36), depriving Romans (and incidentally later historians) of the means of knowing and hence remembering what decisions were being made on their behalf. But forgetting the means by which Octavian was brought to power was only half the problem; the other half was how Rome's past was to be remembered – a past in which the word *libertas*, "freedom," was seen as synonymous with *res publica*.[55] In this too the new emperor would play a role.

In the Augustan period the degree to which Rome celebrated its past was unprecedented. In some sense this is unsurprising; periods of renewal after revolutions are often marked by intense recollection.[56] The paradox of the Augustan period was that it sought to assert the continuity of the Republic while at the same time claiming a new beginning. How could that which had not ended nonetheless begin anew?[57] Without entering into debate about the extent to which Augustus influenced the details of this celebration, there is little doubt that it served the

---

[55] Wirszubski (1968), 5.

[56] Connerton (1989), 6–7; Le Goff (1992), 9.

[57] This, in itself, is a problem for memory, since "new beginnings" – birth – imply "forgetting" or *lack* of memory. Weinrich (2000³), 34–5 ("die Geburt bedeutet Vergessen"). Weinrich's is a fascinating investigation of the history of "forgetting" in Western culture.

new *princeps*' wishes to embrace and extol the Republican past both as 1 repository for moral *exempla* and to advance the notion that the augustan regime was merely the logical (and even fated) end toward which the Republic had been headed all along. Thus in the *Res gestae* he baldly claims to have preserved for memory many *exempla* from Rome's past.[58] And certainly many Romans living under the Augustan regime would not have imagined, as we do, that the Republic had "ended." To appreciate the vigor with which Augustus sought to connect the present with the past one need again only think of the Forum of Augustus, as we shall see in Chapter 5. In this space, as in much of Augustan literature, the Republican past is artificially linked with Aeneas and Troy, a revealing example of how memory comes to be manipulated in this period.[59] Caesar's heir was merely a pawn in the divine plan to restore the Republic to its former moral and political grandeur, to rescue it from the headlong dive it had been in since the late second century.

Republican history therefore figures prominently in the literature and art of the Augustan period. Building projects such as the Forum of Augustus furnished stunning, persuasive, visual prompts to induce the viewer to make the connection between past and present. For the literate, poetry and prose often accomplished the same thing. Vergil's *Aeneid*, of course, not only established the divine credentials of the new regime, but also made space, specifically in Book 6 and on the Shield of Aeneas in Book 8, for a survey of memorable characters and moments from the Republic, all part of the ordained plan for Rome. Horace mines Republican history for themes and *exempla*; even

---

[58] *Legibus novis me auctore latis multa exempla maiorum exolescentia iam ex nostro saeculo reduxi et ipse multarum rerum exempla imitanda posteris tradidi*, "Through new legislation that I authored I have reintroduced to our age many *exempla* associated with our ancestors though currently in disuse, and I have myself handed down to posterity *exempla* for many situations which are worthy of imitation" (*RG* 8.5). See Eder (1990), 82.

[59] Cf. esp. Prop. 4.1a.39–54, where the *animi ... Deci Brutique secures*, "the courage of Decius and the [sc. consular] axes of Brutus," both men quintessential Republican icons, are said to have had their origins in the flight from Troy (cf. Verg. *A.* 6.819–24). My thanks to Alessandro Barchiesi for drawing this passage to my attention.

Propertius (but not Tibullus) on occasion drew material from the Republican past.[60]

The present typically measures itself against the past. What distinguishes the recollection of the past during the Augustan period from the Republican, however, is the presence of the *princeps*. Indeed, it becomes seemingly impossible to talk about the heroes of the Republic without prompting, implicitly or explicitly, a comparison with the new emperor.[61] A few examples will suffice.

In *Ode* 1.12 Horace invokes Clio, the muse of history, in order to help him identify a proper subject (*quem virum aut heroa ... /quem deum?*) for his praises. In the list that follows Horace eventually comes to Rome's native sons (33ff.): the kings Romulus, Numa, Tarquinius Superbus; then, icons of the Republic – Cato, Regulus, the Scauri, L. Aemilius Paulus, Fabricius, M'. Curius Dentatus, Camillus. These merit three stanzas. But the point of the poem only becomes clear in the last four stanzas, all devoted to the *real* "hero" – Clio's answer, in effect, to the question posed in the first line – namely, Augustus. His membership in the Republican club is confirmed by an ambiguous reference to "Marcellus" (45, referring to both the famous third-century general and Augustus' nephew), but importantly, he is distanced from and elevated above the rest with the observation that he is second in power only to Jupiter himself. As Nisbet and Hubbard note in their comment on this poem, the Republicans mentioned here are in fact standard moral *exempla*.[62] Without denying them that status (indeed he confirms it), Horace reconfigures them to serve as favorable if ultimately inferior comparanda to the new emperor. We are clearly in the presence of a new ideology, one that has co-opted the moral value of traditional Republican *exempla* in order to affirm the supremacy of a single

---

[60] Horace: (e.g.) *C.* 1.12, 2.15, 3.5; Propertius: 2.1, 3.5, 3.11, 4.1a, 4.1b, 4.10, 4.11. As Most (2003) shows, moreover, even in an Augustan text such as the *Aeneid* which is *not* explicitly about the Roman Republic the themes of memory and forgetting feature prominently, though I would suggest that their presence reflects contemporary, shared concerns about the direction of Roman society and politics.

[61] This is part and parcel of a movement to "[inscribe] Augustus and his new world ... into the values and traditions with which [Augustan] writers were familiar" (Kraus [1997], 74, with refs. in n. 122). See also Wallace-Hadrill (1987), 223.

[62] Nisbet and Hubbard (1970), 144. Also on this poem, and its role in "constituting the new ideology," Feeney (1998), 111–13.

authority. Such a use of these *exempla* would have been unthinkable prior to Actium.[63]

Ovid, too, participates in a co-opting of history. Narrating the commemorations that take place on the Ides of January, he invites his reader to contemplate the *tituli* that were typically attached to the busts of famous men kept in family atria (*perlege dispositas generosa per atria ceras*): there one could encounter the Scipios, Julius Caesar, T. Manlius Torquatus, Pompey, the Fabii, and others (*F.* 1.587–616). But their honors pale in comparison with those accorded Augustus; they are human, he on a par with Jupiter (ibid. 607–8). Again, historical allusion *apart* from the emperor has become increasingly difficult to achieve. The impact is perhaps best appreciated when one considers the wholesale recasting of Republican history attempted by Livy.

It surely cannot be coincidence that the Augustan period gave rise to the single most comprehensive account of the Roman Republic Rome ever produced. Livy's massive history, a stunning achievement by any standard, set Republican history in the context of the new regime. Over 250 years of monarchy are rapidly dispensed with in Book 1, the analogies between Rome's monarchy and the emerging new regime being perhaps too obvious and discomfiting, leaving 141 Books to devote to the glories of the Republic and the first half of the Augustan regime. Livy clearly writes under the shadow of the new emperor, and numerous studies of various aspects of the narrative show that the present reality of the new Principate is never far from the historian's mind, especially as he draws central characters such as Romulus, Camillus, or Scipio or narrates certain politically charged events such as the rule of the decemvirate in the fifth century.[64] Regardless of the degree to which Livy's work played into – or possibly subverted – the Augustan desire to revive

---

[63] One might usefully compare Horace's pre-Actian allusions to Republican history, e.g., *Epod.* 16 (probably composed in 41 BC or shortly thereafter): there he similarly uses the past to explicate the present, but the poem focuses on the welfare of the community (*omnis ... civitas*, 36) and its relationship to previous history rather than on an individual leader.

[64] For Livy's assimilation of key personalities with Augustus, refs. in Miles (1995), 89 n. 36 as well as his own discussion of Camillus (89–95 and passim); see also Jaeger (1997), 183–4, and Chaplin (2000), esp. 173–202. On decemvirate: Ungern-Sternberg (1986).

Republican values, it is our best example of how reshaping the memory of the Republic went hand-in-hand with the emergence of the Principate.

Many of the issues outlined thus far, and the whole problem of the memory of the past and especially of the Republic, converge in the preface to Livy's history. Both Mary Jaeger and Gary Miles have recently offered full, insightful discussions of the role of memory in Livy's *History*,[65] and much of what I have to say mirrors their own conclusions. Livy himself defines his project as the preservation or the "looking after" (*consuluisse*) of memory: *iuvabit ... rerum gestarum memoriae principis terrarum populi pro virili parte et ipsum consuluisse* (*Praef.* 3). Famously, he equates the experience of reading his *History* with gazing at a monument:

> hoc illud est praecipue in cognitione rerum salubre ac frugiferum, omnis te exempli documenta in inlustri posita monumento intueri; inde tibi tuaeque rei publicae quod imitere capias, inde foedum inceptu foedum exitu quod vites. ceterum aut me amor negotii suscepti fallit, aut nulla umquam res publica nec maior nec sanctior nec bonis exemplis ditior fuit, nec in quam civitatem tam serae avaritia luxuriaque inmigraverint, nec ubi tantus ac tam diu paupertati ac parsimoniae honos fuerit. adeo quanto rerum minus, tanto minus cupiditatis erat: nuper divitiae avaritiam et abundantes voluptates desiderium per luxum atque libidinem pereundi perdendique omnia invexere.

> This is what is especially healthy and profitable in the study of history, that you gaze upon models of every sort as though they were set on an illustrious monument. From there you may choose for yourself and your state what to imitate and what, shameful in both its inception and outcome, to avoid. But either my passion for the task I have undertaken has deceived me or no country has ever been greater or purer or richer in good citizens and noble deeds; in no society have greed and luxury taken so long to arrive, in no society has the respect accorded plain living and frugality been so great or so long-lasting. Indeed, the less we had, the less covetous we were. But lately our wealth and unbounded desires have produced greed and the desire to destroy and lose everything for the sake of luxury and lust.   (*Praef.* 10–12)

---

[65] Esp. Miles (1995), chap. I "History and Memory in Livy's Narrative"; Jaeger (1997), chap. I "The History as a Monument."

Apart from neatly demonstrating the almost palpable connection between text, monument, and memory, Livy sheds light on the reason why the Republic needs to be remembered. The memory conveyed by his history equips the reader with a sense of wrong and right as determined or exemplified by the actions of one's predecessors; it also equips us with the capacity to make sense of, and correct, the present. His history aims to accomplish, in short, precisely what gazing on the busts of one's ancestors is meant to accomplish. He invests the Republican past, as one might one's ancestors, with considerable authority: no age is "greater," "more hallowed," or "richer." History here is envisaged as a tomb which, as any Roman tomb, needs to be revered, cultivated, and respected; remembering the past, like remembering the dead, is seen as a process entirely central to the Roman's aristocrat's sense of self-worth and identity.

As I have argued, this is hardly new or unique to Livy. Cicero's observation, made several decades earlier, about the importance of memory to the Roman nobility reads rather like what Livy had in mind: *valet apud nos clarorum hominum et bene de re publica meritorum memoria, etiam mortuorum*, "the memory of distinguished men who have served the Republic well, even though they be dead, holds great importance for us" (*Sest.* 15). Sallust will make a similar assertion in the *Bellum Iugurthinum*, with specific reference to the power of history (*res gestae*) in this regard: *scilicet non ceram illam neque figuram tantam vim in sese habere, sed memoria rerum gestarum eam flammam egregiis viris in pectore crescere neque prius sedari quam virtus eorum famam atque gloriam adaequaverit*, "Certainly it is not the waxen image that has such power over them; rather, the memory of their deeds produces in noble men a desire to fan that flame and not to rest until their own virtue has equaled the fame and glory [of their ancestors]" (*Jug.* 4.6).

But Livy, like Horace and Ovid, labors in the shadow of the *princeps*, and this too is precisely the difference between Livy and Cicero. Cicero did not have to contend with a ruling authority that had a serious vested interest in how the memory of the past would be construed and presented. This is true, at least, for the greater part of Cicero's political career; Cicero's later relationship with Caesar, especially as captured in the *Caesarianae*, will anticipate the senator/*princeps* model under the Principate. In Livy's case the fact of the emperor, and his deep interest in manipulating memory, problematizes the historian's project in a way that his predecessors could not have imagined.

It is not, moreover, a problem that goes away with the passing of Augustus in AD 14. Rather, it intensifies as the reality of the Republic's demise becomes ever more apparent and the possibility (and some might say the desirability) of a *res publica restituta* fades from view. In many respects Livy's invitation to "gaze" upon the monument that is his *History* remains an open one; his own work testifies to the necessity of a constant reevaluation of one's relationship to the past. Livy himself seems to anticipate this in the phrase *tuae rei publicae*, as though the relevance of his narrative is not confined to his *res publica*, but to all *res publicae* to come. As one moves through the early imperial period, however, with each successive regime we see the memory of the Republic addressed anew and refashioned to reflect (or take issue with) the new ideology.

One measure of the extent to which the Republic and its memory remained a politically sensitive point resides in the degree to which the whole question arises with the accession of each successive emperor. At his accession in AD 14, Tiberius pleaded with the Senate to take back control of the state. They politely declined (Tac. *Ann.* 1.11–13; cf. 4.9). In the two days following the assassination of Caligula in 41, however, the Senate and consuls did propose to restore the Republic (*Capitoliumque occupaverant asserturi communem libertatem*, Suet. *Cl.* 10.3), declaring that the memory of the Caesars was to be abolished (*abolendam Caesarum memoriam*, Suet. *Cal.* 60); the consul who led the charge, Sentius Saturninus, is made by Josephus to lament the fact that he has no memory of the Republic – but his fleeting taste of freedom has made him long for it all the more.[66] But Claudius, less generous than Tiberius, decreed that these two days of madness be wiped from memory, *memoriae eximere* (Suet. *Cl.* 11.1). A year later, Camillus Scribonianus claimed the restoration of the Republic to be the aim of his rebellion (Dio 60.15.3). Nero slyly promised to honor the *antiqua munia senatus*, "the

---

[66] Ἐμοὶ δὲ τῆς μὲν πρότερον ἐλευθερίας ἀμνημονεῖν ἔστι διὰ τὸ κατόπιν αὐτῆς γεγονέναι, τῆς δὲ νῦν ἀπλήστως πιμπλαμένῳ μακαριστούς τε ἡγεῖσθαι τοὺς ἐγγενηθέντας καὶ ἐντραφέντας αὐτῇ...', '"I do not remember our earlier *libertas*, because I was born after it. But as I fill myself insatiably with our present *libertas*, I count those who were born then and nourished by it to be the most blessed of people..."' (*AJ* 19.169). On Sentius' 'Republican' character see Vell. Pat. 2.92; on accounts of the episode, Noè (1984), 111–20; MacMullen (1966), 29–32. Further on these attempts to "restore the Republic" Sion-Jenkis (2000), 155–7.

ancient authority of the Senate," to keep the affairs of the imperial household (*domus*) distinct from those of the *res publica* (Tac. *Ann.* 13.4.2). He reneged. Nearly thirty years later Galba, Nero's short-lived successor in the year 68, claimed, *si immensum imperii corpus stare ac librari sine rectore posset, dignus eram a quo res publica inciperet*, "If the huge body of the Empire could stand on its own and be stable in the absence of a single ruler, I would be the right person with whom the Republic might make a new beginning" (Tac. *Hist.* 1.16.1). But of course the Republic did not. In the year 100 Pliny, somewhat disingenuously, credited Trajan with having restored the Republic – *libertas reddita* (*Pan.* 58.3; the phrase is discussed further in Chap. 4). No one, much less Pliny, believed that. Nor, evidently, did Calpurnius Crassus, a descendant of the great Republican Crassi, who hatched a plot against the seemingly blameless Trajan.[67]

The arena in which anxiety over the loss of the Republic is played out is literature. In some sense, the Empire's writers take over from the Republic's orators the task of preserving memory, a phenomenon anticipated by Cicero's own retreat into writing in the 40s. This constitutes a crucial distinction between the Roman and Greek view of memory, and one which renders this project rather different from similar, recent attempts to write the memory of fifth- and fourth-century Greece:[68] Greeks conceived of writing as the enemy of memory, Romans embraced it as one of the most reliable guarantors of memory – *litterae ... una custodia fidelis memoriae rerum gestarum*, as Livy puts it (6.1.2)[69] – and provided us with a considerably more varied array of literary evidence than that left by classical Athenians. One reason for this lies in the fact that writing becomes the chief means of wresting control of memory from the hands of the ruling authority. The choice is either to collude with the official position or view of the past – to remember or forget what

---

[67] Dio 68.3.2, 16.2. Cizek (1983), 182; Bennett (1997), 40.

[68] I think especially of Loraux (1997) and Wolpert (2002).

[69] Carruthers (1990), 9. The *locus classicus* for antipathy toward writing as a means of remembering is Plato *Phaedr.* 274C–275B; cf. (ironically) Caes. *Gal.* 6.14. Cicero, by contrast, regards memory itself as something on which we "write" (*de Orat.* 2.360); and laments the failure of many Greeks to use writing to preserve memory (e.g., *Brut.* 28, 39 and passim). On these passages, Le Goff (1992), 63–4.

the emperor preferred to remember or forget – or to set one's own agenda.

What, that is, does one do when confronted with an emperor who, asked if he remembers, says "*non memini*"? Or worse, what does one do when the emperor seeks to snuff out memory by burning a text? Tiberius had done both. In AD 25 the historian Cremutius Cordus was brought to trial on a charge of treason: he had written a history that was rather too flattering of Brutus and Cassius, the Republican assassins of Julius Caesar.[70] Tacitus assigns to him a defiant speech in the Senate, following which he starved himself to death. Part of the speech bears repeating:

> "num enim armatis Cassio et Bruto ac Philippenses campos obtinentibus belli civilis causa populum per contiones incendo? an illi quidem septuagesimum ante annum perempti, quo modo imaginibus suis noscuntur, quas ne victor quidem abolevit, sic partem memoriae apud scriptores retinent? suum cuique decus posteritas rependit; nec deerunt, si damnatio ingruit, qui non modo Cassii et Bruti, sed etiam mei meminerint." egressus dein senatu vitam abstinentia finivit. libros per aediles cremandos censuere patres; <s>ed manserunt, occultati et editi. quo magis socordia<m> eorum inridere libet, qui praesenti potentia credunt exstingui posse etiam sequentis aevi memoriam.

'Surely I am not making speeches to incite the people to civil war, as though Brutus and Cassius were armed and on the fields at Philippi? Or is it not the case that they, despite being dead for seventy years, exercise through literature a hold over a part of our memory, in the same way that they are known to us through their statues, which not even the victor abolished? Future generations give everyone their due honor; nor will there be lacking, even if I am condemned, people who will remember Cassius, Brutus – and even myself." Then he walked out of the Senate and starved himself to death. The Senate decreed that the aediles should burn his books. But they survived, hidden and then republished. For this reason one is more inclined to laugh at the foolishness of those who imagine that today's regime can extinguish the subsequent generation's memory.   (*Ann.* 4.35.2–5)

---

[70] For Cordus, in addition to the Tacitus cited here, Dio 57.24.2–4; Suet. *Tib.* 61.3, *Cal.* 16.1. For full discussion of the episode in Tacitus, Moles (1998).

Cremutius, as the shrewd Tiberius knew, is exactly right about the threat posed by the memory of Brutus and Cassius. Robbed of his writing, Cremutius resorts to the last means left him to exert control, taking his own life. This trial anticipates the tug-of-war over Republican memory that would be played out under the remaining Julio-Claudian emperors and the Flavians, capturing the anxiety that could be generated by narrating the past as well as suggesting its potential consequences. Tacitus, with the benefit of hindsight, presents it as a lesson in the incapacity of a regime to control memory. One might well ask, however, why Tacitus himself chose *not* to write a history of the Republic. The answer to that question will be made apparent in the chapters ahead.

CHAPTER

2

Res publica Tiberiana

On August 19, AD 14, at about three in the afternoon, Rome's first emperor quietly passed away at his family home in Nola, in the same room as his father had died.[1] Preparations had been made for the event, above all to ensure that Augustus' death would not give rise to a constitutional crisis. His adopted son Tiberius would be his heir, both to a substantial portion of the estate and to the name "Augustus."

Augustus' corpse was still warm when Tiberius made it clear that controlling memory would be as high on his agenda as it had been on his stepfather's. When the Senate requested that some of their members be allowed to convey the body of the dead emperor to his funeral pyre, Tiberius balked and pointedly instructed that this would not be necessary. Remembering the disturbances accompanying the funeral of Julius Caesar over half a century earlier, he issued an edict forbidding the cremation of Augustus in the Forum rather than in the Campus Martius. Tacitus quotes the edict: "*ne, ut quondam nimiis studiis funus divi Iulii turbassent, ita Augustum in foro potius quam in campo Martis, sede destinata, cremari vellent*", "[he warned them,] 'Do not repeat the disturbances – due to over-enthusiasm – at the funeral of Julius Caesar by pressing for Augustus to be cremated in the Forum instead of the Campus Martius, his appointed place of rest'" (Tac. *Ann.* 1.8.5; cf. Dio 57.2.2). Directly after quoting the edict, as he describes the funeral itself, Tacitus imagines what people thought when they noticed that an armed guard had been assigned to the procession. Just as Tiberius had feared,

---

[1] Suet. *Aug.* 100, Tac. *Ann.* 1.9.1

the scene conjures memories of Julius Caesar, both in those who had experienced the event first-hand and in those to whom such memories had been passed down:

> die funeris milites velut praesidio stetere, multum inridentibus qui ipsi viderant quique a parentibus acceperant diem illum crudi adhuc servitii et libertatis improspere repetita<e>, cum occisus dictator Caesar aliis pessimum, aliis pulcherrimum facinus videretur: nunc senem principem, longa potentia, provisis etiam heredum in rem publicam opibus, auxilio scilicet militari tuendum, ut sepultura eius quieta foret.

On the day of the funeral soldiers stood as though to provide protection, an act mocked at length by those who had either seen or learned from their parents about the day that saw slavery as yet fresh and freedom unsuccessfully recovered, when the dictator Caesar was murdered. To some the event was the worst of crimes, to others a thoroughly splendid accomplishment. Now, it was said, in spite of a protracted reign and also providing his heirs with the means to suppress the Republic, the old emperor Augustus even needed a military guard to guarantee that his burial would be undisturbed.

(Ann. 1.8.6)

Before we turn to the revealing nexus of memories featured in this episode, it is worth pointing out just how fraught with difficulties Tacitus' narrative is. Dio tells us that Augustus had left explicit instructions about his funeral (56.33.1); this information is missing in Tacitus, who alleges that it is the Senate and Tiberius who make the arrangements. Moreover, only in Tacitus do we find the supposed "edict." Apart from the fact such an edict seems unlikely, since Augustus had left instructions which both Tiberius and the people surely would honor – including the instruction that he should be cremated at his Mausoleum in the Campus Martius – just how plausible is it that Tiberius would refer to disturbances during Caesar's funeral in 44 BC? Tacitus further suppresses the fact that Augustus' funeral *did* begin in the Forum Romanum (although he was cremated in the Campus Martius at the site of his Mausoleum, Dio 56.42.2). Nor does he tell us that Drusus, Tiberius' son, delivered a eulogy on the rostra at the north end of the Forum; nor that Tiberius delivered another while standing in front of the Temple of Divus Julius on the south. Tacitus wipes that event from memory in his account of Augustus' funeral, not to mention the portents that heralded Augustus' death, all of which were connected in one way or another with Julius Caesar. Tacitus' account of Augustus' funeral has much to do with his interest in characterizing Tiberius as a paranoid charlatan, a man who pretended to respect the Republic but who, in reality, was more a Caesar than Caesar himself. It has nothing to do with an interest in presenting an accurate account of what happened at Augustus' funeral.[2]

In short, this episode in the *Annals* owes much to Tacitus' belief that memory is chiefly what prompts human action; the historicity of his account aside, the notion that a change of regime inevitably invites comparison with previous power shifts seems entirely credible.[3] Memory prompts the issuing of the edict by the emperor, who "remembers" what happened at Caesar's funeral and fears a repetition of that debacle at Augustus' funeral. Memory works on the spectators at Augustus' funeral, who are indeed put in mind of Caesar's – an event they had themselves witnessed or the memory of which had been passed on to them. In short, memory inevitably figures in moments of political transition, for the present always invites comparison with the past. Imperial accessions naturally provided such occasions for memory, a fact Tacitus regularly exploits, establishing the pattern of repetition and self-reflexive allusion which characterizes his vision of history (cf., for example, the *seniores* at *Ann.* 13.3 who compare the newly installed emperor Nero to his predecessors). In this instance, however, Tacitus underscores the ineffectiveness of the memory Tiberius feared; despite their memory of Caesar's funeral, the idea that the people should cause a disturbance, Tacitus observes, is laughable: there would be no point, for the Republic is dead and gone.

The cynicism of Tacitus' crowd at this juncture is all the more striking in that it appears contrived to expose Tiberius' subsequent attempt to persuade the Senate to take back power for the sham it may well have been. If we take Tacitus at his word, Tiberius initially declined to rule and advised a return to the status quo of the old *res publica*:

---

[2] Discussion and full bibliography in Swan (2004), on Dio 56.34.1–42.4.

[3] For a similar instance in Tacitus, cf. *Hist.* 1.50, where the murder of Galba and imminent civil war prompt memories of the civil wars of the late Republic (*exempla . . . repetita bellorum civilium memoria*).

et ille varie disserebat de magnitudine imperii, sua modestia. solam divi Augusti mentem tantae molis capacem: se in partem curarum ab illo vocatum experiendo didicisse, quam arduum, quam subiectum fortunae regendi cuncta onus. proinde in civitate tot inlustribus viris subnixa non ad unum omnia deferrent: plures facilius munia rei publicae sociatis laboribus exsecuturos.

He offered various remarks about the greatness of the empire and his own reserve. Only the mind of Augustus, he claimed, was capable of such a great responsibility; called by Augustus to share in his work, he had learned through experience how hard the burden of supreme rule was and how subject to the whims of fortune. Furthermore, the many admirable men by whom the state was so well-supported ought not to place ultimate authority in the hands of one person: a greater number of men working together would more easily perform the tasks of governing. (*Ann.* 1.11.1)

No one (much less Tacitus) is deceived by this display (cf. 1.11.2), and following some heated pleas to reconsider his position, Tiberius accedes to – or at least ceases to decline – the Senate's request that he assume the role of *princeps* (1.13.5). Lest we reject it out of hand, the Tacitean version is in fact corroborated by an eyewitness to the event, Velleius Paterculus (2.124, quoted and discussed below).

Once before Tiberius had refused to participate in a move to restore the Republic: according to Suetonius, his brother Drusus had urged him via a letter to agitate with Augustus about precisely that. Tiberius, motivated chiefly by dislike of his relation, revealed the contents of the letter, presumably to Augustus.[4] It is not at all clear, however, that Tiberius was politically opposed to the idea itself. Over twenty years later, when he is in a position to do as his brother proposed, he seems to take some steps in that direction. Levick is perhaps right,

---

[4] *Odium adversus necessitudines in Druso primum fratre detexit, prodita eius epistula, qua secum de cogendo ad restituendam libertatem Augusto agebat, deinde et in reliquis* (Suet. *Tib.* 50.1). Drusus was quite outspoken about his desire to restore the Republic, a sentiment that gave rise to the rumor that Augustus may have poisoned him (Suet. *Cl.* 1.4). He was a man who after death enjoyed *magna memoria*, and whose interest in restoring the Republic enhanced the popularity of his son Germanicus (Tac. *Ann.* 1.33.1–2): evidently it was hoped the son would share the father's ambitions (cf. ibid. 2.82.2).

therefore, to maintain that Tiberius was a man who "believed as fervently as his brother in the Republic" – a Republic that needed a *princeps* to protect it.[5] His stance is not so very far removed from that of Augustus. Moreover, his regime *is* marked by considerable respect for the institutions of the past.[6] Thus whatever the reality, maintaining some sense of continuity with the past was as important for Tiberius as it was for Augustus. The literature of the period reflects this as well.

"Tiberian culture" as a whole has received little attention, perhaps because in comparison to, say, the Augustan or the Neronian period, it seems rather barren.[7] And certainly, in comparison to his predecessor and his four decades of rule, Tiberius does not appear to have exerted much influence over the creative imaginings of the writers who worked under his regime. But it can be no accident that most of Tiberian literature is historical in nature, and therefore, by definition (see Chap. 1), explicitly designed to promote memory. Much of this literature is known to us only by reputation, but what we can surmise is that Republican history, especially late, features fairly prominently.[8]

We have already mentioned the historian Cremutius Cordus, whose *History* encompassed the civil war and extended into the Augustan period, thus documenting the transition from Republic to Principate. The same is apparently true of the *History* of the Elder Seneca, whose later career spans the reign of Tiberius. Others, however, took their historical researches still further back. Among them was Verrius

---

[5] Levick (1976), 33. Cf. Suet. *Tib.* 30.1 with Baar (1990), 156–62.

[6] On the Tiberian regime as continuation of the Republic (or at least continuation of Augustan façade): Eder (1990), 122; Levick (1976), 92 (Republican nature of the Tiberian *consilium*), 100, 106 (Senate and provinces); Syme (1939), 427: "The accession of Tiberius marked a restoration of the Republic more genuine in many respects than that proclaimed and enacted by his predecessor"; Bloomer (1992), 148 n. 2. On the political character of the Tiberian regime, skillfully explicated via the celebrated series of surviving documents from the Tiberian Senate, see Rowe (2002). Rowe, (2002), 1, nicely establishes how this "new political culture [took] shape among the still-surviving organs of the Republic."

[7] Summary of views in Bloomer (1992), 148–9. The neglect is not justified: see Schmitzer (2000), 27–9; cf. Goodyear (1984).

[8] This is true of Augustan historiography as well, for which see Timpe (1986), 71–2. Timpe notes a surge in historical writing in the post-Augustan era, but attributes it to the evolution of the Principate and the sort of reactions it spawned (ibid. 73).

Flaccus, a prolific antiquarian who flourished under Augustus (he tutored the emperor's grandsons) and survived well into the Tiberian period. Flaccus was the author of the *Fasti Praenestini* (one very visible, public way of illustrating the continuity of Roman history), though his most ambitious work was a multi-volume compendium of "memorable facts," *rerum memoria dignarum libri* (we know the title from Gellius *NA* 4.5.7), which may parallel the work of his coeval Valerius Maximus. Although his precise dates are disputed, the historian Fenestella also belongs to the Tiberian period; his extensive *Annales* (at least twenty-two books) ranged from the period of the monarchy down to the late Republic (and perhaps into his own day) and is characterized by tremendous historical as well as antiquarian detail. Personal memory figures in two of the fragments, suggesting an interest in asserting connections between the past and present at a personal level we have noticed before.[9] Bruttedius Niger, a friend of Sejanus, had composed a *History* that included an account of Cicero's death. A staunch supporter of Tiberius, in AD 22 he had assisted in the prosecution of C. Iunius Silanus on a charge of *maiestas*, joining with a group of senators in adducing famous Republican precedents (Scipio, Cato, and Scaurus) to bolster their case.[10] In the Tiberian period, too, Aufidius Bassus was composing a much-admired *History* that extended back at least as far as the death of Cicero. Even the emperor himself turned his hand to an apparently autobiographical history.[11] Nor is this urge limited strictly to historiography: the subject matter of Phaedrus' fables, another product of the Tiberian period, reflects a similar preoccupation with history and the past.[12]

While the works of men like Cremutius Cordus may not justify positing anything so grand as a "historiography of the senatorial

---

[9] Elder Seneca: Peter (1967), cxviii. Flaccus: ibid., cviii–cviiii. Fenestella: ibid., cviiii–cxiii; on personal memory in his *Annales*: ibid., fr. 15 (Plu. *Crass.* 5: τούτων [i.e., Crassus' two female slaves] φησὶ τὴν ἑτέραν ἤδη πρεσβῦτιν οὖσαν ὁ Φαινεστέλλας ἰδεῖν αὐτὸς καὶ πολλάκις ἀκοῦσαι μεμνημένης ταῦτα καὶ διεξιούσης προθύμως, "Fenestella says that he saw one of these slaves himself when she was already an old woman, and that he often heard her recalling these matters and eagerly recounting them"), fr. 25 (Plin. *NH* 33.146).

[10] Tac. *Ann.* 3.66.1. On Bruttedius, Peter (1967), cxvi.   [11] Peter (1967), cxviii.

[12] Henderson (2001), 242 n. 19, by indirection notes Phaedrus' preoccupation with history by stressing its absence in Aesop.

opposition,"[13] the overall impression is that inquiry into the past thrived under Tiberius. Certainly there seems to be as yet no concerted effort to *forget* the Republic. The reasons for that are perhaps best sought in the two historical works that *do* survive from that period, the *Historia Romana* of Velleius Paterculus and the *Facta et dicta memorabilia* of Valerius Maximus, both of which view the Tiberian regime as an extension of the now-restored Republic.[14]

Velleius Paterculus: the Roman Republic, part 2

In some respects, Velleius Paterculus is to the Tiberian period what Livy was to the Augustan. Shortly after AD 30 he published a *History of Rome*, which in scope, though hardly in length (the work comprised only two books), resembles that of Livy and encompasses the founding of Rome down to the year AD 29, fifteen years into the reign of Tiberius.[15] A striking characteristic of this comparatively superficial but very interesting *History* is that it presents Roman history as a seamless whole. There are, to be sure, specific moments of transition, the most significant occurring after the Third Punic War, when in the wake of expansion Rome entered a period of unprecedented luxury and idleness.[16] But politically, if one accepts the Velleian view, there was no sharp dividing line between "Republic" and the "Principate" or "Empire." The Roman state continues with one modification, the rise of the *princeps*, first Augustus and then Tiberius. Even this – the co-opting of the hallowed Republican term *princeps* (discussed further below) – supported the

---

[13] So Conte (1994), 382–3; Timpe (1986), 68–76, paints a different picture of Augustan–Tiberian historiography. Conte counts among the representatives of this Tiberian movement Servilius Nonianus and Aufidius Bassus, although both survived well into the Neronian period. The former's historical work appears to have begun with the death of Augustus, whereas the latter's went back to at least the death of Cicero. See Peter (1967), cxxv–cxxviiii; Noè (1984), 78–84. This is not to deny, of course, that there was considerable opposition – or discontent – under Augustus and his successors, but rather that the degree to which it manifested itself in historiography is limited. Further on the question of opposition in the early Principate Raaflaub (1986); Schmitzer (2000), 287 with refs. in n. 3.

[14] Bloomer (1992), 3.

[15] On the somewhat unique nature of Velleius' *History*, see Schmitzer (2000), 29–36.

[16] Vell. Pat. 2.1.1–2, replicating the Sallustian view (Woodman [1969], 787; Schmitzer [2000], 82).

impression of restoration rather than revolution.[17] In Velleius' eyes the chief contribution of the first two emperors was not so much the over-hauling of the political system as the imposition of peace, which allowed the *res publica* to function in relative tranquility. Some years and several emperors later, Tacitus supplies a corrective to this view, but too often the cynicism of his successor has overshadowed Velleius' attempt to chronicle the virtues of the Tiberian Republic.[18] In Velleius' eyes, Julius Caesar, Augustus, and Tiberius are neither revolutionaries nor thinly disguised despots but saviors, new *exempla* for a new society in search of new paradigms... but not new government.

The book divisions reflect Velleius' perception of Roman history. Book 1 chronicles the founding of Rome, its expansion, and emergence as an international power, concluding with the destruction of Carthage in 146 BC. Book 2, on the other hand, begins roughly with the Gracchan period and focuses on the civil discord that gave rise to the war between Caesar and Pompey and, ultimately, the Principate of Augustus and then Tiberius. Structurally, therefore, the work views Roman history as divisible into essentially two parts, one embracing the establishment of the Republic and the period of expansion and the other the century of domestic discord that led to the stabilization of the Republic under the first two emperors. The Principate, never explicitly acknowledged as a "new" form of government, is thus seen to be a means to maintain rather than replace the Republic.

What was the purpose of such a work?[19] In part it seems designed simply to be a shortened parallel to Livy's *magnum opus*;[20] it carries Livy's *History* a bit further to include Tiberius within its compass, and therefore situate the climax of Rome's glory in the Tiberian rather than the Augustan age. Both Livy and Velleius use the past as a foil to the present, but whereas in Livy's preface, at least, one senses some anxiety about the present, no such concerns surface in Velleius. On the contrary,

[17] For the term and its Republican associations, Brunt and Moore (1967), 55, Syme (1939), 10; see also below with n. 27. Velleius' belief in the continuation of the Republic: Eder (1990), 73; Kuntze (1985), 155–68; Laistner (1947), 109; Sion-Jenkis (2000), 22, 161–2, 192.

[18] Schmitzer (2000), 26; cf. Woodman (1977), 52–4.

[19] On this question, Schmitzer (2000), 40–2.

[20] Velleius intended to write another, apparently full-blown *History* (cf., e.g., 2.96.3, 103.4, 114.4), on which see Woodman (1977), on 2.96.3.

Tiberius has relieved whatever unease the Augustan regime may have caused. Tiberian Rome is without doubt a better place.

Velleius' "renarrativization" of Republican history – a process Sturken identifies as the "defining quality of memory" – is of course more condensed than Livy's, and the "memory" it establishes appears to have the very specific purpose of equipping the emperor with a Republican pedigree, of suggesting that Tiberius embodies all that was good about characters from Rome's past and has repudiated all that was bad (a man who, in other words, took the injunctions of Livy's preface with some seriousness).[21] To that end Velleius writes a history whose meaning lies not so much in the lessons learned from events but in the morals and ethics imparted by the people involved in the events.[22] The same is largely true of Livy, except that Livy devotes considerably more time to detailing events than Velleius; Velleius typically cuts to the chase, focusing on certain key *Roman* players and their attributes.[23]

His undoubted admiration of various Republican icons functions as a foil for the encomium of Tiberius to follow. His favorable portrait of M. Livius Drusus, tribune of the plebs in 91 BC (2.14.2–3), conjures a well-born, eloquent, moral man with a praiseworthy goal – the restoration of the Senate to its former glory (*priscum ... decus*) – thwarted only by the short-sightedness of the very body he was attempting to serve (2.13). In Velleius' hands, he becomes, in his association with the old status quo, a proto-typical defender of the Republic who in his dying breath is made to wonder if Rome will ever have another citizen such as he (2.14.2).[24] Velleius evinces unquestioning admiration for characters

---

[21] On "renarrativization," Sturken (1997), 42–3.

[22] A common observation in Velleian studies: for summary of the scholarship and discussion of the emphasis on personality, Woodman (1977), 28–45.

[23] That is, he is usually more concerned with Romans than foreigners; we encounter little of the extensive character description one finds of, say, Hannibal or Perseus in Livy (there are occasional exceptions, such as the extended description of Maroboduus at 2.108, which perhaps results from the fact that Velleius had personal experience with him). But as Schmitzer (2000), 37–71 has shown, in the small portion of what survives of Book 1 devoted to pre-Roman history, he very much views Rome's predecessors through a Roman imperial lens.

[24] Discussion by Schmitzer (2000), 151–2, who suggests that Velleius' portrait is conditioned by respect for (or hesitation to criticize) the Livian ancestors of Tiberius. See also Rowe (2002), 58–9.

such as P. Cornelius Scipio Africanus Aemilianus (a man who enjoys *perpetua memoria*, 2.4.3) or Cato the Younger (2.35), scarcely mentioning the latter's opposition to Caesar and passing over in silence his death, an act appropriated by so many other writers as the final stand of *libertas*. He is, moreover, able to offer balanced assessments of men such as Pompey (2.29) and Marius (2.11.1,12.5–6). Several prominent Republican families are singled out for special comment as well: the Domitii (2.10.2), for instance, and the Caecilii Metelli. The latter are served up as an example of a once famous family whose *fortuna* has now waned (2.11.3; cf. 1.11).

When we finally arrive at the Tiberian portion of the work, therefore, it is difficult to resist the notion that Tiberius looks like a throwback to Republican ideals. Or rather, given his lineage, stressed by Velleius (2.94.1–2), it seems quite natural to see the emperor as merely the continuator of his illustrious Republican family.[25] Moreover, it is of some significance that in Velleius' eyes the Republic offers ample precedent for Tiberius' position. Pompey, for instance, is given "imperial" authority to combat the pirates (*paene totius terrarum orbis imperium uni viro deferebatur*, 2.31.3); nor was he the first to be given such authority – Marcus Antonius had been similarly empowered in 74 BC. This leads Velleius to muse on the wisdom of such a move:

> sed interdum persona ut exemplo nocet, ita invidiam auget aut levat: in Antonio homines aequo animo passi erant; raro enim invidetur eorum honoribus quorum vis non timetur; contra in iis homines extraordinaria reformidant qui ea suo arbitrio aut deposituri aut retenturi videntur et modum in voluntate habent. dissuadebant optimates, sed consilia impetu victa sunt.

> But occasionally the personality [sc. of someone given such authority] can increase or lessen envy, just as it has the potential to mar the precedent. In the case of Antonius, people had calmly tolerated him, for we rarely begrudge honors to those whose power we do not fear; but on the other hand, people are fearful of bestowing extraordinary powers on men who seem likely either to lay those powers down or retain them as they see fit and the restraint of which lies in their

---

[25] Kuntze (1985), 35–6.

goodwill. The optimates argued against it, but sound advice was
defeated by impulse. (2.31.4)

It is therefore not the *principle* of one-man rule to which Velleius objects;
rather, he stresses the need to make the choice wisely. Quintus Catulus –
a memory-worthy man – articulates precisely the dilemma in opposing in
67 BC the proposal to entrust Pompey with the war against the pirates:

> Digna est memoria Q. Catuli cum auctoritas tum verecundia. qui cum
> dissuadens legem in contione dixisset esse quidem praeclarum virum
> Cn. Pompeium sed nimium iam liberae rei publicae, neque omnia in
> uno reponenda, adiecissetque "si quid huic acciderit, quem in eius
> locum substituetis?," succlamavit universa contio "te, Q. Catule." tum
> ille victus consensu omnium et tam honorifico civitatis testimonio e
> contione discessit. hic hominis verecundiam, populi iustitiam mirari
> libet, huius, quod non ultra contendit, plebis, quod dissuadentem et
> adversarium voluntatis suae vero testimonio fraudare noluit.

> Both the leadership as well as the humility of Quintus Catulus are
> worthy of memory. When he had expressed his views and opposed the
> law in an assembly, he remarked that Gnaeus Pompey was indeed a
> great man, but that he was now too much so for a free republic and
> that all authority ought not to be granted to one man; and he added,
> "If something happens to him, whom would you put in his place?"
> The entire assembly shouted, "You, Quintus Catulus!" Then, over-
> whelmed by the universal consensus, and by such an honorable
> tribute on the part of the citizens, he left the meeting. At this point
> one might marvel at the humility of the man and the people's sense of
> justice: Catulus because he no longer opposed the measure, the people
> because they were unwilling to deprive him of their genuine respect,
> even though he was arguing the opposite case contrary to their wishes.
>
> (2.32.1–2)

This is how the Republic should work. Valerius Maximus, incidentally,
provides an equally laudatory version of this episode in the *Facta et dicta
memorabilia* (8.15.9), suggesting that it was seen to have special relevance.

The scene in fact bears some resemblance to the moment Tiberius
accepts the Principate; Catulus' insistence that power ought not to be
given to any one man recalls, for instance, Tiberius' similar remark to the

Senate, at least as Tacitus describes it (*Ann.* 1.11.1, quoted above). As I noted at the outset of this chapter, Velleius provides his own version of Tiberius' accession. Initially, the new emperor urged that he merely be a *civis aequalis*.[26] The Senate had other plans:

> Quid tunc homines timuerint, quae senatus trepidatio, quae populi confusio, quis urbis metus, in quam arto salutis exitiique fuerimus confinio, neque mihi tam festinanti exprimere vacat neque cui vacat potest. id solum voce publica dixisse <satis> habeo: cuius orbis ruinam timueramus, eum ne commotum quidem sensimus, tantaque unius viri maiestas fuit ut nec bonis *** neque contra malos opus armis foret. una tamen veluti luctatio civitatis fuit, pugnantis cum Caesare senatus populique Romani ut stationi paternae succederet, illius ut potius aequalem civem quam eminentem liceret agere principem. tandem magis ratione quam honore victus est, cum quicquid tuendum non suscepisset periturum videret; solique huic contigit paene diutius recusare principatum quam ut occuparent eum alii armis pugnaverant.

In my haste I have no time to relate – nor could anyone who had the time – what people feared at this point in time, the anxiety of the Senate, the confusion of the people, the fear in the city, how narrow a path we tread between safety on the one side and destruction on the other. I must satisfy myself with having publicly uttered only this: the world whose destruction we had feared was, we came to realize, not even disturbed. So great was the authority of this one man that there was no need for arms, neither <on behalf of good people> nor against the bad. Nevertheless there was one struggle, as it were, in the state, that of the Senate and the Roman people locked in a debate with Caesar: they, to persuade him to succeed to his father's position, he, that he should instead be permitted to live as an equal citizen rather than a *princeps* set apart. At last he was overcome more by

---

[26] In Velleius' view the citizens of a "free state" (*civitas libera*) must by definition be *aequales*. Pompey's refusal to accept this fact is what tarnished his reputation in the end (2.29.4) and is the reason why Velleius implies that those who believed he represented the interests of the Republic were deceived (2.48.4). Tiberius brought *aequitas* back to the state (2.126.2, .4).

reason than by the honor, when he perceived that whatever he had not undertaken to protect would perish. To him alone did it befall to refuse the Principate longer than others fought by arms to seize it.

(2.124.1–2)

Now, when Velleius uses the term *principatus* in the last sentence, it is clearly in its *Republican* sense, denoting simply a position of leadership in the state (OLD s.v. 1); if one imagines, that is, that Augustus had been the sole *princeps* Rome had witnessed, then the statement is nonsensical. Roman history is awash with men who sought a similar *principatus* as well as with many *principes*, some of whose careers are chronicled by Velleius himself.[27]

In the Velleian view Tiberius' position is no different from that of many who have gone before, another continuation of a hallowed Republican tradition of recognizing the leading men in the state. He too is *princeps* – albeit the *optimus princeps* (2.126.4), a title also used, not coincidentally, by Valerius Maximus (see n. 54). With no hint of skepticism Velleius declares that Augustus restored the Republic: *prisca illa et antiqua rei publicae forma revocata* (2.89.3). Thus when on his deathbed Augustus entrusts to his successor his *opera*, there is no doubt in Velleius' mind what that legacy entails.[28] And indeed, Tiberius immediately sets out on his own program of "restoration," rescuing from the grave – and thus restoring to memory – justice, fairness, and hard work (*sepultaeque ac situ obsitae iustitia aequitas industria civitati redditae*, 2.126.2). He models his behavior on not only Augustus, but the Scipios as well, in choosing a "partner in his labors," the soon-to-be-infamous Sejanus

---

[27] Timpe (1986), 74; good discussion of Velleius' use of these terms in Kuntze (1985), 164–6. Crassus, earlier regarded as a *princeps rei publicae* in the wake of the conflict with Spartacus (2.30.6, with, however, Watts' [1998] app. crit. ad loc.; for the phrase cf. Cic. *Rep.* 1.34.2), aimed at *principatus* under the first triumvirate (2.44.2); Caesar acquired *principatus* (2.57.1); Gaius Gracchus was a *civitatis princeps* (2.6.2), as was Marcus Antonius (2.22.3); Marius was a *princeps* (2.19.4); Caesar too (2.68.5). Syme (1939), 10, 311–30; Galinsky (1996), 74. The adoption and redefining of the term *princeps* is an informative example of how the Principate co-opts Republican terminology.

[28] Note that the aim of the rebellion put down by Germanicus in the early days of Tiberius was a *nova res publica* (2.125.1): the rebellion's failure implies the continuation of the "old."

(2.127.1). Velleius goes out of his way to defend the standards by which Sejanus – himself of good Republican stock (2.127.3) – was judged, summoning an array of venerable characters from the Republic with whom Sejanus is to be compared: Tiberius Coruncanius, Spurius Carvilius, Cato the Elder, Marius, Cicero, and Asinius Pollio, men who rose from humble origins (most were *novi homines* or "new men") to positions of prominence and respect in Rome (2.128).

These standards come into play on other occasions as well. Velleius lavishes high praise on the consul of 19 BC, Sentius Saturninus, for his "Republican" conduct during his term in office: he employed "time-honored severity and great resolve, emulating the old ways and sternness of the consuls" (*prisca severitate summaque constantia, vetere consulum more [ac severitate]*, 2.92.2), behavior Velleius praises as "comparable to the renown of any of the consuls of days past" (*factum cuilibet veterum consulum gloriae comparandum*, 2.92.5) and which should not be "cheated of memory" (*ne fraudetur memoria*, 2.92.1). This was the man who, on Caligula's death, would lead a movement to restore the Republic (see Chap. 1). Similarly, more than once Tiberius is shown to eschew his imperial authority in favor of more "Republican" procedures (e.g., 2.126.1, 2.129.2).

Time for Tiberius (and Velleius)

Wallace-Hadrill nicely elucidates the way Ovid, in the *Fasti*, "incorporated [Augustus] into the republican year," in effect replicating the emperor's own efforts to insert himself in the "heart of Roman 'time'."[29] While Velleius does not "insert" Tiberius into Roman history, he does conclude his *History* with a detailed, panegyrical account of Tiberius' career, thus making history "end" with Tiberius. This is the "present" by which Velleius measures the "past" chronicled by his *History*. It is perhaps no accident that "time" holds particular interest for Velleius, for through his "time consciousness"[30] we glimpse one way in which he reinforces the notion of continuity and progression from past to present. In the course of making frequent connections between past and present he often measures the precise chronological distance between two events or

---

[29] Wallace-Hadrill (1987), 223–4.   [30] White (1987), 31.

situations – not dates, but distance. In the process he reorients the reader, forcing us to look at Roman history not forward through the past (*ab urbe condita*) but rather backward from the present (e.g., *a temporibus nostris*).[31] Thus a reference to Opimius prompts the observation, addressed directly to his dedicatee Marcus Vinicius, that Opimian wine is no longer to be found, since it has been 150 years between the consulship of Opimius and that of Vinicius (121 BC and AD 30 respectively, 2.7.5).[32] He compares the cost of renting a house fit for a senator in 125 BC with the extravagant rents charged 153 years later in his own day (2.10.1); the year of Cicero's consulship (63 BC) acquires prestige by the fact that Augustus was born in the same year, 92 years ago (2.36.1).[33]

Other times Velleius marks the distance in less precise terms. He identifies the successive owners (among them Cicero) of the house of M. Livius Drusus down to his own day (2.14.3), an instance of the importance attached in the early imperial period especially to well-known Republican owners of houses still in use (discussed further below); he observes that the current Porticus Octaviae still displays the equestrian statues placed in the original structure built by Metellus Macedonicus after 146 BC (1.11.3);[34] Fabrateria in Latium was founded 153 years ago (1.15.4). In one sense such observations merely establish chronological perspective, but rather than splitting the past off from the present, they create a sense of continuity and connection, of what White (drawing on Ricoeur) has called 'within-time-ness'.[35]

---

[31] To mark one occasion – the adoption of Tiberius by Augustus – he employs *both* methods (2.103.3).

[32] Other instances of dating by Vinicius' consulship: 1.8.1, 1.8.4, 1.12.6, 2.65.2; cf. 2.96.2.

[33] Schmitzer (2000), 92–4, discusses additional implications of this conjoining of Cicero and Augustus.

[34] On several occasions Velleius refers to monuments from the Republican period still extant or visible in his day: the Porticus Minucia (Vetus) of 108 BC (2.8.3); an inscription commemorating Sulla's expression of gratitude to Diana in the vicinity of Mt. Tifata (2.25.4).

[35] White (1987), 51–2. In a technical sense (in terms of cognitive psychology, that is) such moves establish the "spatio-temporal spread" within which Velleius' (and thus his readers') memory exists: Gillespie (1992),116–17. One might compare Cicero's attempt to efface the temporal distance between his own time and that of revered ancestors, "who are not far from the memory of this [i.e., the present] age," *qui sunt*

I would cite as another component of that process the extent to which he retrojects himself and his fellow Romans into the past. That is, he envisions past events, no matter how long ago they may have occurred, as having affected "us" (*nos*) (e.g., 2.4.3). It is important to remember the role (however slight) of personal recollection in the narrative. I mentioned in Chapter 1, for example, his reference to the memory of his great-great-great-grandfather at 2.16.2. In addition, he fondly recalls all that he had seen in the course of his service to Marcus Vinicius' father ("with great pleasure I recall so many events, places, people, and cities," *haud iniucunda tot rerum locorum gentium, urbium recordatione perfruor*, 2.101.3, cf. 2.104ff.); mentions the memory of his brother at 2.115.1; and stresses his participation in Tiberius' achievements in Germany (*gessimus*, 2.106.1). Apart from bolstering his historical authority, such recollections bring into play Velleius' long personal connection with and support of the imperial family, another reminder perhaps that this was, after all, being written under the watchful eyes of an emperor.[36]

The way Velleius conjures time is best appreciated via a small excursus devoted to his notion that great talents converge within rather narrow time frames and a single genre. Thus, for example, the heyday of Roman historiography (ending with Livy), he posits, occurred within a single epoch of eighty years. Following additional examples of his theory, he concludes: *sequiturque ut frequens ac mobilis transitus maximum perfecti operis impedimentum sit*, "it follows that the frequent and fickle habit of passing from one preoccupation to the next is the greatest impediment to perfecting anything" (1.17.7). The same principle, it turns out, applies to states, as he argues in the subsequent chapter (1.18). In short, Velleius' preoccupation with time accords with the view that the Roman state is successful, if not "perfect," precisely because it is *not* in the habit of "passing from one preoccupation to the next." Rather it is an unbroken continuum – a continuum that may experience an ebb and flow, but nonetheless a continuum.[37] On this logic Rome has moved not from Republic to Principate, but from Republic to a better Republic.

<haud> procul ab aetatis huius memoria (*Rep.* 1.1.4). In this connection Bettini's (1991), 113–93, discussion of Roman time makes useful reading.

[36] Roller (2001a),181–2, on these personal expressions of "elite gratitude" in Velleius' text.

[37] Other instances of interest in time: 1.7.2–4, 1.8.4, 1.14, 2.29.1, 2.44.4, 2.53.4, 2.90, 2.103.3.

Velleius' cultural gaze

His excursuses on Rome's literary and oratorical lights, something entirely missing in Livy, similarly foster a sense of progression and continuity.[38] Velleius focuses first on characters from the middle Republic (2.9), then on the late Republic and the Augustan period (2.36.2). A reckoning of the deceased writers of the latter period, he imagines, is "foolish" because they are practically in front of our very eyes (*paene stulta est inhaerentium oculis ingeniorum enumeratio...*, 2.36.3; cf. 2.126.1). Roman literary culture is envisioned as a visible plane, with recent writers more readily in sight, earlier writers off in the distance... but the plane they inhabit is the same.[39] Velleius brings this survey down to the present, yet admits that while he admires living writers (*vivorum ... magna admiratio*), a list is too difficult to concoct (2.36.3). The Roman literary tradition is therefore seen to be a relatively unbroken affair, mirroring the political tradition as well.[40]

If it is Velleius' wish to convince his readers that there is no serious "break" between Republic and Principate – indeed, that the Principate is merely a "restored" Republic – what better way to assert that continuation than to argue that the man most closely identified with the Republic, the man who was killed in order to make way for the Principate, is in fact still alive?

"Relics of Cicero"

Syme maintained that "[o]nly a robust faith can discover authentic relics of Cicero in the Republic of Augustus."[41] However, this is perhaps not as true for the Tiberian period as it was for the Augustan. Seneca the Elder,

---

[38] Discussion of these excursuses in Schmitzer (2000), 72–100; Kuntze (1985), 244–53; Hellegouarc'h (1984), 430–2. Schmitzer (2000), 73, offers Livy's excursus on the origins of satire at 7.2.3–7 as a parallel, but Livy focuses on details of the genre rather than on its practitioners.

[39] Compare the view expressed at 2.92.5, where the "present" is something we "see" (and which "overwhelms" us), the "past" something we "hear" (and which "instructs" us).

[40] Schmitzer (2000), esp. pp. 86–7, nicely elucidates the way Velleius ties the political to the cultural.

[41] Syme (1939), 321; on Cicero's general reputation in the imperial period, Pierini (2003).

for instance, devotes *Suasoriae* 6 and 7 (together with the *Controversiae*, a product of the late 30s) to Cicero. And it is through Cicero that Velleius attempts to bridge or even mask the transition from Republic to Empire or Principate. For a loyalist such as Velleius, narrating the triumviral career of the first emperor was an especially tricky business, particularly when it came to the proscription and murder of Cicero. He could scarcely avoid it, yet it is apparent that for Velleius, and for many other Romans, the manner of Cicero's death was a source of genuine anxiety. Here is a relic indeed.

Proscribed by the triumvirs in November of 43, Cicero was hunted down at his villa in Caieta, torn from his litter, his head and hands cut off and carried to Rome to be displayed on a pole in the Forum.[42] Despite the fact that this had occurred some seventy or so years before Velleius wrote his history, the memory of that event remained very much alive, and, as we know from Seneca the Elder, was kept alive in the *suasoriae* practiced in the rhetorical schools.[43] But it was a memory that had been carefully manipulated, as one can see from Velleius' outburst on the murder:

> Furente deinde Antonio simulque Lepido, quorum uterque, ut praediximus, hostes iudicati erant, cum ambo mallent sibi nuntiare quid passi essent quam quid emeruissent, repugnante Caesare sed frustra adversus duos, instauratum Sullani exempli malum, proscriptio. nihil tam indignum illo tempore fuit quam quod aut Caesar aliquem proscribere coactus est aut ab ullo Cicero proscriptus est; abscisaque scelere Antonii vox publica est, cum eius salutem nemo defendisset qui per tot annos et publicam civitatis et privatam civium defenderat. nihil tamen egisti, M. Antoni (cogit enim excedere propositi formam operis erumpens animo ac pectore indignatio), nihil inquam egisti mercedem caelestissimi oris et clarissimi capitis abscisi numerando auctoramentoque funebri ad conservatoris quondam rei publicae tantique consulis incitando necem. rapuisti tu M. Ciceroni lucem sollicitam et aetatem senilem et vitam miseriorem te principe quam sub te triumviro mortem, famam vero gloriamque factorum

---

[42] App. *BC* 4.19–20; Dio 47.8; Plu. *Cic.* 47–9.

[43] For a survey and analysis of the tradition surrounding Cicero's death, Wright (2001); Noè (1984), 44–77. On the declamatory tradition in particular, Roller (1997).

atque dictorum adeo non abstulisti ut auxeris. vivit vivetque per omnem saeculorum memoriam, dumque hoc vel forte vel providentia vel utcumque constitutum rerum naturae corpus, quod ille paene solus Romanorum animo vidit, ingenio complexus est, eloquentia inluminavit, manebit incolume, comitem aevi sui laudem Ciceronis trahet, omnisque posteritas illius in te scripta mirabitur, tuum in eum factum execrabitur, citiusque e mundo genus hominum quam ^{***} cedet.

Then in a fit of madness Antony and Lepidus (each of whom, as we have said, had been declared public enemies), revived the vile practice that originated under Sulla, proscription. Both evidently preferred to make public what they had suffered rather than the punishment they deserved. Caesar resisted, but in vain against these two. Nothing was so shameful at that time as the fact that Caesar was coerced into proscribing someone or that Cicero was proscribed by anyone. The voice of the people was destroyed by Antony's wickedness, since no one defended the safety of the person who for so many years had defended both the public security of the state as well as the private well being of its citizens. Nonetheless, Mark Antony, you achieved nothing – the sheer indignation that bursts forth from my mind and my heart forces me to exceed the scope of my planned work – you achieved nothing, I say, by offering a reward for the destruction of that divine voice and famous head and by goading people with deadly compensation to murder a man who was once the savior of the Republic and a great consul. You stole from Marcus Cicero some anxious time, his old age, a life that, seeing that you were in charge and a triumvir, would have been more wretched than death. Yet you did not so much rob him of the fame and glory of his deeds and his words but rather you increased them. He lives and he *will* live in memory for all eternity, and provided that this body of the nature of things embraces him – whether that body be constituted by chance, providence, or however, and which Cicero alone of almost all Romans saw in his mind and in his intellect and illumined with his eloquence – it will remain intact and have as its companion for as long as it survives the renown of Cicero. All posterity will marvel at Cicero's writings against you, it will decry your treatment of him, and more swiftly will humankind depart from this world than <Marcus Cicero>.   (2.66.1–5)

Here, Octavian – the future Augustus – is excused; blame for the brutality of the deed laid entirely at the feet of Mark Antony, who he claims was motivated by sheer spite. Other, less partisan sources assert Octavian's complicity.

I would draw particular attention to the manner in which Velleius formulates this passage. Woodman astutely notes that it takes the form of a *consolatio*, but at least part of the passage strikes the tone of a *Philippic*. In apparent homage to Cicero's scathing attacks on Antony, Velleius scolds Antony as though he were in fact alive, abusing him in much the same sort of language Cicero used and even lifting a phrase or two from Cicero.[44] This phenomenon – treating and even addressing historical characters as though they were still alive – will receive further discussion below in connection with Valerius Maximus as well as Seneca, both of whom use the device, though this is perhaps the most striking example.[45] The argument, odd though it may seem (despite being quite conventional), is that Cicero is not really dead. Memory will sustain him and continue to give him life: *vivit vivetque per omnem saeculorum memoriam*, "he lives and he will live in memory for all eternity."[46] Substitute "Republic" (*res publica*) for "Cicero" (the *vox publica*, in Velleius' words) – not a far-fetched exercise, given Cicero's identification with the Republic – and one grasps the implications.

Also remarkable is the sheer sense of personal indignation. Why, one might imagine, should an imperial writer like Velleius be so vehement in his defense of the man who fought for the Republic? Of course the problem disappears if you believe that the Republic is in fact *not* dead.

---

[44] Woodman (1983) on 2.66 passim.

[45] Cf. 2.41.1, where Julius Caesar "grabs the pen" of Velleius Paterculus and forces him to write more slowly (*scribenti manum inicit et quamlibet festinantem in se morari cogit*).

[46] Pliny the Younger picks up on this phrase in his discussion of the death of Verginius Rufus: *Vivet enim vivetque semper, atque etiam latius in memoria hominum et sermone versabitur, postquam ab oculis recessit* (*Ep.* 2.1.11); and indeed, Pliny relates to the deceased as though he were alive (*Verginium cogito, Verginium video, Verginium iam vanis imaginibus, recentibus tamen, audio adloquor teneo* (ibid. 12). For Velleius fame and good deeds ensure a sort of continued life after death: cf. his remark about the death of Metellus at 1.11.7: *hoc est nimirum magis feliciter de vita migrare quam mori*. For the conventionality of the idea – and the possibility that Velleius at 2.66.5 imitates Cicero himself at *Marc.* 28 – Woodman (1983) ad loc.

What he has cleverly managed to do is get around a very sticky problem. As I have suggested, the event could hardly be ignored, but nor could he follow the tradition that made Octavian a willing if not enthusiastic collaborator in the murder of the Republic's staunchest defender. So he perverts history just a bit, blaming Antony, exonerating the future emperor, expressing deep sympathy for Cicero. In so doing he perpetuates a very particularized memory of Cicero, as a man to be remembered as the victim of another man bent on personal domination (Antony), as a man who had done and said many unspecified memorable things, but above all as a man famed for his eloquence.[47] But he was assuredly not to be remembered as a man whose political or philosophical views should be emulated or even studied.[48] That, after all, was why he had been killed, as a more forthright historian could have told you. But that piece of information is excised from Velleius' memory of Cicero.

In a sense, then, Velleius has striven to restore some measure of dignity if not relevance to Cicero by memorializing him in this fashion. But if, as I have suggested, his outburst on Cicero reinforces the notion that the Republic continues, that just as Cicero "lives" so too does the Republic live, at the same time his special pleading highlights the damage the Caesarian and triumviral periods were felt to have inflicted on the Republic; the need to argue for Cicero's continuing influence and the continuity of the Republic must imply that there were those who believed just the opposite, that with the death of Cicero so too died the Republic. While we should not dismiss Velleius' views about the "Tiberian Republic" as insincere or contrived, it is nonetheless evident that in writing his history, and especially of (what we call) the late Republic, he recognized the desirability of presenting a memory that made the Republic seem politically close to the state overseen by Tiberius and respected its traditions and icons. This urge to sculpt memory, so apparent in his handling of Cicero's death, is equally on display in Valerius Maximus. Yet as we shall see, while he shares with Velleius similar views about the continuity of the Republic under Tiberius, Valerius comes to that conclusion by a different route.

---

[47] Velleius' respect for Cicero is evident elsewhere as well: cf. 2.34.3–4, 45.2–3. Cf. Val. Max. on Cicero's death at 5.3.4, with Bloomer (1992), 203–4.

[48] *Pace* Schmitzer (2000), 188, who suggests that Cicero's interest in *concordia* found an ally in Tiberius, thus explaining in part Velleius' favorable portrait of the orator.

Valerius Maximus: remembering memories

Valerius' work, an immense compilation of nearly 1,000 anecdotes entitled *Facta et dicta memorabilia* or *Memorable Deeds and Sayings*, similarly bears witness to the interest in historical memory under Tiberius. Composed in the 20s and early 30s AD, this text emulates the less ambitious collections of *exempla* by Varro and Cornelius Nepos, and, of course, contains stories commonly heard in declamatory schools.[49] But apart from providing a useful window onto imperial rhetoric and education, the *Facta et dicta memorabilia* mean to preserve memory, as the title implies. Valerius invariably talks about his task in terms of *memoria* – drawing from *memoria*, preserving *memoria*, and in some cases denying *memoria*.[50] As in Velleius' *History*, this memory is deliberately and explicitly selective, featuring a carefully chosen set of individuals and events in the Republican past as well as a few non-Roman ones. His avowed purpose is to list not everything that is praiseworthy but rather what "ought to be remembered" (*propositi ... nostri ratio non laudanda sibi omnia, sed recordanda sumpsit*, 4.1.12).

Valerius Maximus and Velleius Paterculus further share the view that the Tiberian period was the logical, divinely defined point toward which Roman history was headed (much as many Augustan writers had envisioned their own period). Bloomer has stressed precisely this teleological aspect of Valerius' work, while suggesting that he was driven by a panegyrical impetus.[51] Certainly, the degree to which he operates in the shadow of Tiberius is immediately apparent in the preface to Book 1:

Vrbis Romae exterarumque gentium facta simul ac dicta memoratu digna, quae apud alios latius diffusa sunt quam ut breviter cognosci possint, ab inlustribus electa auctoribus digerere constitui, ut

---

[49] As Bloomer (1992), 5–7 observes, however, Cicero was Valerius' "methodological predecessor"; see further on the precedents for the *Facta et dicta*, ibid. 18–19; for its function as a resource for declamation, ibid. 254–9.

[50] E.g., 1.1.16, 1.6.9, 1.8.6, 2.7.6, 3.7.3, 3.8.6, 5.1.8, 5.4. ext. 3, 8.3.2. Notionally, at least, he conceives his function as similar to that of Ennius, who imparted the *lumen litterarum* to the *memoria* of Scipio (8.14.1).

[51] Bloomer (1992), 185; for comparison of the two authors, ibid. 192–3; more fully Jacquemin (1998). See also Millar (1993), 4–5

documenta sumere volentibus longae inquisitionis labor absit. ... te igitur huic coepto, penes quem hominum deorumque consensus maris ac terrae regimen esse voluit, certissima salus patriae, Caesar, invoco, cuius caelesti providentia virtutes, de quibus dicturus sum, benignissime foventur, vitia severissime vindicantur: nam si prisci oratores ab Iove Optimo Maximo bene orsi sunt, si excellentissimi vates a numine aliquo principia traxerunt, mea parvitas eo iustius ad favorem tuum decucurrerit, quo cetera divinitas opinione colligitur, tua praesenti fide paterno avitoque sideri par videtur, quorum eximio fulgore multum caerimoniis nostris inclutae claritatis accessit: reliquos enim deos accepimus, Caesares dedimus.

The city of Rome and foreign nations have produced both deeds and sayings that are worthy of memory. They are too widely scattered among other writers to be learned in a short time, and so I have decided to compile a selection from well-known authors so that those who wish to locate examples may be spared time-consuming research. ... You, therefore, I invoke for this undertaking, to whom mortals and gods of one accord have willingly entrusted the rule of sea and land, [Tiberius] Caesar, the fatherland's most reliable salvation, by whose heavenly prudence the virtues of which I am about to speak are most kindly encouraged and vices most severely punished. For if the orators of old properly began with Jupiter Best and Greatest, if the finest poets have taken their beginnings from some divine power, my humble person would have recourse to your favor all the more appropriately, in that while the divinity of others is deduced from what is believed about them, your divinity is seen by tangible proof to be equal to the star of your father and grandfather, by whose exceptional splendor much illustrious brilliance has been added to our ceremonies: for we have inherited the other gods, but we have added the Caesars.   (1. *praef.*)

I first draw attention to the first two words: *urbis Romae exterarumque gentium facta simul ac dicta memoratu digna*. His preference for the term *urbs Roma* is not unprecedented, to be sure (cf. Sal. *Cat.* 6.1), and would be duplicated later by Tacitus in the opening words of the *Annales*, but the text to which this should be compared is the preface of one of Valerius' main sources, Livy.[52] In the latter's opening salvo, where the

---

[52] Bloomer (1992), 59–77; Chassignet (1998), esp. 67–72.

preservation of memory is also identified as the primary goal, it is not the city who is named as the text's central character, but the *populus Romanus* or, to be precise, the *res populi Romani* (*Praef.* 1).[53] Valerius' desire to subsume the individual Roman under a generalizing and depersonalizing rubric *urbs Roma* is consistent with what comes next, the dedication to Tiberius. Again the comparison with Livy is instructive: in *his* preface, Augustus is conspicuous by his absence. With Valerius, however, we move slightly away from Livy's rhetorical and seemingly "Republican" stance to one that more explicitly acknowledges the influence of the emperor over literary productions . . . and by extension, over memory. Clearly, in this preface, Valerius takes care not to raise any individual Roman above Tiberius, while acknowledging that his task, the preservation of memory, depends on the inspiration, not to say good will, of the emperor. The recent case of Cremutius Cordus had perhaps made clear the risks associated with such activity.

Despite this, the degree to which Tiberius is excluded from this work is somewhat surprising. Not once is he named again; apart from a few passing references,[54] the only other substantial mention occurs toward the end of the work, in an outburst rather reminiscent of Velleius' tirade about the death of Cicero and in which Valerius upbraids Sejanus for attempted "parricide."[55] In a memory-erasing move, he omits Sejanus' name:

> Sed quid ego ista consector aut quid his immoror, cum unius parricidii cogitatione cuncta scelera superata cernam? omni igitur impetu mentis, omnibus indignationis viribus ad id lacerandum pio magis quam valido adfectu rapior: quis enim amicitiae fide extincta genus humanum cruentis in tenebris sepelire conatum profundo debitae exsecrationis satis efficacibus verbis adegerit? tu videlicet efferatae barbariae immanitate truculentior habenas Romani imperii, quas princeps parensque noster salutari dextera continet, capere potuisti?

---

[53] A crucial distinction, signaling a significant departure from Livy (*pace* Bloomer [1992], 15).

[54] Once as *optimus princeps* (2. *praef.*), twice as *salutaris princeps* (2.9.6, 8.13. *praef.*), twice as the brother of Drusus (4.3.3, 5.5.3). Valerius' references to the emperor's brother – among the rare allusions to contemporary events – seem prompted by his sense of *pietas*. For Valerius' take on Tiberius, Bloomer (1992), 227–9.

[55] For the argument (by which I am unconvinced) that the conspiracy referenced here may *not* be that of Sejanus, Millar (1993), 4 with refs.

aut te compote furoris mundus in suo statu mansisset? urbem a Gallis captam et trecentorum inclutae gentis virorum strage foedatum Alliensem diem, et oppressos in Hispania Scipiones et Trasumennum lacum et Cannas bellorumque civilium domestico sanguine manantes + furores + amentibus propositis furoris tui repraesentare et vincere voluisti. sed vigilarunt oculi deorum, sidera suum vigorem obtinuerunt, arae pulvinaria templa praesenti numine vallata sunt, nihilque quod pro capite Augusti[56] ac patria excubare debuit torporem sibi permisit, et in primis auctor ac tutela nostrae incolumitatis ne excellentissima merita sua totius orbis ruina conlaberentur divino consilio providit. itaque stat pax, valent leges, sincerus privati ac publici officii tenor servatur. qui autem haec violatis amicitiae foederibus temptavit subvertere, omni cum stirpe sua populi Romani viribus obtritus etiam apud inferos, si tamen illuc receptus est, quae meretur supplicia pendit.

But why do I criticize those acts or linger on them, when I see that all crimes have been outdone by the plotting of a single parricide? With every impulse of my mind, therefore, I am swept along by the full force of my indignation, by an emotion more pious than powerful, to destroy that deed. For who could utter, with sufficiently effective words, the curse owed an attempt to bury the human race in blood-soaked shadows preceded by snuffing out the trust of friendship? No doubt you, who are wilder than savage and barbarous brutality, could have held the reins of the Roman empire, which our leading citizen and parent keeps in safe hands. Or had you achieved the aims of your madness, would the world have stayed in its place? Would Rome have been captured by Gauls, the day of the Allia stained with the slaughter of 300 men from a famous family, the Scipios defeated in Spain, Lake Trasimenus and Cannae dripping with native blood spilled in civil war? all insanity, which you wanted to bring forward to the present and surpass through your mindless plans. But the eyes of the gods were awake, the stars maintained their vigor, altars, sacred couches, the temples were protected by a divine presence. And nothing which ought to keep guard over the head of

---

[56] This reading, tenuous at best, was accepted by Briscoe in his 1998 Teubner edition (the text used here) but rejected (I think rightly) by Shackleton-Bailey in the 2000 Loeb edition, who prefers Perizonius' emendation to *augusto*.

Augustus [see n. 56] and our fatherland allowed itself to be lulled; and most of all, the author and protector of our security saw to it with his divine counsel that his most excellent services would not collapse with the ruin of the whole world. So peace persists, laws are in force, the true course of both public and private obligations is preserved. Moreover, he who tried to subvert these things by violating the bonds of friendship has been destroyed together with his whole family by the might of the Roman people and suffers the penalty he deserves, even in the underworld ... if he has been accepted there.   (9.11. ext. 4)

It is fascinating that the chaos Valerius imagines would have been induced had Sejanus succeeded is pictured in terms of a reversal of several key events in Republican history, clear instances of the "insanity" (*furores*[57]) that Sejanus would have "made manifest" or "brought forward to the present" (*repraesentare*) and "surpassed" (*vincere*) by means of his "mindless plans" (*amentibus propositis*).[58] (Recall that Isidore defines people who are *amentes* as *immemores* or "without memory": see Chap. 1 n. 7.) The murder of Tiberius (for that is what he is talking about) would have repercussions not only in the *present* but also in the *past*, as though the act had the potential somehow to "change" history ... and therefore memory.

But it is precisely through the stability and effective governance brought to Rome by Tiberius that evil men like Sejanus are thwarted, thus allowing history and memory to remain intact. It is Valerius' job to transmit that memory – not to show what has changed, but rather to suggest the constancy and continued efficacy of Roman values. So like Velleius, but more explicitly in a moral rather than a political and historical sphere, Valerius Maximus observes no real split between Republic and Principate, merely the ascension of a *princeps*, a man who has "saved" rather than "changed" the state, the *certissima salus patriae* (1. *praef.*).[59]

---

[57] The text, however, is uncertain here: Briscoe (1998) app. crit. ad loc.

[58] Coudry (1998), 47, for discussion of the significance for Valerius of the events here enumerated.

[59] Thus he is the *salutaris princeps* (see n. 27). On Valerius' efforts to efface the distinction between past and present, Bloomer (1992), 11–12, 205–6, 216, 223.

Principle of selection

The *Facta et dicta memorabilia* documents the traditions Tiberius rescues or preserves, and does its part in handing down what in Valerius' view is "worthy to be remembered." Not everything, it turns out; much may safely be forgotten. Bloomer has fully discussed the organization and thrust of the work and, to some extent, what drives the shape and tenor of individual anecdotes.[60] I am interested here in considering briefly some of the criteria for selection.

In the first place, there are temporal limitations; the bulk of the historical events to which he alludes occurred prior to the Augustan period and the battle of Actium in 31 BC. To appreciate the implications of this, imagine a compilation of the deeds of famous Americans that included no one after 1940. That is roughly comparable: with few exceptions Valerius mentions no event in the sixty years or so prior to the composition of his work.[61] In short, the criterion for inclusion here was essentially that you had to be dead and have lived during the Republic.

As we shall presently see via a passage cited below, Valerius will explain the apparent neglect of both the triumviral and (more interestingly) Augustan period. But the gap, and the handy chronological compartmentalization it seems to produce, is rendered far less obvious than it might be through the elision of time. In contrast to Velleius, who, as we saw, is quite precise about marking time, Valerius seldom provides concrete chronological clues.[62] When he does, the references are usually vague (e.g., *vetustas* vs. *saeculum nostrum*, 5.5.3; cf. 8.13. *praef.*, *avorum nostrorum temporibus*, 6.8.1). The stories he tells are in some sense "timeless," and indeed, given their moralistic aim, it simply does not matter *when* a particular event occurred.[63] In Valerius' moral universe, time – just

---

[60] Bloomer (1992), 17–58 and passim; cf. Skidmore (1996), 83–92.

[61] Bloomer (1992), 204. Perhaps not coincidentally, Bayley (1966), 68–9, remarks that in many classic nineteenth-century historical novels (e.g., Pushkin's *The Captain's Daughter*) a sixty-year "event horizon" represents the ideal distance in time between the narrator and his subject: at this remove in time, the past is not yet seen as "something over and done with." (I owe this observation to Denis Feeney.)

[62] As Bloomer (1992), 29–30, has demonstrated, moreover, there is no attempt to observe chronological order within a given chapter.

[63] Valerius' *exempla* therefore lack the sort of context one expects in a historical narrative and in that sense may create a false or incomplete impression of the historical moment

as "life" – is immaterial. The effect is to suggest that the moral values of the Republic and of Tiberian Rome are precisely the same.[64]

That moral universe, however, is fashioned as much by exclusion as it is by inclusion. In his selectivity, Valerius does for Tiberian Rome what Chaplin (2000) claimed Livy did for the Augustan period, by emphasizing certain *exempla* over others on the basis of their relevance for the times. As Chaplin argues, *exempla* are flexible and mutable, adaptable to different situations.[65] In this Valerius does nothing more than exactly what Augustus himself claimed to have done (*RG* 8, quoted in Chap. 1 n. 58). In his case, as I have noted, the bulk of Valerius' *exempla* or anecdotes is pre-Augustan; he is adamant that his interest lies in *exempla* that are *tradita*, "handed down," rather than *nova*, "new" (1.8.7). Ostensibly, then, his pose is not of someone who *creates* memory (as he might do were he to include men like Agrippa and Maecenas, who at a later period *do* take on the status of *exempla*: see Chap. 3 n. 3) but rather hands it down. But even then there are certain events and characters he refuses to memorialize in his work. The civil war between Pompey and Caesar, for instance, causes him considerable discomfort: it is, he claims, a period whose "memory" is "to be loathed" or "should bear adverse witness" (*detestandam memoriam*, 3.3.2).[66] Unpleasant events, bad people, and reprehensible acts do find their way into his work (e.g., under rubrics such as *De ingratis* or *Dicta improba aut facta scelerata*), but generally with apologies or some special pleading (e.g., 9.2. *praef.*).[67] The "memory" of such people and events must be carefully controlled (e.g., *crudelitas* must not be accorded *silentium*, but rather it must be "recalled" [*revocata*] in order to be restrained, ibid.). It is equally apparent that inappropriate or unethical behavior results in a tarnished memory or the denial of memory altogether. Brutus, for instance, though a man of some quality, caused his memory to be drowned in a sea of "irreversible curses" (*omnem nominis sui memoriam inexpiabili detestatione perfudit*,

with which the *exemplum* is associated. As a guide to Republican history, therefore, the value of the work is circumscribed. See David (1998b), 129.

[64] Levick (1976), 91.

[65] Cf. Farrell (1997), 383, referring (in connection with Roman memory) to the "plasticity" of Roman stories.

[66] Cf. 2.7.12, 2.8.7, 6.2.8. Bloomer (1992), 53–4; Wardle (1997), 328–31.

[67] Bloomer (1992), 163–4.

6.4.5); the magnitude of Pompey's *ruina* is such that though Valerius recalls it he cannot narrate it (. . . *ruinam eius* [sc. *fortunae*] *maiorem esse quam ut manu mea attemptari debeat memini*, 5.3.5); Hannibal would have enjoyed *insignem . . . memoriam* had it not been for his erratic behavior (9.6. ext. 2); the only event in the life of the litigious Carfania worthy of *memoria* was her death (8.3.2); Damasippus' foul character causes his *memoria* to be "constricted" or "damaged" (*perstringitur*, 9.2.3); the Ephesians rightly abolished by decree the memory of the utterly foul man who plotted to burn the temple of Diana (*ac bene consuluerant Ephesii decreto memoriam taeterrimi hominis abolendo*, 8.14. ext. 5) – Valerius colludes in this by concealing the man's name.[68] Given this unease, he religiously separates the good from the bad, clearly more interested in "honorable people," the *honesti*, whose memory must be kept distinct from that accorded "base people" (*infimi*, 5.2.10; cf. 8.14. ext. 3). He therefore tends to privilege positive *exempla* over negative (cf. the sentiment expressed at 5.4. *praef.* or 9.3. ext. *praef.*). "Good words and deeds" enjoy the "endless power" (*viribus aeternis*) of "tenacious memory" (*pertinax memoria*, 6.4. *praef.*).

What is to be gained by reading the *Facta et dicta memorabilia*? In part, moral edification. Valerius' *exempla* serve much the same function as the family *imagines* displayed in Roman atria (at one point he actually equates his *exempla* with *imagines*, 9.11. *praef.*). Together with the accompanying *tituli* (reading, in other words, is a component of the process), these *imagines* prompt the viewer to emulate the virtues of the viewed (*effigies maiorum cum titulis suis idcirco in prima parte aedium poni solere ut eorum virtutes posteri non solum legerent sed etiam imitarentur*, 5.8.3). *Imagines*, and thus *exempla*, also bring the past forcefully into the present, compelling us to recall "old events" as though they were "fresh" (*vetera pro recentibus . . . recordari*, 5.4. ext. 1).[69] But they serve a more public, civic purpose as well. The scrutiny of and respect for the past – specifically, the *prisca ac memorabilia instituta* – will benefit the present. For it is through such activity that his citizen-readers come to grasp the *elementa* or the "building blocks" of their current condition under Tiberius (2. *praef.*). The remembered *exempla* of the past provide

---

[68] As he goes on to explain, despite the Ephesians' efforts, the man's name was nonetheless included in Theopompus' *Histories*.

[69] Skidmore (1996), 84–6.

correctives for the shortcomings of the present; through "gazing" (*respicere*) at the heroes of the past, we are "lifted up" (*exsurgamus*) and "remade" (*recreemus*).[70] The Republican past here is not distinct from an imperial present, but rather constitutive of it.

That continuity is evident in another statement about the benefits of contemplating the past, when Valerius specifically compares the educational systems of Greece and Rome, praising the latter for the degree to which its poetry induces the young "to imitate the noteworthy deeds of their ancestors," *egregia superiorum opera*. This, he argues, is what gave rise to the Camilli, Scipios, the Fabricii, the Marcelli, the Fabii...and the divine Caesars (*inde oriebantur Camilli Scipiones Fabricii Marcelli Fabii, ac ne singula imperii nostri lumina simul percurrendo sim longior, inde, inquam, caeli clarissima pars, divi fulserunt Caesares*, 2.1.10). Thus under a single heading (*imperium nostrum*) Valerius lumps Rome's leading Republican "lights" together with the "Caesars." To be sure, an important distinction is made: the Caesars warrant the epithet *divi* whereas the others do not. This is related to the phenomenon we observed in his Preface to Book 1; and, rather more interestingly, in Horace *C.* 1.12 discussed in Chapter 1, which trots out several of the same characters, thereby suggesting some continuity of perspective between the Augustan and Tiberian periods.

Valerius' living dead

Valerius links past and present in a rather more curious way too. If time is merely relative, then so is life, in Valerius' view, and thus he refers to "dead" characters as though they were in fact alive. This follows from the characterization of his *exempla* as *imagines*, and accords with the Roman view of *memoria* which, as I discussed in Chapter 1, is one means of

---

[70] *Haec igitur exempla respicere, his adquiescere solaciis debemus .... quid ergo modicam fortunam quasi praecipuum generis humani malum diurnis nocturnis conviciis laceramus, quae ut non abundantibus ita fidis uberibus Publicolas Aemilios Fabricios Curios Scipiones Scauros hisque paria robora virtutis aluit. exsurgamus potius animis pecuniaeque aspectu debilitatos spiritus pristini temporis memoria recreemus: namque per Romuli casam perque veteris Capitolii humilia tecta et aeternos Vestae focus, fictilibus etiam nunc vasis contentos, iuro nullas divitias talium virorum paupertati posse praeferri* (4.4.11). Other instances where past virtues are suggested as correctives to present shortcomings: 4.3.7, 4.4.7, 4.8.4

keeping the dead alive. Characters from the Republican past are frequently addressed directly, in the second person; occasionally they actively influence the narrative. This is a species of *enargeia*, a standard rhetorical trope whereby a speaker conjures a visual image in the mind of the listener, employed here in a text. Valerius creates in the mind of his reader, that is, a vivid image of the character actually acting in the text, in "real time." *Enargeia* is in fact closely linked to *memoria*, the vehicle by which these images are summoned.[71] Crassus intervenes, for instance, to make sure Valerius does not pass him by in silence (1.6.11); Cloelia makes him "forget" his task (3.2.2); Bibulus – like Julius Caesar in Velleius (2.41.1, see above with n. 45) – grabs Valerius' pen and forces him to write about him (4.1.15).[72] These are not necessarily empty rhetorical gestures. The fame of these individuals – their memory – has rendered them deathless and therefore able (like Velleius' Cicero and Caesar) to influence events in the present. As he puts it in discussing one famous *exemplum*, even in their tombs such individuals are alive – *tumulis etiam nunc vivitis* (5.4. ext. 3); this is perhaps related to Augustine's view that one's memory preserves not *simulacra*, but *res ipsas*, thus effectively dispensing with the separation implied by death (*Conf*. 10.16). It is important to stress, however, that this privilege is extended exclusively to "admirable" characters; with one exception – Cassius, the assassin of Caesar (1.8.8) – no individual of questionable moral character is ever addressed or allowed to intervene in the narrative.

---

[71] Cf. Quint. *Inst*. 6.2.29–32, with Vasaly (1993), 89–104.

[72] Other exx.: Cato (4.1.14), Romulus (3.2. *praef.*), Scipio Africanus (4.1.10), Scipios as a group (8.15.5). In many instances a character refuses to be "passed over in silence" or, in other words, consigned to oblivion. For the equation of the two (silence and oblivion) in Roman thought, Gowing (2000), 51; see, e.g., Val. Max. 8.2.2. Apostrophes to characters as though alive: Caesar (1.6.13, 6.8.4), Cassius (1.8.8), Postumus Tubertus and Manlius Torquatus (2.7.6), Mars (2.7.7), Aemilius Paulus Macedonicus (2.10.3), Romulus (3.2. *praef.*), Cato (3.2.14), M. Cassius Scaeva (3.2.23), Porcia (4.6.5), *amicitia* (4.7.3–4), Sempronia sister of the Gracchi and wife of Scipio A. (3.8.6), Cimon (5.4. ext. 2), *vetustissimi foci* (5.4.7), unnamed Spanish brothers (5.4. ext. 3), Pudicitia (6.1. *praef.*), Pompey (5.3.5), *mens* (7.2. ext. 1), Cleanthes (8.7. ext. 11). As Bloomer (1992), 160–1, notes, such addresses are a familiar feature of declamatory schools and, together with other rhetorical devices, serve to "collapse the distance between author, text, and reader" (ibid. 252).

Two examples

I would like to consider two examples that illustrate some of the observations made above – about the *exempla* Valerius selects for inclusion,
the way he masks time, and his emphasis on positive over negative
exempla. They show as well how in his evasion of certain details
Valerius perverts memory. What I mean by this is simply that comparison with other sources reveals that he has imposed on the *exemplum* a
meaning rather different from that it may have already possessed. Both
examples are taken from a section in Book 6, which has as its title *Libere
dicta et facta* or, loosely rendered, "outspokenness." The key word of
course is *libere*. Given the equation of *libertas* with the Republic (discussed
in Chapter 1) and Valerius' pointed qualifications of the concept in his
preface, this section holds particular interest. As Valerius explains, he
approves of *libertas*, but only in moderation; extremes are to be avoided.[73]

As one example he tells a short story involving Pompey the Great:

> Cn. Lentulus Marcellinus consul, cum in contione de Magni Pompei
> nimia potentia quereretur, adsensusque ei clara voce universus popu-
> lus esset, "acclamate" inquit, "acclamate, Quirites, dum licet: iam
> enim vobis inpune facere non licebit." pulsata tunc est eximii civis
> potentia hinc invidiosa querella, hinc lamentatione miserabili.

> When complaints were being registered in an assembly about the
> excessive power of Pompey the Great, and everyone was loudly
> proclaiming their agreement, the consul Cn. Lentulus Marcellinus
> remarked, "Protest while you can, Quirites, for soon you will not be
> able to do so with impunity." At that moment, the power of a
> distinguished citizen was beaten down by an odious complaint on
> the one hand and a dire lament on the other.   (6.2.6)

Marcellinus' remark, in Valerius' view, is an example of "free speech,"
whose consequence was the diminution of the power of an *eximius civis*,
an "outstanding citizen." What these two sentences lack entirely, of
course, is any context, in itself a memory-destroying move;[74] we have
no idea, really, of what the people are complaining about, nor is it exactly

---

[73] Bloomer (1992), 54–6.   [74] Fentress and Wickham (1992), 73–4.

clear whether we should regard Marcellinus' remark with approval or not. What matters is that we note the power of Marcellinus' words to have a dramatic result. Now, Pompey the Great was a tremendously problematic figure, given his undeniable reputation as a great general and his association with the defenders of the Republic. But in his several references to Pompey, Valerius manages to deprive him of any real explicit political significance, and thereby safely navigates some tricky waters: to be able to include Pompey (whose memory could scarcely be erased) and yet render him politically innocuous was an accomplishment.[75] This passage is a good example of how he achieves that.

It happens that we do know the context for this story: the year was 56 BC, and Crassus and Pompey had just decided to take sides against Caesar. Pompey had tried to orchestrate his election to a consulship, but was thwarted in the attempt by Marcellinus. Cassius Dio relates the story as an example of one of many ways in which Pompey double-dealt with Caesar (39.28.5). Valerius, by contrast, has stripped it of at least *that* meaning, and returned to us instead an *exemplum* which, deprived of an historical framework, can serve only as a lesson in the power of words spoken with excessive *libertas* to bring someone down.[76]

One final example. An anecdote about Cato the Younger immediately precedes the story about Pompey and Marcellinus. Valerius knows that his readers will be looking for a Cato anecdote, especially in a section dealing with *libertas*. Like Pompey, this arch enemy of Caesar who took his own life in 46 BC to evade capture, is simply unavoidable; no character from the late Republic was more controversial or more closely identified with the demise of the Republic, *libertas*, and opposition to monarchy. Indeed, the anecdote acknowledges that identification at the outset:

> libertas sine Catone? non magis quam Cato sine libertate: nam cum in senatorem nocentem et infamem reum iudex sedisset, tabellaeque Cn. Pompei laudationem eius continentes prolatae essent, procul dubio efficaces futurae pro noxio, summovit eas e quaestione legem recitando, qua cautum erat ne senatoribus tali auxilio uti liceret. huic

---

[75] On Valerius' handling of Pompey, Bloomer (1992), 207–26.

[76] As Bloomer (1992), 56, puts it in discussing Valerius' views of *libertas* and associated *exempla*, "Valerius' anecdotes quite obviously commemorate correct behavior and become problematic when the inherited paradigms jar with contemporary codes."

facto persona admirationem adimit: nam quae in alio audacia videretur, in Catone fiducia cognoscitur.

Can there be freedom without Cato? No more than there can be Cato without freedom. For when he was serving as judge in the case of a notoriously corrupt senator and some documents conveying Pompey's support for the man were brought forward (which would without doubt have been very useful for the cad), Cato had them removed from the court, invoking the law which admonished that senators could not make use of such aids. No surprise, given the character of Cato: for what might seem to be audacity in another person, in Cato is regarded as self-assurance. (6.2.5)

Valerius views this display of *libertas* as a mark of Cato's influence, which in this instance protected him. Here, too, we lack context. But we know from Plutarch (*Cato* 48, *Pomp.* 55) and Dio (40.52.2, 55.2) that this episode occurred in the year 52 BC, when Pompey was consul; and both Plutarch and Dio tell the story as an illustration of Cato's efforts to undermine the excessive power of Pompey at a time when it seemed as though Pompey and Caesar might reconcile. In Valerius, however, Cato's *libertas* is seen not as allied with an effort to safeguard the Republic, but merely as a form of free expression. Thus while he expresses considerable admiration for Cato – indeed, he reveres him as the model Roman citizen (2.10.8; cf. 3.2.14) – at no point does he allude to Cato's opposition to Caesar.[77]

Such seemingly small tweakings of memory – good examples of the "plasticity" of Roman stories remarked by Farrell (see above with n. 65) – reflect an effort to maintain that connection with the Republican past while at the same time softening some of its potentially risky meanings. The *Facta et dicta memorabilia* marks a transition to a period when, whatever Tiberius might claim or even wish, the simple fact of the emperor's power was having a profound effect on the way authors such as Valerius Maximus and Velleius Paterculus presented the Republic.

---

[77] One finds, for instance, quite a different emphasis on Cato in (e.g.) Cic. *Off.* 1.112. For general discussion of Cato in Valerius Maximus, see Bloomer (1992), 187–91; Freyburger (1998), 113–14. Cf. Valerius' treatment of Cicero which, as Bloomer (1992), 194, discusses, serves to "forget" the "historical optimate . . . in lieu of a more serviceable abstraction"; cf. Pierini (2003), 31–3.

While both might seek to preserve memories of the Republic, the memories they serve up require some manipulation. This is merely the foreshadowing of a development we shall observe in subsequent chapters: as the time and distance between the Republic and the Principate grew, it would become increasingly difficult *not* to acknowledge that politically, morally, and culturally Rome was turning into a very different place.

If they share similar views about the worth of Tiberius and the degree to which the Republic continues under his watchful eye, a distinction between Velleius and Valerius lies precisely in the character of Tiberius in their work. Tiberius is not only present in Velleius' *History*, he constitutes its climax, its point. Rather than attempting to distance the emperor from the Republic, Velleius conjoins the two, effacing any perceived separation between them. Whereas Tiberius comes at the end of Velleius' *History*, he stands at the very beginning of Valerius' *Facta et dicta memorabilia*, lending both authority and approval to the project ... and then essentially disappearing from it (a move Tiberius might have appreciated, given his reluctance to rule). Yet the gap Valerius seemingly creates by limiting the selection of *exempla* to the pre-Augustan period is rendered largely invisible through the absence of dates and context. Distinctions of genre alone cannot explain this difference; Velleius could easily have terminated his history with the death of Augustus, Valerius could easily have adduced later *exempla*. It is the precisely the authority of Republican *exempla* Valerius wishes to exploit in order to renew their moral relevance for Tiberian Rome – even if it is true that the Principate no longer offers precisely the same scope to engage in the sort of activities that Republican aristocrats enjoyed;[78] and for Velleius, it is important to have his account of the Republic include, indeed end with Tiberius. Despite their differing uses of Tiberius, in both authors the principles of exclusion and inclusion are very much at work, fashioning a memory of the Republic for an era that has neither fully dissociated from nor fully replicated it.

Remembering Tiberius

To return, then, to Tiberius himself. As we have seen, early in his regime Tiberius revealed his own anxiety over memory and his attempts to

---

[78] I am not *fully* persuaded by Bloomer's (1992), 55, conclusion that Valerius' *exempla* are "parables not paradigms."

control it. The trial of Cremutius Cordus, alluded to in Chapter 1, becomes in Tacitus the quintessential moment when that anxiety comes to a head. The question of how *Tiberius* is to be remembered becomes an issue, in Tacitus' narrative, directly after the conclusion of Cordus' trial in AD 25. Faced with a request from the Spanish legation for permission to construct a shrine to Tiberius and Livia, the emperor explains his refusal:

"Ego me, patres conscripti, mortalem esse et hominum officia fungi satisque habere, si locum principem impleam, et vos testor et meminisse posteros volo; qui satis superque memoriae meae tribuent, ut maioribus meis dignum, rerum vestrarum providum, constantem in periculis, offensionum pro utilitate publica non pavidum credant. haec mihi in animis vestris templa, hae pulcherrimae effigies et mansurae; nam quae saxo struuntur, si iudicium posterorum in odium vertit, pro sepulchris spernuntur. proinde socios cives et [deos et] deos ipsos precor, hos ut mihi ad finem usque vitae quietam et intellegentem humani divinique iuris mentem duint, illos ut, quandoque concessero, cum laude et bonis recordationibus facta atque famam nominis mei prosequantur." perstititque posthac secretis etiam sermonibus aspernari talem sui cultum. quod alii modestiam, multi, quia diffideret, quidam ut degeneris animi interpretabantur. optimos quippe mortalium altissima cupere; sic Herculem et Liberum apud Graecos, Quirinum apud nos deum numero additos. melius Augustum, qui speraverit. cetera principibus statim adesse: unum insatiabiliter parandum, prosperam sui memoriam; nam contemptu famae contemni virtutes.

"As for me, senators, I ask you to remember – and I want posterity to remember – that I am a mortal, performing mortal tasks, and that I shall consider it enough to have fulfilled my duties as *princeps*. People will more than adequately serve my memory, provided they consider that I have conducted myself in a manner worthy of my ancestors, mindful of your affairs, steady in the face of danger, undaunted by opposition when it came to the public interests. In your minds these shall be my temples, these my glorious and enduring images. For those things built of stone, should the judgment of posterity turn into hatred, come to be despised as mere tombs. Therefore I beseech our allies and citizens as well as the gods themselves: may the former grant me a calm mind, one cognizant of both human and divine law,

63

until the end of my days; the latter, that, whenever I pass on, they would accord my deeds and my reputation honor and good memories." And thereafter he persisted in scorning veneration of himself, even in private conversation. This fact some attributed to his modesty, many to his diffidence, a few to a base spirit. For the best of mortals, it was said, aim at the highest: thus did Hercules and Bacchus earn a place among the gods with the Greeks, as did Quirinus with us; Augustus did better precisely because of his aspirations. Other benefits come to emperors as a matter of course. One thing, however, they must constantly tend to: that their memory be favorable. For to disdain one's reputation is to disdain virtue. (4.38)

Even here, some eleven years into his reign, Tiberius continues to play the Republican card. As ironic as the term may seem, especially in the hands of Tacitus, Tiberius' claim to be *princeps*, like Velleius' use of *principatus*, is a purely Republican move. (The irony is apparent, for when invoked by the nameless commentators in the latter part of the passage quoted – that is, outside of Tiberius' speech – the term clearly means "emperors"). This is confirmed both by the insistence on his own mortality as well as by the appeal to the verdict of his "ancestors." Memory is a mental activity, assured by good deeds (cf. Velleius in n. 46), not something secured through monuments. This seemingly veiled reference to – and repudiation of – the large Mausoleum Augustus had constructed in the Campus Martius are surely not to be taken seriously, but it is nonetheless representative of Tiberius' desire to be viewed as an *aequalis civis*.

This preoccupation with memory on the part of Tiberius – and apparent as well, I have argued, in the historiography and literature of the period (thus not entirely a figment of Tacitus' imagination) – reflects a larger concern in Tiberian society about the relevance of the Republican past for the present. The cynicism with which Velleius and Valerius have typically been read may well be unwarranted. Rather, their work should be seen less as unintentional obituaries for Republican history and values, more as an attempt to recuperate that past before it was too late.

Tiberius' obituary, on the other hand, provides a fitting conclusion, for imperial death scenes tell us much about how an emperor was to be remembered. It was, for instance, of some importance to his biographers to note that Augustus had died in the same room as his father had. Such favorable coincidences suggested a comforting sense of continuity and connection, a sort of circularity. Thus when we are told that Tiberius died on March 16 in AD 37 in the famous villa at Misenum that had once belonged to the Republican voluptuary Lucullus, the memory of Lucullus becomes linked with the memory of Tiberius; the life of the former is understood as in some sense an iteration of the latter's.[79] At least some of the associations could be flattering and desirable: Lucullus was, after all, a successful general (like Tiberius), joined in a second marriage to the niece of Cato the Younger, allied for most of his career with the cause of the optimates. But our sources incline toward a less complimentary read, of a dissolute man who retired to a private and secluded pleasure-palace on the Bay of Naples. That association seems quite deliberate. A list of the villa's owners reads like a who's who in late Republican history – Marius (the original builder), Sulla's daughter Cornelia (from whom Lucullus purchased the property in the mid-60s BC), Julius Caesar. Despite the fact that Lucullus was neither the first owner of the villa nor perhaps even the most famous, it is nonetheless the association with *Lucullus* that the sources wish to stress in narrating the emperor's death. The association was a contemporary one: Tiberius' use of the villa had been commemorated by Phaedrus in 2.5, the fabulist, too, evidently alive to a suggestive linking of these two men.[80]

Thus the *princeps* who wished to be remembered for the extent to which he embodied Republican virtues is instead associated with one of the worst examples the Republic had to offer, a man on whom Velleius fixes the blame for the contemporary obsession with luxury (2.33.4) and who receives mere passing reference in Valerius Maximus.

The emperor's dying moment was itself rich in symbolic possibilities. We are told that as death was near Tiberius removed his ring as though to give it to someone (presumably Gaius) and then placed it back on his finger, clenching his fist lest it should be removed.[81] The act of a man refusing to relinquish power? or of one making a final attempt to prevent power from passing to the hands of a single individual?

---

[79] Tiberius' death: Tac. *Ann.* 6.50, Suet. *Tib.* 73 (the Elder Seneca cited as the source). On the villa, McKay (1972), 12–18; D'Arms (1970), 23–8, 184–6.

[80] Henderson (2001), 22–3.

[81] Suet. *Tib.* 73.2; at *Cal.* 12 a different version, where Caligula attempts to remove the ring but Tiberius resists, whereupon he is suffocated.

Whatever the truth of the matter, with the death of Tiberius the *res publica* passed into the hands of a man who was not reluctant to be declared a god . . . and at whose hands the *principatus* would be revealed for the sham it was. A throwback not to the Republic, but to the monarchy (Suet. *Cal.* 22.1).

"Caesar, now be still"

In the *De clementia*, addressed to the nineteen-year-old Nero, Seneca expresses relief that the freshly minted emperor has shown that he will not 'forget himself':

> Magnam adibat aleam populus Romanus, cum incertum esset, quo se ista tua nobilis indoles daret; iam vota publica in tuto sunt; nec enim periculum est, ne te subita tui capiat oblivio.

> The Roman people were taking a big gamble, since it was unclear where that noble talent of yours would lead; now the prayers of the people are assured, for there is no risk that you will suddenly forget yourself. (*Cl.* 1.1.7)

The *De clementia*, in which this passage appears, and the *De beneficiis*, the source of the passage quoted at the beginning of Chapter 1, are the two most substantial texts written by Seneca in the first couple of years of Nero's reign and prior to his retirement in AD 62; both most likely date to 55 and 56, the second and third years of the Neronian Principate.[1] The *De clementia*, explicitly, and the *De beneficiis*, implicitly, offer advice to the young emperor.[2] Whatever one may conclude about the nature and aim of that advice, Seneca considers what the emperor remembers – or forgets – to be of some importance. As it turns out, this is true not only of the emperor; Seneca regards memory as vital to individuals and society at large. But memory of what? At least in the case of the *De clementia*,

---

[1] For the dates, Griffin (1976), Appendices A1 and A3.
[2] Griffin (2000), 535–51, discusses the two texts.

Seneca is quite clear about this. Outlining the purpose of the text, he claims that it will function as a mirror – a *speculum* – for Nero, a looking glass into which the emperor can peer and see himself (*Cl.* 1.1.1). *That* will be his memory, the record of what he must remember. The text, therefore, contains and equips Nero with memory. Yet somewhat surprisingly, in the *De clementia* Seneca hardly ever refers to any person or event prior to the Augustan period; this is quite a different approach from that of Valerius Maximus who generally stops short of the Augustan period in recording what he considered memorable.[3] Evidently, for Seneca there was little from the Republican past that warranted remembering, at least in connection with the subject of mercy. And indeed, *clementia* was a peculiarly imperial virtue, largely unnecessary in a free *res publica* of equals under the law.

Generally speaking, the diminishing appeal of the Republican past in these two texts anticipates the situation in the Neronian period. As I suggested in the last chapter, with a widening chronological gap between Republic and Principate and as the Principate itself acquired a "history" that warranted memory and memorialization (in effect displacing or at least overshadowing the Republican past) and emerged as a separate entity from the Republic, the ways in which it was remembered, and the value accorded that memory, underwent change. This coincided, of course, with a regime that did not represent itself, at least to the degree that the Tiberian did, as a continuation of the Republic. In contrast to the Tiberian period when, as we saw, a fairly substantial interest in the Republican past manifested itself in historiography proper as well as in Valerius' compilation of historical *exempla*, the rich Neronian literary and artistic tradition dwells very little on that past.

This chapter examines the most striking exception to that general truth – Lucan's *Pharsalia* – in juxtaposition to his uncle Seneca's *Epistulae morales* (*Moral Letters*), a text which, in its deployment of Republican *exempla*, stands in stark contrast to both Lucan's work and

---

[3] References in the *De clementia* to events and characters from the Republic are essentially two: Sulla at 1.12.1–3 and Vedius Pollio at 1.18.2. Compare the tendency evident in the exchange between Seneca and Nero in AD 62 (when Seneca's influence was waning) in Tac. *Ann.* 14.53: advising the emperor of the wisdom of retirement, he invokes *magna exempla ... fortunae ... tuae*, namely, Agrippa and Maecenas (cf. 14.52.4).

its Tiberian predecessors, especially the *Facta et dicta memorabilia* of Valerius Maximus. One difference between the two sets of comparanda examined in this and the previous chapter will be immediately apparent. Whereas Velleius Paterculus and Valerius Maximus present a fairly united front – and a very positive picture of the emperor and his relationship to the past – Lucan and Seneca offer two essentially contrasting perspectives on what I see as a fundamental devaluation of Republican history in the Neronian period.[4] It is surely no coincidence that, as Sion-Jenkis has stressed, Seneca is the first imperial writer to concede *explicitly* that the Augustan Principate marked a real change in the character of the *res publica*.[5] Moreover, in comparing the two texts discussed in this chapter, one should bear in mind that they were composed at roughly the same time, between 61 and 65; that both uncle and nephew had experienced something of a falling out with Nero; and that both, by virtue of being implicated in the Pisonian conspiracy against the emperor, took their own lives in 65, though Lucan's complicity seems rather more certain than Seneca's.[6]

History and memory in Seneca: a Neronian perspective

As a barometer of changing attitudes between the late Republic and the Neronian period, the question of history and memory in Seneca merits special consideration. As one might expect, Seneca recognizes the value of both history and memory and, like Cicero, posits a close connection between the two. His interest in history has been most succinctly documented by Emilio Castagna (1991). Castagna observed that it is possible to construct a fairly full history of the Republic from the extensive works of Seneca. A few of his conclusions bear repeating. Seneca is seldom interested in history or historical writing per se; he seems to have, that is,

---

[4] On the whole my observations complement rather than duplicate Roller's (2001a) illuminating comparison of the pair (chaps. 1 and 2).

[5] Cf. Sen. *Ep.* 71: *Quidni ille mutationem rei publicae forti et aequo pateretur animo? Mutatio*, of course, is the operative word; *res publica* continued to be the term used simply to designate the "state", though the double-sided nature of the term could prove problematic. For discussion, Sion-Jenkis (2000), 23, 51, also 55–63 (collecting other instances of a similar acknowledgment in imperial literature).

[6] On the conspiracy, Griffin (1984), 166–70; MacMullen (1966), 26–7.

no clearly developed philosophy of history. He has some well-defined likes and dislikes: Cato the Younger, for instance, clearly occupies a privileged position in Seneca's moral universe. Caesar more often than not is criticized, Pompey is the object of sympathy. But there is also considerable ambiguity and inconsistency, as in his treatment of Scipio Africanus, another frequently adduced *exemplum*. What Castagna did not explicitly discuss, perhaps because the point is obvious, is that Seneca is chiefly interested in individuals rather than in events or institutions. In contrast to Cicero, for instance, he seldom engages in debate about right and proper forms of government. Rather, he fixes his attention on morals and ethics, on how men should *conduct* themselves rather than how they should *govern* themselves, and to that end he adduces examples from the history of the Republic and from other periods as well.[7] Moreover, he rarely records the historical details of an individual's actions, but (like Valerius Maximus) merely remarks whether they behaved well or badly, with clemency or cruelty, with anger or in compassion, with bravery or in cowardice.

But the most important deduction to be made from Castagna's study – and this is corroborated by other studies of Seneca's *exempla* – is that references to Republican personalities figure most prominently in what Seneca wrote under Claudius; they decrease noticeably in the works written after his retirement under Nero in 62 – more specifically, the *Epistulae morales*, which are written entirely in that period and together with the *Naturales quaestiones* constitute the last of Seneca's writings until his suicide in 65.[8] Few scholars have found this particularly interesting, but in a period (the Neronian) when, according to Tacitus and other sources, the members of the aristocracy were being specifically targeted as "Republicans" – the so-called "Stoic opposition" – it must have some significance that Seneca seems to appeal less often to the Republic.[9]

---

[7] Griffin (2000), 533–5. Thus MacMullen (1966), 63–4, characterizes Senecan Stoicism as "inward and philosophic," in search of "a freedom that is no longer political but moral."

[8] Castagna (1991), 91–8; Mayer (1991), 159–60.

[9] Griffin (1976), chap. 5, does observe shifts in Seneca's use of historical *exempla* over time. Stoic opposition: cf. Cossutianus Capito at Tac. *Ann.* 16.22.4–5 or Tigellinus at 14.57.3, accusing, respectively, Thrasea Paetus and his supporters and Rubellius

His views on the merits of history – and of Republican history in particular – come into sharper focus if we consider his views on memory, a subject to which he had given considerable thought. In certain respects his views are conventional, and have much in common with the sort of things we find in Cicero and, perhaps most tellingly, in an important source for Roman memory, his own father, Seneca the Elder, who in the preface to Book 1 of the *Controversiae* addresses the subject at some length. Like Cicero and his father, Seneca holds that the memory of the past needs to be cultivated and passed on; failure to recollect and recollect often will cause us to forget that which we should remember (*Ep.* 72.1, *Ben.* 3.2.3). Writing, he understands, plays a crucial role in the preservation of memory. He is insistent about this. Letter 21, for example, remarks how Cicero preserves the memory of Atticus; interestingly (because he seems to make no distinction in this regard between an orator and a poet), Seneca adduces Vergil as a second example. Like Cicero, Vergil is also a preserver of memory:

> nomen Attici perire Ciceronis epistulae non sinunt. nihil illi profuisset gener Agrippa et Tiberius progener et Drusus Caesar pronepos; inter tam magna nomina taceretur nisi <sibi> Cicero illum adplicuisset. profunda super nos altitudo temporis veniet, pauca ingenia caput exerent et in idem quandoque silentium abitura oblivioni resistent ac se diu vindicabunt. quod Epicurus amico suo potuit promittere, hoc tibi promitto, Lucili: habebo apud posteros gratiam, possum mecum duratura nomina educere. Vergilius noster duobus memoriam aeternam promisit et praestat:
>
> > fortunati ambo! si quid mea carmina possunt,
> > nulla dies umquam memori vos eximet aevo,
> > dum domus Aeneae Capitoli immobile saxum
> > accolet imperiumque pater Romanus habebit.

Cicero's letters prevent the name of Atticus from perishing. Atticus would have gained nothing from having Agrippa as his son-in-law, Tiberius as his granddaughter's husband, and Drusus Caesar his great-grandson. He would lie silent in the midst of such great names had he not bound Cicero to him as a friend. A deep flood of time will

Plautus of sham Republicanism. Griffin (1976), 171–7; Brunt (1975); Sullivan (1985), 115–52; MacMullen (1966), 21–3, 46–70, and passim.

overwhelm us; few are the talents who will rise above it and, despite the inevitability of departing at some point to the realms of silence, resist and for a long time overcome oblivion. That which Epicurus was able to promise his friend, I promise you, Lucilius. I shall find favor among our descendants; I can take with me names that will endure. Vergil promised and secured undying memory for two men:

> Blessed are you both! if my poetry has any power,
> no day will ever erase you from the memory of time,
> so long as the house of Aeneas inhabits the unmovable citadel
> of the Capitoline and the Roman father wields power. [*A.* 9.446–9]
> (*Ep.* 21.4–5)

Apart from demonstrating something we shall see Seneca has in common with Lucan – a belief that poetry is just as capable of transmitting historical memory as prose (incidentally, Lucan will allude to this same episode in Vergil) – this passage confirms that his letters, like Cicero's, will similarly preserve memory. That memory will be not merely of Lucilius, but perhaps more importantly, of Seneca's own thought and as a subset of that, of what he considered "memorable" about certain historical characters.

In Seneca's opinion, part of the reason these "memory caretakers" matter is because they preserve for us individuals whom we may find of particular service. Thus we acquire, by virtue of the historical record (a phrase I use loosely), *exempla*; from among them we are to choose those who may make particularly good models for us (e.g., *Ep.* 52.7–8).[10] This, of course, is precisely what we look for in texts such as Valerius Maximus' *Facta et dicta memorabilia*. Seneca imagines these "good" people as inhabiting our minds and our memories; like Valerius, he often addresses his *exempla* as though they were present and alive.[11] In the contemplation of the "memory" of one of these individuals, and as though they are watching us, we order and arrange our own life:

---

[10] Maso (1999), 77–8. Further on Senecan *exempla* Roller (2001a), 88–97.

[11] E.g., *Epp.* 25.6, 67, 71.15, 87.9; for the similar practice of Valerius Maximus see discussion in Chap. 2. Thus Castagna (1991), 106, is not quite right to assert that in the Senecan model "la memoria non ridà vita al passato." In the absence of their *praesentia*, the *memoria* of great men is the next best thing (*Ep.* 102.30).

accipe, et quidem utilem ac salutarem, quam te adfigere animo volo: "aliquis vir bonus nobis diligendus est ac semper ante oculos habendus, ut sic tamquam illo spectante vivamus et omnia tamquam illo vidente faciamus." hoc, mi Lucili, Epicurus praecepit ... aliquem habeat animus quem vereatur, cuius auctoritate etiam secretum suum sanctius faciat. o felicem illum qui non praesens tantum sed etiam cogitatus emendat! o felicem qui sic aliquem vereri potest ut ad memoriam quoque eius se componat atque ordinet!

Listen to this useful and salutary piece of advice, which I want you to fix in your mind: "You should choose and keep before your eyes someone good, and live as though that person were watching you and do everything as though they were looking." This is Epicurus' advice, Lucilius ... The mind should have someone whom it respects, by whose authority it renders even its innermost shrine still more sacred. Happy is the person who can correct [us] not only when he is actually present but even when he exists in our thoughts! Happy is the person who is able to respect someone to such an extent that he also composes and regulates himself in accordance with his memory of that model.   (*Ep.* 11.8–9)

It is important to bear in mind, however, that we are entirely free to pick and choose: if Cato is relevant to our purposes, choose him; if not, choose someone else (ibid. 11.10). When we read the *Epistulae*, however, the choice is of course ready-made for us; what we get is a very selective perspective on the past – what *Seneca*, in short, considers memorable. In *that* sense his own writings provide a snapshot of memory in the Neronian period. To be sure, every reader will bring to the reading of Seneca and his *exempla* some prior knowledge of these characters, but Seneca's text nonetheless presents us with its own fixed picture or memory, the contemplation of which in turn makes it part of our own memory.

At the same time however – and this is where he significantly parts company with Cicero – he also considers memory the enemy of innovation. This is most clearly explained in Letter 33, where he distinguishes between "memory" and "knowledge":[12]

---

[12] Cf. the distinction between *memoria* and *sensus* at *Ep.* 95.61: both are processes by which we "comprehend" things that are *aperta* (i.e., obvious or readily available information).

quousque sub alio moveris? impera et dic quod memoriae tradatur aliquid et de tuo profer. omnes itaque istos, numquam auctores, semper interpretes, sub aliena umbra latentes, nihil existimo habere generosi, numquam ausos aliquando facere quod diu didicerant. memoriam in alienis exercuerunt; aliud autem est meminisse, aliud scire. meminisse est rem commissam memoriae custodire.

How long will you take your orders from someone else? You give the orders; utter something that will be entrusted to memory; offer something from your own [talents]. That's why I consider them to lack eminence, all those [philosophers] I've just mentioned, who never created anything themselves, but simply acted as interpreters of other people's creations and hid beneath someone else's shadow; who never dared at any time to act on that which they had studied for so long. They exercised their memory in someone else's work. But memory is one thing, knowledge is another. Memory merely guards that which has been consigned to memory.   (*Ep.* 33.7–8)

It is one thing, that is, to summon up information learned through past experience – this is what memory does; it is quite another to formulate new knowledge. To put it another way, Seneca places strict limits on what is to be gained from history, from memory, from the past. His own experience, his first-hand knowledge, displaces history as the *principal* source of wisdom.[13] And that may well be part of the explanation for why in the *Epistulae* he seems to dwell less often on the past than he might. But contributing to this decision must also be a sense that the Republic now simply has less to offer. Thus in distinct contrast to predecessors such as Valerius Maximus or Velleius Paterculus, Seneca has no interest in perpetuating the myth of a restored Republic. It is never for *that* reason that he alludes to the Republic or to characters and events from the Republic.[14]

Before turning to some specific examples of Seneca's use of Republican history in the *Epistulae*, it may be useful to consider a rather more typical example of what one finds in this collection. As I have remarked, the *Epistulae* generally avoid specific references to the Republic to a greater degree than those works composed prior to the reign of Nero. The way Seneca deploys *exempla* in his earlier work in fact more closely resembles the practice (but not necessarily the aim) of Valerius Maximus.

---

[13] Maso (1999), 49–51, 81.   [14] Maso (1999), 62, 66–8.

Poverty, for example, is a favorite *topos* for both authors. Valerius Maximus devotes a whole section of Book 4 to the subject (4.4–11), with anecdotes drawn entirely from the Republic about people such as Cornelia, Valerius Poplicola, Menenius Agrippa, C. Fabricius, Q. Aemilius Papus, Atilius Regulus, L. Quinctius Cincinnatus, Cn. Cornelius Scipio Calvus, M. Scaurus. In some of the *Dialogues*, composed under Gaius and Claudius in the 40s and published perhaps not more than a decade after the appearance of Valerius' *Facta et dicta memorabilia*, Seneca similarly turns to the question of poverty. When he speaks in praise of it in the *Consolatio ad Helviam matrem* (*Dial.* 12.10–12), he adduces by name three Republican characters famous for their frugal way of life: Menenius Agrippa, Atilius Regulus, Scipio Africanus – two of these three appear in the Valerius passage cited here as well, and for the third Seneca merely swaps Cn. Scipio for the more illustrious nephew. Indeed, it seems clear that here Seneca has his eye on Valerius, on whom he occasionally draws for some of his material.[15] Written in exile and an (albeit implicit) expression of resignation to the whims of the emperor, the *ad Helviam* obviously puts Republican history to quite a different use and under vastly different circumstances than the *Facta et dicta memorabilia*. Nonetheless, that history still *has* a use.

Yet some years later when, in the 60s and under Nero, he comes to write of poverty in the *Epistulae* – which he does with some frequency – he rarely makes reference to specific *exempla*.[16] This is the case, for instance, in Letter 18. Here he offers advice in accordance with the teachings of philosophers, *ex praecepto magnorum virorum* (18.5). He cites no Republican *exempla*, as he had done in the *ad Helviam*. He does, however, at the end quote Vergil *Aeneid* 8.364–5, referring to the visit of Aeneas to the humble hut of Evander. As it happens, Valerius Maximus similarly evoked this site in the passage referenced above (4.4.11), as did Seneca himself in the *ad Helviam* (9.3).[17] At this point, however, in a text written under Nero rather than Claudius, while redeploying the paradigm of Roman frugality from the distant and

---

[15] Bloomer (1992), 63–77, on Seneca's use of Valerius Maximus.
[16] For references to poverty in the prose works, Motto (1970), 172–3.
[17] See Chap. 2 n. 70.

archaic past, he now excludes explicit reference to its Republican exemplars.[18]

The effect of such exclusions or silences should not be overlooked, for they finally suggest a movement away from the moral universe of the Republic, which was seen to have some relevance in the Tiberian period. If in talking about a character from the past Seneca preserves a memory of that character, in *not* talking about someone he denies him or her memory. Not surprisingly, just as "memory" is explicitly identified with history and with writing, silence is explicitly identified in Roman thought with the act of negating memory (see Chap. 2 n. 72). Thus Seneca specifically instructs us not to bother with the memory of "bad" people, because by definition they make bad models.[19] Predictably, therefore, the *Epistulae* on the whole exclude unsavory characters such as Catiline or Mark Antony, for instance. Yet by the same token, the many available positive *exempla* from the Republic appear less frequently in Seneca's Neronian period than in the work produced prior to 54. Such references, then, when encountered, appear to manipulate history and memory all the more pointedly precisely because they are comparatively unexpected.

Cato, Scipio, and Seneca's Republicanism (Epp. *14 and 86*)

Two letters in particular may be used to illustrate Seneca's use of the Republican past. The first, Letter 14, concerns the care we take for the body, and the moral lesson is simple: since we need to take care of ourselves, we should avoid those things that might put us at risk. Specifically, *odium, invidia,* and *contemptus* (*Ep.* 14.10). How do we learn to avoid those things? Through philosophy, which in effect requires retiring from an active political life. A life in politics and the *sapiens,* the wise man or philosopher, are evidently incompatible.

---

[18] Examples of this sort of thing are not hard to find. At *Dial.* 6.13 (the *Consolatio ad Marciam*), for instance, written under Gaius (Griffin [1976], 396–7), Seneca cites the examples of Aemilius Paulus and Horatius Pulvillus (and alludes quite specifically to Marcius Rex), apparently drawing on Val. Max. 5.10.102. Yet returning to this topos in the *Epistulae* under Nero, he simply mentions, without naming them, *innumerabilia exempla* (*Ep.* 99.6). See Bloomer (1992), 65.

[19] E.g., *Ep.* 94.28 and passim. As discussed in Chap. 2, Valerius Maximus expresses a similar view (e.g., 5.2.10, 5.4. *praef.,* 8.14. ext. 3, 12.9.3. ext. *praef.*).

About two-thirds of the way into the Letter, an interlocutor, presumably Lucilius, interrupts to say, "Well, wait a minute … what about someone like Cato the Younger? He voluntarily puts himself in harm's way during the civil war, yet is he not a *sapiens*?" This is in turn countered with a remark by (apparently) another, imaginary interlocutor:

> "quid ergo?" inquis "videtur tibi M. Cato modeste philosophari, qui bellum civile sententia reprimit? qui furentium principum armis medius intervenit? qui aliis Pompeium offendentibus, aliis Caesarem, simul lacessit duos?" potest aliquis disputare an illo tempore capessenda fuerit sapienti res publica: "quid tibi vis, Marce Cato? iam non agitur de libertate: olim pessum data est. quaeritur utrum Caesar an Pompeius possideat rem publicam: quid tibi cum ista contentione? nullae partes tuae sunt. dominus eligitur: quid tua, uter vincat? potest melior vincere, non potest non peior esse qui vicerit."[20] ultimas partes attigi Catonis; sed ne priores quidem anni fuerunt qui sapientem in illam rapinam rei publicae admitterent. quid aliud quam vociferatus est Cato et misit inritas voces …?

> "What then?" you say, "Does Cato seem to you to engage in a moderate sort of philosophy? he who combats civil war by expressing his opinion? who puts himself in the middle of the weapons wielded by two maddened leaders? who while some people are causing offense to Pompey and others to Caesar, defies both at once?" Someone might dispute whether or not the Republic ought to have been entrusted to a wise man at that point in time: "What do you expect, Marcus Cato? Freedom is no longer at stake; it fell by the wayside long ago. The question is whether Caesar or Pompey should be in control of the Republic. What do you have to do with that dispute? It is none of your business. A master is being selected. What does it matter to you which one wins? The better man may win, but once he has won, he cannot but be the worse." I've touched on Cato's final role. But even his earlier years were not such as to permit the wise man to have any part in the plundering of the Republic. What else could Cato do but shout and utter useless words …? (*Ep.* 14.12–13)

---

[20] For the punctuation adopted here, Griffin (1968), 373–5.

Cato is discussed as though he were alive (note the present tense), as though the civil war were still an ongoing event.[21] Somewhat surprisingly, Seneca – usually so well disposed toward this his favorite *exemplum* – suggests that in this instance the situation did not call for a *sapiens*. And then, rather abruptly, he – or the second interlocutor – fires a blunt question at Cato, again as though this were still a current topic of debate: *quid tibi vis, Marce Cato?* "What are you after, Cato?" Anticipating the answer – *libertas* – he responds, "But that is a thing of the past. This is no longer a struggle for *libertas*, but about who will possess the Republic – Caesar or Pompey."

Miriam Griffin (1968) questioned the punctuation adopted by Reynolds in the Oxford Classical Text edition of the *Epistulae*. She preferred to have inverted commas placed (as I have put them) around *quid tibi vis, Marce Cato? ... qui vicerit* to indicate that this was a remark by the *aliquis* in the previous sentence rather than by Seneca himself, arguing that the whole section replicates a *topos* commonly found in rhetorical schools, and should not necessarily be construed as reflecting a negative judgment on the part of Seneca about Cato. She may well be right about this, but the editorial confusion underscores how seamlessly Seneca can move from a past event to the present. Moreover, regardless of who utters these words, they seem readily applicable to Seneca's own situation. In Seneca's worldview, as many scholars have noted, *libertas* – the *libertas* that was seen as virtually synonymous with the Republic – *was* a thing of the past; the question was therefore which *dominus* would be in control; the wise man has no part in this choice. So while this may draw inspiration from a common rhetorical *topos*, the literal blurring of time in this section forces us to confront the dilemma as though it demands a resolution *now*, in the present rather than in the past.

It is worth noting, too, that in this letter, at least, Seneca does not qualify what he means by *libertas*. There is no attempt, that is, to invest this word with a new relevance, to appropriate it in the service of the notion of a restored Republic. This differs from what Valerius Maximus was observed to have done (and later Pliny the Younger will do). Valerius' Cato, like Seneca's, is identified with *libertas*, but as we saw,

---

[21] Cf. Bartsch (1997), 141 on the present tense in Lucan.

in context the word is narrowly construed as the right to speak one's mind; it hardly stands for a political system or way of life. The meaning of this word undergoes considerable modifications over the course of the early Principate – this is why it constitutes, as I observed in Chapter 1, a real linguistic *lieu de mémoire* – but Seneca has surprisingly little to say on the subject.[22] He may hardly be said to mourn its loss in any serious way. In contrast, Lucan's *Pharsalia* continually foregrounds the loss of *libertas* and forces us to ruminate on the consequences.

In vignettes such as we encounter in Letter 14, Seneca perpetuates a very particularized memory of Cato, a memory of an essentially depoliticized Cato.[23] Cato's relevance in Neronian Rome – the reason Neronian readers should remember him – lies not in his political views, but rather in the manner in which he conducted himself in trying circumstances. While it is true that Seneca admires Cato, nowhere does he admire him for opposition to Caesar. He repeatedly comes back to Cato's fortitude, but never suggests that we should take up the cause of *Catonian libertas*, that is, the Republic. In short, the memory of Cato Seneca most wishes to preserve is that of a moral *exemplum*, not as an exemplary opponent of absolutism.[24] It is the latter, however, that we will find in Lucan.

Valerius' Cato and Velleius' Cicero, we should remind ourselves, are similarly depoliticized: these authors, like Seneca, locate the importance of Cato and Cicero in qualities other than their politics. The difference is that whereas neither Valerius nor Velleius equates the deaths of Cato or Cicero with an end of the Republic (and therefore of *libertas*), Seneca does not share with them the vision of an unbroken Republic; on the contrary, as here in Letter 14 and elsewhere, he regards the Republic as finished. This is the fundamental shift between the Tiberian period and the Neronian, at least as far as Seneca is concerned.

A further distinction lies in the ends to which Seneca puts such characters. While the "refashioning" of standard Republican *exempla*

---

[22] On *libertas* in Seneca, Viansino (1979), 174–87; Wirzubski (1968), 146–7.

[23] E.g., Wirzubski (1968), 127–8, though in general he is surely correct that Seneca had little use for Cato's politics (as I argue further below).

[24] Rudich (1997), 119. Further on Cato in Seneca, Griffin (2000), 545; (1976), 182–201 and passim; Castagna (1991), 97; Sullivan (1985), 117–20; Narducci (2001); Sion-Jenkis (2000), 87–8; George (1991), 243–5 and the discussion of *Ep.* 14.

is commonplace in Seneca, one begins to suspect that Seneca's "take" on the icons of the past has a good deal to do with his own self-presentation.[25] Consider, for instance, Letter 86 and the description of a visit to the villa of Scipio Africanus at Liternum in Campania.

Seneca has a particular fondness for the villas of famous people, and as several recent studies have pointed out, Roman aristocratic houses are very much a locus of memory, capturing in their design and ornamentation the character of the owner.[26] Seneca is keenly aware of the connection between houses and memory, and he typically adduces them as a vehicle to explore some aspect of the owners' or previous owners' life. This particular villa was apparently well known, and may have been something of a tourist attraction.[27] Here, in 184 BC, Scipio lived out the final year of his life in voluntarily imposed exile in order to avoid being brought up on bribery charges in Rome.

When *we* think of Scipio Africanus – or for that matter when Romans think of Scipio Africanus – the enormously successful general who defeated Hannibal comes to mind. Romans tended to want to forget the final year of his life, which was generally regarded as a somewhat dodgy end to an otherwise brilliant career. Livy, our best source for this and himself a "tourist" to Scipio's villa (38.56.3), curtly dismisses Scipio's exile, concluding that he was "a memorable man – but more memorable for his military skill than his peacetime accomplishments" (*vir memorabilis, bellicis tamen quam pacis artibus*, 38.53.9).

Several details in the letter suggest that Seneca is consciously rebutting Livy (and in effect therefore the preferred Augustan memory of Scipio), and perhaps this very sentence, for it is precisely Scipio's exile that impresses Seneca. Prompted to reminisce about Scipio by not only the house but the tomb of Scipio himself, which was apparently located on the villa grounds, and an altar dedicated to his memory, he suggests that Scipio's self-imposed exile was not a defiance of the law but an act of great magnanimity, for he had relieved the state of the embarrassment of

[25] As Roller (2001a), 93, neatly demonstrates in his discussion of Senecan *exempla*, more often than not Seneca deploys Republican *exempla* to unmask them, to identify "shortcomings in this mode of inferring value."

[26] Esp. Bodel (1997), Baroin (1998), Treggiari (1999), Hales (2003); and with particular reference to Seneca and *Ep.* 86, Henderson (2004), esp. 93–118.

[27] McKay (1972), 207; D'Arms (1970), 1–2, 12–13.

prosecuting his great self.[28] He even puts in Scipio's mouth a short speech defending his decision. This speech also occurs in Livy's narrative, though Livy reports the speech in indirect discourse and most interestingly has it uttered *not* by Scipio but by his supporters (38.50.8). But this is not all that interests Seneca. Following the defense of Scipio's exile, Seneca describes the house, lingering in particular on its somewhat spartan bath. He conjures an image of the venerable Scipio in one corner of the dingy bath, washing from his body dirt accumulated while working on his farm – thereby notionally aligning him with another great Roman who endured a voluntary exile, Camillus. Other notable Republican Romans are said to have bathed this way: Cato the Elder and Fabius Maximus, for instance. This leads naturally to a comparison of the decadent lifestyle and sumptuous baths of Seneca's own generation with the simplicity and virtue of the Republican past.[29]

Seneca therefore plays with Scipio's memory in two ways. He provides us with a different "take" on Scipio's exile; rather than attempting to apologize for it, as Livy does, he turns it into a final act of magnanimity on the part of Scipio; and he adds to the store of memory about Scipio by picturing him in his bath. In the process he demystifies Scipio: in place of the great and even mythic Roman general, the subjugator of Hannibal, we glimpse him in a private, seemingly ordinary moment, detached from the very circumstances that in most Romans' eyes made him extraordinary. Both twists are transparently self-serving, given the fact that Seneca writes this letter in his own kind of self-imposed exile, during which he famously lived an austere existence.[30] Both letters I have discussed take standard historical *exempla* known essentially for rebelliousness (in the case of Cato) and military success (in the case of Scipio) and deftly turn them into arguments for political quietism.[31] Quietism, however, is hardly what drives Lucan's *Pharsalia*.

---

[28] Cf. *Ep.* 51.11, where he says that Scipio's exile was more honorable at Liternum than at Baiae.

[29] Maso (1999), 69–70. Seneca's use of Scipio in this way also seems in line with Roller's observation (2001a), 97–108, that in his deployment of *exempla virtutis* Seneca typically downplays military success as a worthwhile goal for the imperial aristocrat.

[30] E.g., *Ep.* 83, 108; Tac. *Ann.* 15.45.

[31] Cf. Sullivan (1985), 142–3 on the character of the *Epistulae*. In a shrewd discussion of *Ep.* 86, Henderson (2004), 101, succinctly summarizes Seneca's manipulation

"Optima civilis belli defensio oblivio est"
Lucan's memorializing history

This remark, attributed to the censored Augustan declaimer Labienus (Sen. *Con.* 10.3.5), has special point when one considers Lucan's project. For if indeed the best defense against civil war is to forget, what may be said of a work whose explicit purpose is to *remember* a civil war? Insofar as he could, Valerius Maximus had studiously avoided mentioning the travails of the civil wars of the late Republic; Velleius put the best spin possible on an admittedly dicey moment (given his loyalties) in Roman history. The risks of writing of the period in general were articulated by no less than the emperor Claudius, who abandoned a planned history of triumviral Rome (*post caedem Caesaris dictatoris*) because he felt it was no longer possible to write freely and truthfully about the past (*neque libere neque vere ... de superioribus*, Suet. *Cl.* 41.2). And certainly, as a rule Neronian historians seem not to have been particularly interested in going back further than the Augustan period.[32] But Lucan's epic brings front and center, in a way nothing Seneca (or any other imperial author for that matter) wrote ever did, what was certainly the most controversial moment in late Republican history, the civil war between Caesar and Pompey. The *Pharsalia* or *De bello civili* completely rewrites the history of this war, promoting a very different memory from that transmitted by Caesar himself or by any subsequent historian.

But Lucan's project is as broadly etiological as Vergil's or Livy's; if they sought to explain the rise of the Roman people, Lucan fixed his attention on the rise of the Principate, locating its genesis unambiguously in the civil war. Despite the seemingly infinite number of ways in which the poem may be read, most would agree that if not the work of an out-an-out dissident, the *Pharsalia* clearly would have made many uncomfortable. My interest in the poem lies in the way it treats memory, as a point of comparison with what we have seen in Seneca. Although Lucan does not of course discuss history and memory in the same explicit terms as Seneca, memory is one of the poem's central concerns.

of Scipio: "he has shifted, metamorphosed, ancient legend to make Roman modernism."

[32] E.g., Pliny the Elder, Servilius Nonianus, and Cluvius Rufus, all of whom wrote histories of the post-Augustan period; Aufidius Bassus went back at least to the death of Cicero but probably no further. Discussion in Chap. 2.

Caesar's entry into Italy

One of the most telling memory moments in Lucan's poem occurs early on. About two-thirds of the way into Book 1, we read that the rumors preceding Caesar's descent into Italy fill the minds of the people with an overwhelming fear. Despite the fact that they *know* Caesar – and evidently remember him to be a reasonable man – on this occasion imagination wins out over memory. And so, influenced by a fear that their memory *ought* to tell them is unfounded, they envision someone who is rather different from what they remember. As Lucan puts it, *nec qualem meminere vident: maiorque ferusque / mentibus occurrit victoque inmanior hoste*, "The man (i.e., Caesar) they see is not the man they remember: in their minds he appears bigger, wilder, more brutal than the enemy he has conquered" (1.479–80).

Since we know that Lucan's Caesar is indeed a pretty nasty piece of work, the irony of this scene is apparent. The man they *imagine* turns out *not* to be the man they knew or remembered: Caesar *is* "big, wild, and certainly brutal." Fiction and reality are reversed. Memory, it appears, is not entirely reliable, and certainly not the memory transmitted by the standard historical account, that of Caesar himself. The Caesar of Lucan's *De bello civili* in fact bears little resemblance to that memorialized in Caesar's *Commentarii de bello civili*. Now, as has been recognized, Caesar's own *De bello civili* was an important source for Lucan. And we should not be surprised to discover that in Caesar's account of this moment, cheering, eager crowds greet him as he makes his way south to Corfinium and eventually to Rome.[33] In *Caesar's* text, he is *precisely*

---

[33] Cf. Caes. *Civ.* 1.15, 18. In Lucan the people are "more well-disposed toward Pompey" (*pronior in Magnum populus*, 2.453); the Latin communities are "ambivalent, undecided, wavering in their allegiance" (*urbes Latii dubiae varioque favore / ancipites*, 2.447–8), though in the end "terror easily changed their minds, and fortune spirited away their irresolute loyalty" (*facilis sed vertere mentes / terror erat, dubiamque fidem fortuna ferebat*, 2.460–1; cf. 1.486–7, "it was not only the crowd that panicked, struck by unwarranted terror," *nec solum volgus inani / percussum terrore pavet*, and 3.80–3, 97–8). Note that when *terror* appears in *Caesar's* text, it is the *terror* of the Pompeians at the news of Caesar's approach (*Civ.* 1.14.1). For Lucan's use of Caesar, Fantham (1992), 19–23; and for a perceptive discussion of one especially interesting instance, Fantham (1985). For his "resistance to Caesarian ideology" (59), Roller (2001a), 54–63.

the man they remember and expect ... or rather, the man Caesar *wants* us to remember.

Thus here, and in many other ways, Lucan aims to set the story – and specifically Caesar's story – straight. It is not merely the memory of Caesar that interests Lucan; he engages with, questions, emends, and otherwise modifies the memory of a number of individuals and, more generally of course, the memory of an event that set in motion the demise of the Republic. But while Lucan's epic establishes a sort of counter-memory of the civil war, at various points in the poem memory itself – and some of the problems associated with memory – emerges as a significant theme in its own right.

In Lucan, however, we glimpse an interesting intersection of epic or poetic memory and historical memory. It would be overly facile to suggest that one is characterized by fictional and the other by non-fictional content; as we have seen, in Roman thought history and memory are inextricably linked, yet memory may be just as readily transmitted by poetry as by prose. We have seen that Seneca makes just this point, but as I argued in Chapter 1, his perspective is hardly unique. The important detail is this: memory for Lucan is a quintessentially human phenomenon, prompted and controlled by human actions. It is, in fact, precisely the issue of control that most interests him. Caesar will emerge in this poem as a destroyer of memory; in some sense Lucan seeks to wrest memory from his control. Thus, famously, it is the *cives*, Rome's citizens, from whom Lucan demands the story (1.8), not the Muses, the inspiration for (most significantly) Vergil's memory (cf. *A.* 1.8), and certainly not Caesar.[34] Seen in the light of what Romans considered to be the link between memory and history, Lucan's project is distinctly historical.[35]

---

[34] Conte (1966), 46–7.

[35] With respect to the "historian or poet" debate (a central issue in much of the scholarship on Lucan), see in particular the very useful discussion of Feeney (1991), 250–60 and passim; cf. Lintott (1971); Ahl (1976), 70–1. Syme's (1958), 1.142–3, comparison of Lucan and Tacitus is illuminating; cf. Conte (1985), 103–4. Equally helpful, as an instance of how closely Lucan's treatment of a character approaches that found in a "bona fide" Roman historian, is Leigh's (1997), 116ff., splendid comparison of Livy's Camillus with Lucan's Pompey. My thanks to Stephen Hinds for refining the points I make here.

Memory moments in Lucan

One especial value of memory is that it can motivate and persuade; for that reason, of course, it is a cornerstone of Roman rhetorical theory. We find a splendid example of this in Book 2: with the Roman citizens contemplating the onset of yet another civil war, an old man delivers a rather long speech, the purpose of which is to search "for precedents in memory for their intense fear" (*magno quaerens exempla timori*, 2.67).[36] This constitutes a fairly long and very vivid digression, almost Sallustian in character and function, in which Lucan conjures the memory of the civil war between Marius and Sulla.[37] As if to give his tale added weight, he impresses upon his listeners that this is a personal recollection, his own memory (*meque ipsum memini*, 2.169), for he had buried his brother during the war (having had first to locate the body to match it with the severed head!).[38] The effect of this speech is to evoke his listeners' memory of the horrors of civil war … and to inspire them to avert a repeat performance (rather like Tiberius' appeal to and fear of memory on the occasion of Augustus' funeral, discussed in Chapter 2): *sic maesta senectus | praeteritique memor*

[36] Other characters in Lucan, too, adduce history in making arguments, e.g., Caesar at 1.326, Pompey at 2.531–96 and 7.358–60 (imagining that should dead Roman heroes come alive, they would fight on his side) and passim in this speech; Massiliots at 3.307–55; Lentulus at 5.27–34; and Lucan himself (see next note). A related instance is Erichtho's soldier, who (in obvious imitation of the parallel encounter between Anchises and Aeneas in *Aeneid* 6) reveals to Sextus Pompey the dismay and disapproval of an array of venerable Roman icons he has encountered in the underworld (6.777–820). The weight of this disapproval, of course, goes entirely unheeded (though Lucan never indicates whether or not Sextus ever conveyed this information to his father). Lucan similarly conjures up an image of venerable Romans in criticizing Caesar's behavior with Cleopatra – even they might be tempted by what they saw (10.149–54).

[37] The pair appears from time to time in the course of the poem (e.g., 1.580–4). For their importance in Lucan, Fantham (1992), 28–9; Henderson (1998), 177–81; Conte (1985), 94–6; in imperial literature generally, Sion-Jenkis (2000), 82–3 with notes. For the whole episode discussed here, Conte (1985), 77–83 and passim; Fantham (1992) ad loc.; Narducci (1979), 50–4; Quint (1993), 142–3; Henderson (1998), 177–81. Lucan himself parallels the "historical digression," at 1.158–82, as he sets out (in ways that recall similar digressions in Sallust, Livy, and Velleius) the decline of the Republic that led to civil war.

[38] Presaging, especially, 3.758–61 and the naval battle off Massilia (and of course Pompey's own head loss).

flebat metuensque futuri, "thus the elders in their grief began / to weep, remembering the past and fearful of the future" (2.232–3).[39] As Fantham (1992, ad loc.) has commented, these lines contain a pointed allusion to *Aeneid* 5.716 (*id metuens veterisque memor Saturnia belli*), where, however, Juno is doing the remembering. Again, Lucan shifts the stewardship of memory from gods to mortals. Moreover, *this* memory is a particularly valuable one, for it arms people with knowledge of what will happen when a civil war occurs. Of course it proves to be an ineffectual memory, for the people who most need to hear and heed it, don't (e.g., Brutus in the next line, 2.234, who in the speech that follows seems oblivious to historical precedent).[40] And there's the rub: memory can lead to wise choices, but only if we listen to the people who are telling us the right memory.

Personal recollection mixes with public in this particular episode, and indeed, Lucan seems sensitive to the fact that private and public memory are often intertwined, that one needs the other. Thus there are occasionally moments in the poem when deeply personal "memory moments" are seen to have far broader repercussions. The most compelling instance of this occurs at the beginning of Book 3, when Julia, the daughter of Caesar and wife of Pompey who had died in 54, appears in a dream to Pompey. Julia, whose death in Lucan's view took away the possibility of reconciliation between Caesar and her husband (1.111–20), assures Pompey that Lethe has not robbed her of memory, that she has not forgotten him: *me non Lethaeae, coniunx, oblivia ripae / inmemorem fecere tui*, " 'The memory-destroying waters of Lethe, husband, / have not made me forget you' " (3.28–9); that she will follow him wherever he goes; and that she will not let him forget either her or his relationship to Caesar.[41] This is a decidedly awkward moment for Pompey, because he has of course remarried, to Cornelia, and while Julia may not have forgotten *him*, he has evidently tried to forget *her*. Pompey just does not comprehend, however, and despite the fact that this important memory is banging on his front door,

---

[39] Fantham (1992) ad loc. notes the similarity with Verg. *A.* 1.23.

[40] Cf. Petreius' reproach to his men at 4.212: "*inmemor o patriae, signorum oblite tuorum.*" Had they "remembered" these things properly, they would clearly see the right course of action.

[41] Lucan's language and the translingual pun (*Lethaeae ... oblivia ... inmemorem*) flag his interest in the memory play operative in this scene. I owe this point to Denis Feeney.

he persuades himself that what he has seen is not real, but merely an "empty vision" (*vanus visus*, 3.38): the dead *have* no *sensus*, he insists – and that term clearly includes "memory"[42] – if they do, then "death is nothing" (3.39–40). Fred Ahl ([1976], 291) rightly says of this moment that it is the point at which Pompey "breaks with the past." That, however, turns out not to be salutary. In a sense Pompey rejects his own memory, or rather a part of his past, as manifested in Julia.[43] Of course, he greatly values what Lucan terms the "happy times" (*tempora laeta*, 7.20): in *these* memories he will find comfort and refuge in his famous dream that opens Book 7.[44] However, he seems not to understand that memory, in order to be effective, cannot have the luxury of being so selective. He will come to learn that contrary to what he believes, death really *is* "nothing"; as Lucan observed earlier in Book 1 (1.457–8), death is merely the halfway point in life. Memory conjoins the two, and memory alone has the capacity to counter-act the annihilating effects of death ... or of civil war.

Given Pompey's inadequate grasp of memory, it is interesting that Lucan uses Pompey to make one of his most compelling points about the subject. I refer to the conclusion of Book 8, as Lucan worries that the body of Pompey has never received a proper burial, imagining that perhaps he himself might retrieve the bones (cf. Prop. 1.21 and the plea of the poet's deceased relative). Why *shouldn't* Pompey have a proper burial? Who, after all, he imagines, will fear a tomb? *Quis busta timebit?* (8.840) Well, indeed. But the purpose of tombs – and, as I argued in Chapter 1, of texts such as Lucan's – is to commemorate, to perpetuate the memory of the dead.[45] The failure to give Pompey a proper burial in the first place was *precisely* to consign him to oblivion; to mark his burial with a tomb would achieve exactly the opposite. This leads Lucan to his consolatory observation that tombs do not really matter anyway: physical memorials eventually dis-integrate, robbing people of *physical* evidence of a person's existence (8.865–9). But Pompey's (virtual) "tomb" will suffer no such damage: *nil*

---

[42] OLD s.v. 4. This is clearly implied in passages such as Cic. *Phil.* 6.13. See also n. 12 on Sen. *Ep.* 95.61. On death as the terminator of memory, cf. Lucr. 3.670–8, with Bailey (1947) ad loc.

[43] Ahl (1976), 292, views this as a break with the "*victrix causa* of the Iulii," i.e. a signal that Pompey has now chosen the "losing" side (symbolized in Cornelia, former wife of the son of Crassus).

[44] Ahl (1976), 179.

[45] Henderson (1998), 188; and references in Chap. 1, n. 17.

ista nocebunt / famae busta tuae (8.859); his memory transcends the corrupting influences of time and decay. At least to some degree, the *Pharsalia* constitutes a poetic (à la Horace) *monumentum* for the dead general, compensation for the cult denied to him but accorded to the victor and all his successors. And as if to illustrate the essential deathlessness of Pompey, Book 9 opens with his spirit transmigrating into Cato and Brutus, thereby ensuring continued existence, his memory, at least in some form (9.1–18).[46]

Memory and the past are things we need to pay attention to, Lucan seems to say. This point is signaled in relation to other characters as well. Curio's own reputation, for instance, assures his immortality, the ability to overcome the corrupting influences of time (4.809–24);[47] the Caesarian tribune Vulteius, through his suicide, becomes a *memorabile exemplum* (4.496–7);[48] and equally notable is the Caesarian soldier Scaeva, who, in the final lines of the poem as we have it, is said to have earned *perpetua fama* (10.542–6).[49]

Caesar the memory-destroyer

These are people who *do* things that ensure their memories; but in most circumstances they must ultimately entrust those memories to *other*

---

[46] Cf. Cornelia at 9.70–2; and the example of Appius at 5.227–36. On Pompey's burial and the end of Book 8, Ahl (1976), 189. Ahl (loc. cit., n. 59) observes the similarity between the sentiment expressed here (about the absence of a physical memorial) and the remark of Caesar at 5.668–71 (when his boat threatens to capsize). The latter implies that the memory of Caesar can continue to induce fear ("*desint mihi busta rogusque, / dum metuar semper terraque expecter ab omni,*" 5.670–1). Cf. Ahl (1976), 208.

[47] Note, however, that Curio intemperately trusts in the "memory" of Scipio (symbolized by his pitching camp on the same ground as Scipio had) to bring him victory (4.661–5).

[48] But note that Lucan laments the fact that Vulteius' *exemplum* is not properly understood – this is a memory few interpret correctly (4.574–81).

[49] In a fine discussion of the epic's final lines, Connors (1998), 137–41, shows how "This memory of Caesar remembering Epidamnus ... refigures the epic telos of imperial history as the telos of an individual life" (138), an observation that underscores the degree to which Lucan conceives this conflict in terms of both personal and collective memory. Appius might be included among those whose "memory" is to be valued, though his *bustum memorandum* (5.231) leaves it somewhat ambiguous as to whether he or the actual tomb is to be remembered.

people. A means of avoiding the attendant risks of that is to compose one's own account. This is precisely what Caesar had done. The *Commentarii de bello civili* guaranteed that history would be viewed through its author's eyes. That is, Caesar knew well that controlling memory was crucial to the exercise of power, despotic or otherwise,[50] and writing these "memoirs" – the Greek translation of *commentarii* is ὑπομνήματα – was certainly an attempt to exercise his power, even if the circumstances of their publication remain unclear. Lucan was cognizant of the general's desire to direct memory: when Caesar says at 7.299–300 that victory in the war will give him the power to control *quae populi regesque tenent*, he refers not merely to physical possessions. But if Caesar's ostensible role in his own work is as a preserver of memory, Lucan presents him in the *Pharsalia* as just the opposite, as a man with a penchant for ignoring or, still worse, destroying memory.

The problem of Caesar and memory is best captured in one of the most celebrated scenes in the poem, Caesar's visit to Troy in Book 9 in the course of hunting down Pompey in Egypt.[51]

> circumit exustae nomen memorabile Troiae
> magnaque Phoebei quaerit vestigia muri.   965
> iam silvae steriles et putres robore trunci
> Assaraci pressere domos et templa deorum
> iam lassa radice tenent, ac tota teguntur
> Pergama dumetis: etiam periere ruinae.
> aspicit Hesiones scopulos silvaque latentis   970
> Anchisae thalamos; quo iudex sederit antro,
> unde puer raptus caelo, quo vertice Nais
> luxerit Oenone: nullum est sine nomine saxum.
> inscius in sicco serpentem pulvere rivum
> transierat, qui Xanthus erat. securus in alto   975
> gramine ponebat gressus: Phryx incola manes
> Hectoreos calcare vetat. discussa iacebant
> saxa nec ullius faciem servantia sacri:
> 'Herceas' monstrator ait "non respicis aras?"

---

[50] Chap. I, n. 3.

[51] The visit to Troy is well discussed by Bartsch (1997), 131, and Ahl (1976), 214–22; Rossi (2001) teases out additional nuances.

He walks around a name to be remembered – torched Troy –
and looks for the vestiges of Apollo's great wall.
Now barren woods and trees, robbed by rot of their limbs,
weigh down upon the houses of Assaracus and grasp the temples
of the gods with their weary roots; and all of Pergamum is covered
with thickets: even the ruins are ruined.
He gazes on the rock of Hesione and the bedchamber of Anchises,
lying hidden in woods; on the grove where the judge sat,
on the place from where the boy was snatched, on the summit
where the Naiad Oenone grieved: no rock is nameless.
In his ignorance he had crossed the stream wending its way through
dry dust:
this was the Xanthus. Incautiously he stepped in the deep
grass: a local Phrygian warned him not to tread on the shades
of Hector. Stones lay strewn about,
preserving no semblance of any holy place:
His guide says, "Don't you see the altars of Hercean Zeus?"

(9.964–79)

What Caesar finds in fact is nothing – there are no ruins to visit, merely decay and desolation – no visible remains to prompt his memory. All that survives is the name; only this is *memorabile*.[52] More accurately, Caesar simply does not know what he is looking at. *Inscius*, "ignorant", as Lucan calls him, he needs the local guide to warn him not to "tread on the shade of Hector."[53] This prompts a rare outburst from Lucan himself, to assure Caesar that the world will not soon forget him:

---

[52] Lucan is aware of the capacity of names to preserve memory: cf. 4.654–5 and the tale of Antaeus told by the *rudis incola*: "*hinc, aevi veteris custos, famosa vetustas / miratrixque sui, signavit nomine terras,*" " 'hence [i.e., from Antaeus] has tale-bearing antiquity, the guardian of the ancient past who marvels at itself, marked the land with his name.' "

[53] Cf. again the local in 4.591–2: *nominis antiqui cupientem noscere causas / cognita per multos docuit rudis incola patres*, "the uncultured local revealed to him, since he wished to know the origins of the ancient name, the lore handed down by many ancestors"; also the "bards" of 1.447–8. Caesar in Lucan seems incapable of "knowing" anything (cf. the *nescia virtus* of 1.144, with Ahl [1976], 259), in contrast to Cato. Memory for him is ineffectual: despite the lessons of Hannibal at Cannae (who gave Aemilius Paulus an honorable burial), Caesar refuses to accord the same

o sacer et magnus vatum labor! omnia fato   980
eripis et populis donas mortalibus aevum.
invidia sacrae, Caesar, ne tangere famae;
nam, siquid Latiis fas est promittere Musis,
quantum Zmyrnaei durabunt vatis honores,
venturi me teque legent; Pharsalia nostra   985
vivet, et a nullo tenebris damnabimur aevo.

How great and holy is the task of poets! from death
you snatch everything and you bestow upon mortals eternal life.
Caesar, do not envy their sacred memory:
for if the Latin Muses are allowed to promise anything,
for however long the honors of the Smyrnaean poet last,
our descendants will read me and you. Our Pharsalia
will live and we shall be consigned to darkness by no age.

                                                        (9.980–6)

This echoes a similar remark made in Book 7 prior to Pharsalus
(7.205–13),[54] and in both passages Lucan asserts his own role as the
preserver of memory. It is not, to be sure, a role he particularly relishes:
Henderson astutely remarks the double meaning of *sacer* as "sacred/
cursed," pointing out that Lucan feels nothing but disgust at his subject.[55] But while he cannot (and does not wish to) snuff out Caesar's
memory, he can influence it. He demonstrates this shortly after the
passage in Book 7, as he *declines* to memorialize the most heated part
of the battle of Pharsalus, preferring to consign it to the darkness, to
silence (*tenebris, tacebo*, 7.551–6). As I noted above, silence is one means
of denying memory. Thus Lucan, too, controls memory; and like
Caesar's guide, Lucan directs us toward what we need to remember
and equally what we need to forget. Here at Troy, explicitly, he sets
himself in opposition to Caesar in *Caesar*'s role as preserver of memory,
at the same time aligning himself with Vergil as a preserver of memory

honor to the dead at Pharsalus – yet he "remembers" (*meminit*) that they are fellow-
citizens (7.797–803).

[54] Ahl (1976), 212–19, compares the ruins of Troy with the ruins of Pharsalus. At some
level, however, Troy also stands in for Rome (Narducci [1979], 47–8), suggesting
that just as the memory of Troy persists, so too does that of Rome, despite the
"forgetfulness" of despots such as Caesar. Cf. Edwards (1996), 64–6.

[55] Henderson (1998), 184–6.

(among other things, the passage quoted recalls Vergil's lines on Nisus and Euryalus, perhaps not coincidentally quoted by Seneca in Letter 21, discussed above, in his own musings about memory) as well as with Homer and the memory of Homer (in line 984). Epic and historical memory converge, with Lucan placing a foot firmly in both camps. In his historical guise, when he says that future generations will "read me and you" – and notice he puts the "me" first – he alludes to Caesar's own account of the war which his poem has seriously questioned.[56]

And even in this moment, Lucan exercises some memory control. This episode concludes not with Lucan's outburst, but rather with a prayer offered by Caesar himself upon finishing his visit to Troy. Despite needing the guide to identify what he is looking at, Caesar is fully aware of the importance of Troy ... and of the importance of its memory to his own legacy. Thus he invokes the "gods of the ashes" (*di cinerum*, 9.990) who inhabit the site and the memory of his Trojan ancestors (9.990–9) in order to ensure that his own memory will be viewed in the context of this long, glorious tradition. In Caesar's view, *this* memory clearly must be perpetuated. But this is of course not in the least what Lucan intends to memorialize. Vergil had done that, and while Lucan exploits in this scene the Julian myth of Troy, he will not collude with Vergil in promoting it. Rather history (and Lucan) now demands that Caesar's record be called to account and properly remembered, not in the context of a trumped-up myth but on its own. Again he directs us to the question implicit throughout the text: whose memory do you want to believe? – that of the historian Caesar? or of the poet Lucan?

By the time Caesar reaches Troy, as readers we are already well aware of Caesar's destructive capacity.[57] Indeed, somewhat remarkably, given the extent to which the illusion of a restored Republic persisted well into the early imperial period, Lucan has no doubt that Caesar's victory marked the death of the Republic and the demise of *libertas*, the moment at which, as he famously puts it, *omnis voces, per quas iam tempore tanto / mentimur dominis, haec primum repperit aetas*, "this was the moment when we first discovered all those expressions with which we have lied to

---

[56] For discussion of this episode and some of the points made here, Martindale (1993), 49–53; Hardie (1993), 106–7; Narducci (1979), 76–7; Bartsch (1997), 147.

[57] Johnson (1987), 74–6; Narducci (1979), 91–109.

our masters for so long" (5.385–6).[58] The best illustration of this point – and of Caesar's role as a destroyer of memory – is found in Book 7, shortly before the troops engage on the battlefield at Pharsalus:

> hae facient dextrae, quidquid nona explicat aetas,
> [ulla nec humanum reparet genus omnibus annis]
> ut vacet a ferro. gentes Mars iste futuras
> obruet et populos aevi venientis in orbem   390
> erepto natale feret. tunc omne Latinum
> fabula nomen erit; Gabios Veiosque Coramque
> pulvere vix tectae poterunt monstrare ruinae
> Albanosque lares Laurentinosque penates,
> rus vacuum, quod non habitet nisi nocte coacta   395
> invitus questusque Numam iussisse senator.
> non aetas haec carpsit edax monimentaque rerum
> putria destituit: crimen civile videmus
> tot vacuas urbes.

> These hands will bring it about that the ninth age [i.e., Lucan's era], whatever it may accomplish,
> [– no age can repair the human race in all the years –],
> shall be free from war. This war will destroy future
> nations and carry off people of an age yet to come,
> robbing them of their birth. At that time all the Latin name
> will be but a myth: Gabii, Veii, Cora –
> covered in dust, hardly even their ruins will be able to be observed.
> The lares of Alba, the household gods of Laurentum,
> the countryside empty, which no senator will inhabit except
> unwillingly, on a night appointed, complaining that he does so
> under the orders of Numa.
> It's not greedy time that has worn away and left the memorials of
> these things to rot: we witness the criminal consequence of civil war,
> so many empty cities.   (7.387–99)

---

[58] Lucan's aside at 5.385–94 comes at the moment when in the fall of 49 Caesar returned to Rome from Spain and southern France and had himself appointed dictator and then consul for the year 48, the year in which Pompey would be defeated at Pharsalus. For Lucan this is the moment at which the Republic died and the Empire began to take shape. See Ahl (1976), 56–8; Sion-Jenkis (2000), 85–6.

This devastation caused by Pharsalus recalls the ruins of Troy (see n. 54), but both scenes equally put us in mind of the crumbling landscape of Italy with which the poem opens (1.24–32).[59] Caesar in general brings destruction and silence to Rome/the world (cf. 5.27ff.), annihilating both people and places – not only people and places of the *past*, but of the future as well; the war wipes out not only the Republic, but the very means by which the memory of the Republic could be passed on from one generation to the next. Thus Lucan will observe a few lines later (7.580ff.) that on the battlefield where Libertas made its final stand, Caesar killed all the Lepidi, the Metelli, the Corvini, the Torquati – the great families of the Republic, *patriae perit omne decus* (7.597).[60]

Lucan's counter-memory?

I have said that Lucan's poem constitutes a counter-memory to the accepted view of the war between Pompey and Caesar. But it is a little more complicated than that. As is indicated by those several episodes in which memory figures explicitly, Lucan calls into question the Ciceronian theory of "history" as the "lifeblood of memory" – or rather, I should say, he substantially qualifies it. Nero's is *not*, Lucan seems to insist, the Rome of Cicero or of the Republic, and just as all else has changed, so too has the seemingly simple act of remembering. However else they might function in the poem, these episodes problematize memory, dramatize its essential fragility, and expose how open it is to misinterpretation or to no interpretation at all. The elderly citizens *do* remember the horrors of Marius and Sulla, but no one listens to them; Julia too remembers – her memory proving more powerful than

---

[59] Ahl (1976), 215–16. Lucan's reference to Veii (very much a Republican site of memory, in its associations with Camillus) in line 392, moreover, may contain a contemporary reference to the notion, popularized in a scurrilous poem, that Nero's Domus Aurea (or the reference may be to the Domus Transitoria) risked gobbling up Veii (Suet. *Nero* 39.2).

[60] Cf. 7.432–48 with Ahl (1976), 42. Observe too the aside at 7.617–47, where he says (639) that *plus est quam vita salusque / quod perit*. "We" are victims of that defeat as well (and so is memory). However, at the end, Pharsalus stands as a "memorial" to what has happened there: see 7.846ff. One might compare the plundering of the temple of Saturn in Book 3, envisioned by Lucan as a sort of "robbing" or desecration of Roman history (3.154–68).

Lethe – and tries to bring Pompey to his senses, but Pompey refuses to heed this memory, remembering instead only that which he chooses to remember. Cato becomes a vessel of memory, when Pompey's spirit transmigrates into him: Cato will lose the war, but ultimately be memorialized, at least in Latin literature, to a far greater degree than Julius Caesar. And then there is Caesar himself, a man whose destructive behavior annihilates memory and who is himself incapable of grasping the importance of what he sees because he, too, lacks memory (see n. 53). But the poem itself constitutes the greatest triumph of memory, restoring to the public conscience, to *collective* memory, an event that brought an end to the Republic.[61] The resistance to Caesarism is of course bound up in the concept of *libertas*; Lucan, as Tacitus after him, deemed *libertas* and Caesarism to be fundamentally incompatible. In Lucan's view, *libertas* depends on memory, on the capacity and opportunity to *remember* – for in the absence or suppression of memory, we lack the necessary motivation to fight for freedom.[62] In a world dominated by a memory-destroying Caesar, *libertas* cannot exist.

Lucan's interest in memory seems to have caught the attention of his eulogist, Statius. He calls him *memor gentis* – a man with a "memory for his people" (*Silv.* 2.7.52); and envisions his enforced suicide at the hands of Nero as a dip in Lethe (*iussus praecipitem subire Lethen*, "undergoing oblivion," ibid. 100–4). But like his Julia, Lucan negated Lethe's effects, in his case by virtue of his poem. Certainly, the passages examined here suggest that Lucan gave the question of memory some serious thought. While he celebrates in his poem the deathlessness of memory and its capacity to confer immortality, he cautions that the preservation and handing-on of memory requires vigilance. Some memories – depending on who is doing the remembering – may be deceitful; while pretending to preserve the past (as Caesar did in his own work), they have the capacity

---

[61] Cf. Quint (1993), 133: "The *Pharsalia* gives back to the vanquished republicans their story of resistance and keeps that story alive in historical memory."

[62] This connection of *libertas* and *memoria* is not unique to Lucan: cf. Tac. *Hist.* 1.1.1: *nam post conditam urbem octogingentos et viginti prioris aevi annos multi auctores rettulerunt, dum res populi Romani memorabantur, pari eloquentia ac libertate,* "Many authors of course have written of the previous 820 years following the founding of Rome, at a time when the affairs of the Roman people were being consigned to memory with both eloquence and freedom." On Lucan and *libertas*, Ahl (1976), 55–7, 278–9 and passim; Wirszubski (1968), 124; Fantham (1992), 13.

to destroy it (as Caesar does in Lucan's). It is that engagement with memory, I have suggested, that makes the *Pharsalia* a work of Roman history.

In this enormously complex and rich poem, the issue of the past, of memory, is central. Rudich and others are quite right, of course, to say that Lucan feels no nostalgia for the Republic.[63] But Lucan does foreground as one of the risks of civil war, although perhaps a risk especially associated with extreme autocrats such as Caesar, the loss of memory. At the same time his poem reminds us (as will the historian Tacitus several decades later in his account of the trial of Cremutius Cordus) that the memory of individuals and of momentous events can seldom be eradicated – at least as long as there are people like Lucan who are prepared to transmit and, where necessary, emend their memory.

Neronian Republicanism

We should not overlook what Seneca and Lucan have in common. Both, for instance, feel perfectly free to fictionalize history to suit their purposes. What they present us with are not "real" memories any more than "real" history. While we might agree with Rudich that this is the "price of rhetoricization," the fact is that history in the hands of a Roman is endlessly mutable and dynamic – otherwise it would risk becoming irrelevant.[64] This is more than simple revisionism; it goes to the heart of how memory is, to revert to Le Goff, mastered and controlled. Yet the ends to which these two authors wish to manipulate the memory of the past are starkly different, and this is not merely a question of genre. Lucan throws history in your face, overwhelms you with it, in some sense makes you a participant in it. Seneca's use of Republican history, on the other hand, is quite deliberately selective and, we should recall, fairly limited; in the majority of the *Epistulae* it does not figure at all. He tiptoes around some of the difficulties Lucan brings to the fore, which is why Seneca's use of the past in the *Epistulae* does not really smack particularly of dissent; rather he seems consciously to transform potentially problematic *exempla* into paradigms for survival in a society in which

[63] Rudich (1997), 126–7 and passim; but cf. Sullivan (1985), 143–4.
[64] Bartsch (1997), 137: "It reasserts the individual's right to make sense out of the past".

freedom has been seriously curtailed. By contrast, it is very difficult to resist reading Lucan's *Pharsalia* as anything but a provocative commentary on the genesis of a Julio-Claudian autocracy and Nero.[65]

The political context in which these texts were produced differed radically from that of the Tiberian period; and so, of course, did the relationship of Seneca and Lucan to Nero differ dramatically from that of Velleius Paterculus and Valerius Maximus to Tiberius. Although the latter two authors evidently both supported and enjoyed the support of the emperor, they are for the most part politically unengaged. Seneca, by contrast, occupied a position of considerable influence in the imperial court to the extent that he was able to formulate and shape policy for some time.

Perhaps the most striking distinction between the Tiberian and Neronian periods is that at no point under Nero do we hear of any suggestion that the Republic be restored.[66] Seneca may well have had something to do with that. It needs to be borne in mind that the architect of the Neronian regime, at least in the beginning, was none other than Seneca. Having either fully grasped the political realities of the day or simply concluded that the Republican past really had little to offer the new regime, Seneca envisioned instead a new direction for the Principate.[67] In that regard, the *De clementia* is a particularly useful text. As I pointed out earlier, in that "how-to-be-a-good-ruler" handbook references to the Republic and to Republican *exempla* are noticeably few; the chief *exemplum* Seneca offers up instead is Augustus (cf. Suet. *Nero* 10). Indeed, the very *fact* of the *De clementia* signals a departure from the Republic, where the "clemency" of a "ruler" would be moot.[68] We find further evidence for the distancing of the Republic from the new regime in Nero's accession speech summarized by Tacitus in Book 13 of the *Annals* and said to have been authored by Seneca. While in that speech Nero promises to restore the *antiqua munia* of the Senate,

---

[65] For detailed treatment of the differing "ethical discourses" found in Seneca and Lucan, see Roller (2001a), chaps. 1 and 2, esp. 124–6.

[66] Note that a potential participant in the Pisonian conspiracy was rejected precisely because it was feared he might want to restore the Republic (Tac. *Ann.* 15.52.3). Martindale (1984), 66; Mayer (1978), 86. On the lessening interest in "restoring the Republic," Raaflaub (1986).

[67] Sullivan (1985), 117–20, 129–34.

[68] For the "paradigms" of the *De clementia* and their function in defining the relationship between Nero and the nobility, Roller (2001a), 239–47.

the political plan offered up makes it clear who is to be in charge.[69] This seems to have been an entirely happy arrangement – provided the emperor did not forget himself.

In a regime whose theme was innovation, not restoration,[70] celebrating the Republican past simply had no place in the agenda. It is no accident, I think, that the Republican past, much less the civil war, figures in no serious way in Neronian literature or in Neronian historiography (such as we know it). This is why, of course, Lucan's *Pharsalia* seems so out of place; and why Eumolpus' own poetic version of the civil war in Petronius' *Satyricon* seems so simultaneously comical and unnerving.[71] Ironically, if we believe Cassius Dio (62.29), the only person to have addressed Republican history directly was Nero himself: he contemplated writing a 400-book epic on Roman history. (One of the project's advisors, interestingly enough, was none other than Cornutus, Lucan's teacher.) If the Republic were to be remembered at all, it would be as the emperor wanted it remembered. And this is doubtless why there is nothing in the Neronian building program to parallel the Forum of Augustus or the Ara Pacis, monuments that celebrated the continuity of Rome's past and its traditions; nor would one mistake Nero's Domus Transitoria or its successor, the Domus Aurea, as throwbacks to Republican austerity.

Nero may have carried this too far, however, for increasingly he seems to have expressed open hostility to the memory of the Republic. Cassius Dio tells us, for instance, that Nero used to hold games and entertainments in which the senatorial and equestrian descendants of the great Republican families – families memorialized throughout the city (including the Catos and the Horatii) – were forced to act, sing, play the part of gladiators, the chief aim being to allow the spectators to witness the degradation visited upon the relatives of the Republic's most famous icons (61.17). The act seems oddly reminiscent of Caesar's slaughter of

---

[69] *Ann.* 13.4; Griffin (1974), 21ff.

[70] Cf. the peasant at Cal. Sic. *Ecl.* 7.44–7: *certe / vilia sunt nobis, quaecumque prioribus annis/vidimus, et sordet quicquid spectavimus olim,* " 'We certainly regard as worthless that which we saw in times past, and whatever spectacles we once enjoyed seem cheap.' " Note too that in *Ecl.* 1.63ff. the new Golden Age is a return to the time of Saturn and of Numa, not (of course) to the Republic. Even if Calpurnius Siculus is not Neronian, his work still reflects the early imperial (post-Tiberian) ambivalence about the Republic. See Narducci (1979), 28–9, on this poet and Lucan.

[71] For detailed analysis, Connors (1998), 100–46.

Republican families on the battlefield at Pharsalus as described by Lucan and discussed above. A further instance of the mockery Nero made of the past was the so-called liberation of the Greeks in AD 67, often viewed as a desecration of the real liberation effected by Flamininus in 196 BC.[72] Even his building program could be seen to inflict destruction on particularly Republican sites of memory (see n. 59 on Veii).

The act most explicitly connected with Nero's desecration of the past is the great fire of 64. It is surely of some significance that the one prose narrative Lucan is known to have composed was an account of this very fire, the *De incendio urbis*. The fire was symbolically and literally a destruction of the old to make way for the new. All accounts of the event remark the altered landscape of the city. Tacitus enumerates some of the many old buildings that were lost in that fire and hints at the damage done to Roman memory as a result,[73] but Suetonius provides the most telling remark:

> per sex dies septemque noctes ea clade saevitum est ad monument-orum bustorumque deversoria plebe compulsa. tunc praeter immen-sum numerum insularum domus priscorum ducum arserunt hostilibus adhuc spoliis adornatae deorumque aedes ab regibus ac deinde Punicis et Gallicis bellis votae dedicataeque, et quidquid visendum atque memorabile ex antiquitate duraverat.

> For six days and seven nights the conflagration raged, forcing the people to seek refuge in monuments and tombs. Then, in addition to a huge number of apartment complexes, the houses of ancient generals, decorated with war trophies, burned, together with temples vowed and dedicated during the monarchy and then the Punic and Gallic wars, and anything noteworthy and memorable from the past.

> (*Nero* 38.2)

Thus all visible remnants of what was memorable of old were consumed by the fire – *quidquid visendum atque memorabile ex antiquitate duraverat* – and

---

[72] Cf. Dio 63.8 with Alcock (1994b), 103. Strikingly, the inscription of the speech Nero delivered on this occasion omits reference to Flamininus' "liberation" (Smallwood [1984] no. 64 = ILS 8794); the memory of that Republican event is therefore detached from Nero's iteration of it, even though in the historical tradition the two are linked (e.g., Plut. *Flam.* 12.8; Dio 63.8).

[73] *Ann.* 15.38–44, esp. 15.41.1; cf. Dio 62.16–18.

yet it is in memorializing structures (*monumenta* and *busta*) that the people are forced to take refuge.[74] My point here is not simply that Nero's actions suggest at the very least disregard for the sanctity of the past, but that authors often assess them in connection with some aspect of the Republican past, with memory.

It is not too much of a stretch of the imagination to see in these events parallels with the sorts of issues I have suggested are raised by Lucan. And read against the background of the Neronian regime, Lucan's concern with memory – how it can be destroyed, manipulated, etc. – now looks rather more like an attempt to counter a political agenda that sought to devalue the past. Seneca, ironically, had a hand in setting that agenda – though he would never countenance the wholesale annihilation of memory. Writing, for both Lucan and Seneca, was the one way to assure its perpetuation, yet the memories of the Republican past they sought to promote served very different purposes.

Both, we may be sure, were aware that the emperor would take a deep interest in what they wrote. And it is always tempting to imagine how Nero might have read Seneca and Lucan. Lucan's Caesar, of course, is often viewed as a foil for Nero; as Ahl reminds us, Lucan refers to Julius Caesar and all of his successors by that one name alone.[75] While the purpose of this may not necessarily be to collapse all distinctions between the Julio-Claudian emperors, Lucan's Caesar does embody the characteristics of an undesirable despot, characteristics that the historical record suggests Lucan's own Caesar, Nero, shared. Like Julius Caesar, Nero proved not to be the ruler Romans "remembered"; in contrast, that is, to the relatively benign and competent emperor they encountered at the outset of his reign, in the end he proved to be someone else – someone "bigger, wilder, more brutal" (Lucan, 1.479–80, discussed above).[76] As his reign drew to a close, what Seneca feared in the *De clementia* had in fact happened: Nero forgot himself, had become

---

[74] Cf. Tac. *Ann.* 15.41. At *Hist.* 3.72 Tacitus similarly views the fire of AD 69 as a "destruction of the past" and especially of the Republic (*gloria operis libertati reservata*). On this, Edwards (1996), 74–82; the fire in general, Champlin (2003), 121–6 and *passim*.

[75] Ahl (1976), 55; cf. Henderson (1998), 177, 195–6; Roller (2001a), 37–8.

[76] Ironically, it is worth noting, the memory of Nero proved to be very long-lived, beginning with the several "false Neros": see Champlin (2003), 10–12.

something that he initially was not. What he remembered – what he reinstantiated – was the Caesar Lucan had hoped to avert. But it was only because of memory that one could tell the difference. With the death of the last Julio-Claudian emperor, however, Caesar was, as Shakespeare's Brutus had bidden him to be, at last still (*Julius Caesar* 5.5.50). And with him, so it must have seemed, the Republic.

Rome's new past

"Not this time," or "dignus eram a quo res publica inciperet": Galba and the Flavians

Upon the death of Nero and shortly after his accession, in AD 69 Galba met with his chosen successor, Piso Licinianus, to discuss the handover of power. In the speech Tacitus concocts for him, Galba remarks on Piso's illustrious Republican heritage: he was descended from Pompey the Great and Marcus Crassus, as well as being affiliated with the Sulpicii and Lutatii. Piso himself, Tacitus adds, seemed to look and act the part of an "old school" Roman (*vultu habituque moris antiqui*, *Hist.* 1.14). But far from adducing these as advantages on which to capitalize, Galba deems Piso fit for rule *in spite* of such qualifications. In the political arena, it seems, such things no longer possess any meaning (cf. 1.15); when it comes to choosing a *princeps*, what matters instead are "outstanding character and patriotism" (*praeclara indoles ... et amor patriae*). Galba, whose coinage had declared the restoration of "freedom" (*libertas restituta*),[1] then makes a surprisingly frank admission:

> "Si immensum imperii corpus stare ac librari sine rectore posset, dignus eram a quo res publica inciperet: nunc eo necessitatis iam pridem ventum est, ut nec mea senectus conferre plus populo

---

[1] See Boyle (2003), 4–5, with refs. in n. 11; Wirszubski (1968), 124. Clearly, of course, not the restoration of the Republic, but "freedom" from the tyranny of Nero – another example of the constantly shifting meaning of this word throughout the imperial period (see Chapter 1).

Romano possit quam bonum successorem, nec tua plus iuventa quam
bonum principem. sub Tiberio et Gaio et Claudio unius familiae
quasi hereditas fuimus: in loco libertatis erit quod eligi coepimus."

"If the huge body of the Empire could stand on its own and be stable
in the absence of a single ruler, I would be the right person with whom
the Republic might make a new beginning. But by now we have long
since come to the point where my advanced years can confer upon the
Roman people no more than a good successor – nor can your youth
do more than supply a good emperor. Under Tiberius, Gaius, and
Claudius we (sc. emperors) were like the heirs of one family; that we
now begin to be chosen will take the place of *libertas*."[2]

(*Hist.* 1.16.1)

More the product of Tacitean hindsight than Galba's perspicacity, the
remark nonetheless accurately reflects the political reality of post-
Augustan and especially Neronian Rome (though Nero himself is pointedly omitted from the list). The choice of words is telling: the shift to
monarchy was made under evident duress (*necessitas*); it happened some
time ago (*iam pridem*); some degree or rather some simulacrum of
libertas is nonetheless achievable, provided that emperors are chosen
on their merits rather than determined by birth; the Republic has given
way to the Principate – thus Galba speaks not of "restoration" but of an
unrealizable "new beginning" (*inciperet*), at the same time emphasizing
that he cannot and will not be a sort of new Brutus, a bringer of *libertas*
in the wake of the Julio-Claudian monarchy's demise.[3] "Not *this* time,"
he seems to say.

This is the linchpin of Tacitus' "Republicanism". It is not the case that
Tacitus urges a return to the Republic or feels a misplaced nostalgia for
it; rather, what one wants is a *princeps* enlightened enough to recognize
that the Senate should still play a role in governance and must enjoy
sufficient freedom to express its views without fear of reprisal or retribu-
tion. It should be stressed that this is a significant advance from the position that equated the Republic with *libertas* and the demise of the former
with the loss of the latter. It is this "have-your-cake-and-eat-it-too"

---

[2] I take this to mean, that while Galba will not restore the Republic (true *libertas*),
what he offers is the next best thing.

[3] My thanks to Denis Feeney for an illuminating discussion of this passage.

attitude that seems to emerge in the latter half of the Principate. In Trajan, Tacitus and Pliny – the authors of the two texts examined in this chapter and both active members of the senatorial class – found such an emperor.

The intervening Flavian period, however, possessed a rather different political character from that of either the early decades of the Principate or the subsequent reigns of Nerva and, more significantly, Trajan. In some respects an odd and abbreviated iteration of the Julio-Claudian,[4] the Flavian dynasty nonetheless shows little of the sort of schizophrenic attitude toward the Republic we observed of the earlier period. In this respect Galba's speech anticipates the situation of the Flavian period, when the urge to claim a "return to the Republic" has subsided, the reality of and necessity for the Principate at last largely accepted.[5] While the spirit of Republicanism does occasionally rear its head – principally during the reign of Domitian[6] – for the most part it no longer seems politically expedient for the incoming emperor to claim to be "restoring" anything. Indeed, one of the hallmarks of the Flavian period is its capacity to individuate itself, to dissociate itself from both its recent and distant past.[7]

To be sure, Flavian culture still makes capital out of the Republican past, though missing is the revolutionary fervor of a Lucan or the Republic-perpetuating tendencies of a Valerius Maximus or Velleius Paterculus. Flavian epic takes on Greek myth and legend: Statius' *Thebaid* and *Achilleid*, or Valerius Flaccus' *Argonautica*. While these may be every bit as "political" as Senecan tragedy, as one scholar has analyzed the *Argonautica*, at least, "the old possibilities and freedoms of

---

[4] Boyle (2003), 5–6.

[5] As Boyle (2003), 5–6, discusses, as a paradigm Augustus and the Augustan regime held more importance for Vespasian than the Republic (cf. D'Ambra [1993], 33). He further speculates (ibid. 7) that the theme of the Flavian period might best be described as *principatus restitutus*, the theme of *libertas restituta* (and whatever vestiges of Republican meaning that motto might retain) now abandoned.

[6] Note, for instance, the continuing association of well-placed Stoics such as Helvidius Priscus with Cato and Brutus (cf., e.g., Tac. *Hist.* 4.8.3). For the Republican opposition under Domitian, MacMullen (1966), 61–8 and passim.

[7] Boyle (2003), 29–35, esp. 32: "Despite its allusions to the first principate, Flavian Rome seemed adjacent to that tradition: set apart, uprooted, arbitrary, multiplicatory, erasory, replaceable."

the republic are no longer seen as viable."[8] And of course, Flavian epic also turns to Republican history. The *Punica* of Silius Italicus – apart from Lucan's the most ambitious epic on a topic in Republican history to have survived from the Principate – merits more attention than is given to it here (especially in light of the many interesting ways it treats memory). But Silius' decision to write an epic poem on the Republic's most significant military achievement – in stark contrast to an epic on the horrors of civil war – is a celebration of Roman imperialism, not of Roman (or rather *Republican*) *libertas*. Without doubt, it memorializes the Republic, but averts its gaze from the troublous final years of the Republic and focuses instead on an event that could be seen, much as Silius' beloved Vergil had done in the *Aeneid*, as presaging the future greatness of the empire.[9]

Republican *exempla* occasionally crop up in Martial, sometimes in thought-provoking ways. He places Nerva, for instance, in a poem featuring a number of standard Republican models (Camillus, Fabricius, Brutus, Sulla, Pompey, Caesar, Crassus, and Cato), imagining their reactions to the new Caesar: so impressed would they be, that they would happily accept him as their ruler – even Cato would become *Caesarianus* (*Ep.* 11.5). Martial does have a sense of the absurd, here playing on the familiar trope of the emperor who surpasses even the greatest of his Republican forebears (we observed this in Horace and Ovid, and shall encounter it again in Pliny's *Panegyricus*). But on the whole, as Dyson and Prior so aptly remark, "The memory of the Republic and its associated places and structures no longer intrudes much on the consciousness of a rising literary star."[10] Much the same could be said of Statius. Even in the poem where he might be expected to make the most of the setting (the Roman Forum) and the subject to exploit the Republic, *Silvae* 1.1 on the equestrian statue of Domitian, the references to Republican topography and history are little more than props; he summons neither Republican places nor events with which he wishes to connect the emperor in any meaningful way. The city and

---

[8] Zissos (2003), 672.

[9] For Silius' respect for Vergil, Pliny *Ep.* 3.7.8, with Hardie (1993), 64–5. For Silius, especially for the ways in which he engages with the past, see now Tipping (1999), and forthcoming.

[10] Dyson and Prior (1995), 254.

culture we encounter in these two poets are largely and unapologetically imperial.

Of course I do not want to suggest that references to the Republic under the Flavians are devoid of meaning (indeed, the Republic in the Flavian period is a worthy subject unto itself[11]). Clearly, such references attest a continued desire to preserve some memory of the Republican past as well as the persistence of that memory. But the texts we encounter in this period lack the sort of overtly political (or deliberately depoliticizing) attitude toward the Republic one associates with earlier imperial literature; in that sense, the Flavians offer no real parallels to Velleius Paterculus, Valerius Maximus, Seneca, or Lucan. Republican *exempla* have become for the most part window dressing, functioning in much the same way as the Republican portrait types favored by Vespasian.[12] Such allusions underscore character and respect for tradition, not political values. Thus Suetonius comments on Vespasian's reverence for the past, displayed in his desire to preserve physical reminders of pre-imperial Rome (especially inscriptions), but in the same breath remarks many *new* buildings erected by the emperor, who in this respect was more ambitious than any of his predecessors (*Vesp.* 8).

This collocation of old and new characterizes the work of a central figure in Flavian and early Trajanic culture, Quintilian. As is true of Silius, considerably more could be said about the way Quintilian memorializes the Republic. I shall restrict myself here, however, to some brief observations about the way he sets the stage for the two texts on which I shall concentrate in this chapter. The *Dialogus*, in particular, is often read as a reaction to Quintilian, specifically to his *De causis corruptae eloquentiae*;[13] the *Panegyricus*, the product of one of Quintilian's most famous pupils, perhaps best shows Quintilian's training in action.

The career of this imperial rhetorician and teacher spans a considerable period of time: he would have been nineteen when Nero came to power in AD 54 and he died early in the reign of Trajan, ca. AD 100. He left us one of the most precious of imperial texts, the *Institutio oratoria*, an

---

[11] E. g., Gallia (2003), which I have not seen.

[12] Boyle (2003), 4, 16; Kleiner (1992), 172–9. This revival of Republican fashion goes back, of course, to Augustus, who appeals to it as one means of visually underscoring his embodiment of Republican virtues: Zanker (1979), 354, 358.

[13] Brink (1989).

extensive manual for the training of the orator from birth through manhood. Like the *De clementia* and the *Panegyricus*, this text provides advice – advice directed, however, not at the emperor, but at the Roman aristocrat, redefining for the imperial senator the skill upon which the Republic (in Cicero's view) had depended. Its central question, there-fore, is what does it mean to be an orator under the Principate? what does such a person need to know?

The answer is a rather different one from that given by Seneca to the young Nero in the *De clementia*. Quintilian's well-educated orator will need to acquire a firm knowledge of Republican history and oratory. Therefore, just as they were for Cicero – the Republican personality who looms largest in this text – memory and mnemonic technique are of fundamental importance for Quintilian. The *Institutio* is a crucial source for the subject (see Chap. 5 with n. 18). Clearly, memory – remembering the past – continues to be vital to Roman culture and society, as both the *Dialogus* and the *Panegyricus* will underscore. Indeed, Quintilian con-cludes the *Institutio* with just this point. In the absence of orators, everything becomes silent; and with silence, comes the loss of memory (*Ipsam igitur orandi maiestatem, qua nihil di inmortales melius homini dederunt et qua remota muta sunt omnia et luce praesenti ac memoria posteritatis carent ... petamus*, 12.11.30). On more than one occasion we have observed this connection in Roman thought with silence and mem-ory (see Chap. 2 with n. 72). The difference for Quintilian, of course, lies in the uses to which that memory is to be put.

Quintilian's orator, like Cicero's, needs to be able to access a vast store of *exempla*, among them Republican *exempla*. These stories, preserved in Rome's *monumenta*, teach all manner of virtues; to learn about bravery, justice, loyalty, restraint, frugality – what better teachers could one have, he says, than the Fabricii, the Curii, the Reguli, the Decii, and the Mucii (*Inst.*12.2.29–30)? This history sets the moral com-pass by which the imperial orator must steer his course; and like his Republican counterpart, he will be concerned about his own memory (12.2.31). At the same time, however, Quintilian insists on the necessity of knowing more recent history, of acquiring a "supply of recent *exem-pla*" (*exemplorum copia ... novorum*, 12.4.1). Thus while standing firm on the continuing importance of *exempla* in Roman education (and especially in the training of an orator), Quintilian recognizes that *recent* history has a value that should not be overlooked. Times and tastes have changed; this is why the style of Cato and Gracchi, for instance, is unsuited for modern times (2.5.21–2). This aligns him with the Senecan view that, as we saw, privileges the recent over the distant past, at least in his Neronian period, but significantly distinguishes Quintilian from Valerius Maximus and the rejection of "new" (*nova*) *exempla* (Val. Max. 1.8.7, discussed in Chap. 2).

Yet Quintilian's actual *practice* betrays him a bit. When, for example, he seeks suitable models for *accusationes* (prosecutions), he summons names only from the Republic. Among these "state leaders," *principes in re publica viri* (for they are the ones best equipped for such a task), are Hortensius, the Luculli, Sulpicius Rufus, Cicero, Julius Caesar, and both Catos (*Inst.*12.7.3–4) – all solidly from the Republican age. By contrast, when he comes to cite paragons of different *styles* of oratory (*species*), Republican and imperial characters stand comfortably side by side, Scipio Africanus with the Neronian Seneca, Julius Caesar with the Flavian Julius Secundus (whom we shall meet in the *Dialogus*), Q. Hortensius with Trachalus, et al. (12.10.10–12). While it seems highly implausible that Quintilian could not summon from his memory well-known examples of imperial prosecutors, Maternus, as we shall see, will argue that prosecutions in the imperial period are unnecessary. It is telling, however, that Quintilian does not make this point himself. But we are clearly in the presence of an author fully acclimated to the political and social culture of the Principate.

Joy Connolly neatly summarizes the purpose of Quintilian's *Institutio*: "his attempt to sanitize oratory for manly use, certainly part of Cicero's purpose, was part of a larger effort to ease oratory's exit from the political sphere, highlighting its ideological role as a gatekeeper to elite society – the only path open to oratory under autocracy."[14] In the *Dialogus*, Tacitus addresses this point explicitly; in Pliny's *Panegyricus*, we shall see it in action.

If, then, Quintilian in particular and Flavian culture in general depoliticize the Republic, the *Dialogus* and the *Panegyricus* from the Trajanic period will seem at first glance to "reactivate" the Republic. Indeed, the imperial text that most directly articulates the tension between Republic and Principate is Tacitus' *Dialogus*. Yet although the *Dialogus* is a

---

[14] Connolly (forthcoming), chap. 6.

product of the early Trajanic period, its "action" appropriately occurs early in the reign of Vespasian, as though in reflection of the distancing of the Republic observable in the Flavian period. The *Dialogus*, that is, hardly pleads for a return to the Republic, but rather offers a compelling explanation for why that is no longer necessary. I read this text in conjunction with Pliny's *Panegyricus*. While seeming to embrace the Republic and its traditions (*libertas*, allusions to Republican *exempla*, etc.), Pliny does so in the service of an unabashedly imperial panegyric. Both texts may therefore evoke the Republic, but they also characterize a period when the memory of the Republic shows signs of enervation.

The Republic revisited: Tacitus' *Dialogus*

One of Tacitus' early works – and, as Barnes would have it, the "most problematical"[15] – the *Dialogus* recounts a gathering of several men that occurred most probably in the year AD 75. Its date of composition is of course some time later, probably (depending on whom one believes) in AD 102.[16] The central (and not unprecedented) topic of conversation is the current state of eloquence or oratory: is it on the decline or not (*Dial.* 1)?[17] While there is general agreement that contemporary, i.e., imperial, oratory is *different* from the oratory of the Republic, no *consensus* emerges as to whether one is "better" or "worse" than the other.[18] Despite that absence of consensus (and Tacitus' well-known mistrust of the Principate as an institution), it would be a mistake to read the *Dialogus* as an indictment of the Principate as the villain that marginalized the skill by which Romans had chiefly measured power and success in the past. True, the text connects the demise (or changing nature) of oratory with the loss of *libertas*. It turns out, however, that this is not a bad thing. Rather, the *Dialogus* proposes an unprecedented rapprochement of Republican and imperial values that implies that the Republic is indeed "past". This conclusion is not new, of course – Seneca

---

[15] Barnes (1986), 225.

[16] Mayer (2001), 22–7, summarizes the arguments.

[17] On decline as a common rhetorical topos, Luce (1993), 13; Williams (1978), 6–51, thoroughly discusses the phenomenon.

[18] *Pace* Brink (1993), 338–9. If one thing is certain about the *Dialogus*, it is that no one single point of view prevails (Luce [1993], 33–6).

had already said as much – but as we have seen, each new regime (whether it be that of Vespasian, in whose reign the piece is set, or that of Trajan, in which it was written) has had to come to grips with the problem of the past.

The *Dialogus* parades its Republican roots in some very obvious ways, none more so than the way it deals with Cicero. As we have seen, throughout the early imperial period Cicero is in many respects equated with the Republic and its demise. The anxiety over Cicero operative in Velleius is missing in Seneca and indeed is generally absent in Neronian literature, one indication of the waning "guilt" associated with and the significance attached to Cicero's murder.[19] In the late Flavian and early Trajanic periods, however, Cicero's star seems to rise a bit with Quintilian and the younger Pliny, to the extent that scholars often talk of an emerging neo-Ciceronianism. Yet if, as Winterbottom has argued, Cicero takes on the status of an *exemplum* in this period, it is by virtue of his talent as a stylist and his pedagogical value, not as a model for political activism or resistance.[20] Nonetheless, the *Dialogus'* obeisance to Cicero is neither *pro forma* nor entirely apolitical in intent.

In some sense, the theme of the *Dialogus* could be reduced to this simple question: why do we not emulate Cicero? In many respects the *Dialogus* does just that. Its very title places it firmly in the genre Cicero single-handedly transformed; and as if to dispel any doubts about its roots, the *Dialogus* pointedly eschews the obligatory nod toward Plato evident at the beginning of most Ciceronian dialogues. The *Dialogus* is quintessentially Ciceronian and Roman. Various Ciceronian texts have been adduced as models or at least sources of influence – the *de Oratore*, the *Orator*, and the *De re publica*, for instance.[21] And stylistically, of course, the language is so heavily influenced by Cicero that it even prompted serious doubts about Tacitean authorship.

---

[19] For Cicero's influence on Seneca (less than one might imagine) see now Setaioli (2003). Surprisingly (given his involvement in the events), Cicero appears only once in Lucan's *Pharsalia*, in a notoriously unhistorical and not terribly flattering moment: Lucan has him confront Pompey on the morning before Pharsalus, though we know that he was not present at the battle (7.83ff.). Ahl (1976), 160–3.

[20] Winterbottom (1982), 241 (Cicero as *exemplum*); cf. Brink (1989), esp. 475 (the "non-political" nature of neo-Ciceronian oratory), 486–8 and passim (pedagogical value).

[21] Esp. Michel (1962); Koestermann (1930); Koutroubas (1987).

For the most part, however, the debt to Cicero has not been satisfactorily explored – or rather, scholars have not fully examined why Tacitus felt obliged to invoke Cicero at all. In one sense the answer seems obvious: as both Rome's greatest orator and the man who had brilliantly *written* about oratory, Cicero seemed a logical choice. What Tacitus does not evoke, at least in any explicit fashion, is the Cicero who was historically and symbolically associated with the end of the Republic. Rather, the *Dialogus* (as does much of Seneca's work, for instance) employs the Ciceronian form and even the Ciceronian ethos, while at the same devaluing the political significance of his life and career. Cicero never did achieve precisely the same status as a moral and ethical *exemplum* on the order of, say, Cato the Younger, but in the early Principate, as we saw, he was not merely a paragon of style. In contrast to his predecessors, however, Tacitus takes his cue for the *Dialogus* not from Cicero's career or even his oratory (these are what impressed Velleius, for instance), but from one of the least appreciated of Cicero's texts, the *Brutus*. If Cicero stands for anything in the *Dialogus*, it is as the representative of a political system that was grounded in memory and the author of a text that identified the survival of the Republic with preservation of memory (and therefore with orators). Tacitus takes issue with Cicero's fatalism; a counterpoint to the *Brutus*, the *Dialogus* assures its readers that there is life – and memory – after the Republic. Thus as I shall argue here, the *Dialogus* rejects Cicero in more ways than one: an act of memory itself, the text questions the value of remembering the Republic at all.[22]

In purely formal terms, the influence of the *Brutus* has been recognized. Gudeman and others, that is, have noticed several echoes of that text in the *Dialogus*; it is, moreover, the only Ciceronian text named in the piece (*Dial.* 30.3).[23] The connections are a bit more palpable, however, than a few borrowed phrases. Commentators have not observed, for instance, that the very first sentence of the *Dialogus* plays on an unusual

---

[22] Goldberg (1999), 224, neatly puts it thus: "to explore, as the *Dialogus* certainly does, the collapse of Ciceronian values is not necessarily to regret that collapse."

[23] For Tacitus' debt to the *Brutus*, Gudeman (1894) on 30.12 and passim (p. 291); it is most easily traced via the Index Locorum, s. Cicero *Brutus* (pp. 395–6). For the *Dialogus*' debt to Cicero generally, Mayer (2001), 27–31 (mostly interested in matters of style), and Luce (1993), 12–13 with references.

phrase from the *end* of the *Brutus*, as though one text were picking up on the other. His age, Tacitus remarks, is bereft of eloquence – *aetas … laude eloquentiae orbata* (*Dial.* 1.1); so too does Cicero speak of "orphaned eloquence" – *orba eloquentia* (*Brut.* 330). There is an important distinction: for in Tacitus' view it is the times that have lost eloquence, in Cicero it is eloquence that has lost its chief supporters (chief among them Hortensius). The phrase nonetheless forges an unmistakable link between the two texts. I will return to the *Brutus* to suggest other ways in which the *Dialogus* mirrors it, but let me turn first to the *Dialogus* itself.

The *Dialogus* presents itself as Tacitus' memory – the phrase he uses is *memoria et recordatio* (*Dial.* 1.3) – of a gathering of several men that occurred at some point in the reign of Vespasian, probably in the year AD 75;[24] Cicero, too, using the same phrase (*memoria et recordatio*, *Brut.* 9), explicitly alleges that the *Brutus* is *his* recollection of a similar meeting in 46 BC.[25] At this gathering, the four principal participants in Tacitus' piece – Curiatius Maternus, Marcus Aper, Julius Secundus, and Vipstanus Messalla – held a wide-ranging discussion about the decline of eloquence in the early Principate.[26] It is on the character of Maternus that I wish to concentrate.

At first glance, Maternus certainly looks like a flaming Republican. The reason Aper and Secundus have come to visit, in fact, is out of concern for Maternus, who had authored and just recited in the presence of the emperor a tragedy entitled the *Cato*, doubtless reenacting the famous, defiant suicide of Caesar's arch-opponent in 46 BC during the civil war. Maternus' performance had caused quite a stir, prompting concern for his well being. Why, his friends wonder, had he so flagrantly taunted the imperial court with the memory of a man so closely identified with pro-Republican and therefore anti-imperial sentiment? It is worth noting that Maternus is said not merely to have *played* Cato, he actually for a time *became* Cato and "forgot" himself (*sui oblitus*):

Nam postero die quam Curiatius Maternus Catonem recitaverat, cum offendisse potentium animos diceretur, tamquam in eo

---

[24] On the date, Mayer (2001), 16 with n. 43.

[25] It should be noticed that in distinct contrast to the *Brutus*, where Cicero is a central character, Tacitus is merely a witness to the proceedings. On this "self-effacing" move – which I see as distinctly imperial – Luce (1993), 37.

[26] For the prosopography of these individuals, Mayer (2001), 44–7.

tragoediae argumento sui oblitus tantum Catonem cogitasset, eaque
de re per urbem frequens sermo haberetur, venerunt ad eum Marcus
Aper et Iulius Secundus...

It was the day after Curiatius Maternus had given a reading of his
Cato, by which it was said that he had irritated the feelings of certain
powerful people, because in the subject of his tragedy he had forgotten himself and thought only of Cato. While all Rome was discussing
this, Marcus Aper and Julius Secundus came to him... (*Dial.*2.1)

It is hard to know how best to render Tacitus' *cogitasset* – one might be
tempted to say that Maternus "channeled" Cato. As Gudeman (1894, ad
loc.) glosses it, the term here signifies "that the object of your thought
takes complete possession of you." We have observed this phenomenon
before, the imagining of characters from the Republic actually "coming
alive" and influencing or directing events in the present.[27] This was one,
very effective way of "memorializing" the dead, of giving them not
symbolic but actual life.

This is dangerous stuff, or so Aper and Secundus surmise: Maternus'
performance is said to have "caused offense" (*offendisse* in 2.1, *offensas*
in 3.2) to "those in power" (*potentium animos* in 2.1), to have set tongues
wagging (*frequens sermo* in 2.1, *fabulae malignorum* in 3.2), and to have
provided fodder for those inclined toward an unfavorable interpretation
of Maternus' choice of subject (*pravae interpretationi materiam*). That
choice, Secundus claims, is simply not "safe" (*securiorem*, 3.2). It is
essential to observe, however, that while these inferences are made by
two very smart men (cf. *Dial.* 2.1), they are nonetheless inferences – and
vague, unsubstantiated inferences at that; while it is true that Cato had
long been the poster boy for Republicanism and anti-imperial sentiment,
by the Neronian period he had lost much of his bite as the incendiary
exemplum he had once been (see Chap. 3). Stoics embraced him as a
model for how to escape tyranny, not overthrow it. The concerns of Aper
and Secundus may therefore be misplaced and even anachronistic, and
we are provided with no justification for them. It is hard to imagine that

---

[27] Cf. relevant discussions in Chaps. 2 and 3. In the present instance (as Stephen Hinds
points out to me), cf. Cic. *Amic.* 1.4–5, where Cicero similarly claims to have
"become" Cato in the *De senectute*.

Maternus meant to be subversive ... or that the emperor Vespasian would have regarded the recitation of his *Cato* as much of a threat.

Maternus, in fact, seems quite unruffled by their concern (cf. *Dial.* 13.5–6, 41.4). The two men proceed to ask him why, instead of writing political dramas about dead Republicans, he does not redirect his energy to oratory (*Dial.* 3) – which, ironically, given its subversive potential under the Republic, now seems to be the safer occupation. Maternus' answer is perhaps not entirely what one expects. He defends not the choice of subject (from which one might infer that for him the choice is entirely unproblematic and without risk), but rather the medium: poetry. This, it turns out, is what interests him, for in poetry this experienced and well-respected lawyer can express what for him is a "more sacred and more noble eloquence" than that currently practiced in the forum (*sanctiorem ... et augustiorem eloquentiam*, 4.2). Thus while at first glance it *looks* as though Maternus is going to be made the mouthpiece of Republican values (what else would one expect from someone who wrote a *Cato*?), he ends up being quite the opposite.[28]

This episode serves as a preface to the ensuing discussion on the decline of oratory, the (evidently) central theme of the work. As one might anticipate, much of what follows centers on Cicero, the Republican orator par excellence. Aper, with the naïveté of youth, attempts to argue that the span of time from Cicero's death in 43 BC to his own time (the dramatic date of the dialogue being ca. AD 75) is really only the length of one lifetime (*Dial.* 17).[29] It is not entirely clear why this is an important distinction for him, except that by bringing Cicero within the compass of his own existence, he reduces the famous statesman's status just a bit. For Aper it is a question of the new versus the old, not of Republic versus Principate. Cicero, in Aper's view, is simply passé (cf. 19, 22). He rejects the relevance of the dead outright – it is much more pleasant, he says, to discuss the new and contemporary, rather than the old and forgotten paradigms, the *remota et oblitterata exempla* (8.1; cf. 22, and 15). Aper, in fact, reveals himself to be the arch-enemy of

---

[28] Further on the character of Maternus (and on the *Dialogus* in general) Bartsch (1994), 98–125 and passim.

[29] Or *centum et viginti anni* (120 years) as he reckons it. Gudeman (1894), 185–7, supplies evidence that this number represented for Romans "the limits of a man's lifetime."

memory who cannot understand what he perceives to be an obsession with the past. For him the *imagines ac tituli et statuae* whose sole purpose is to preserve memory are useless chunks of stone (8.4).

This is a shocking point of view – leading Brink to label Aper and his realistic views as "amoral" and "acultural"[30] – for it goes against the grain of the deep-seated Roman reverence for the dead and for the past. It is a stark assertion that the value of *exempla* is temporary and short-lived, that all forms of commemoration in time become valueless.[31] Messalla attempts to counter Aper's remarks, asserting that *eloquentia* has without question "declined" (*descivisse ab illa vetere gloria*, 28.1–2), lauding Republican practices, adducing (*Brutus*-like) examples of famous Republic orators (34.7–35.2), and ultimately praising Cicero (it is Messalla who cites the *Brutus* at 30.3). As Brink has called him, he is the "aristocratic traditionalist," the one fervent Ciceronian in the whole piece.[32] But Messalla comes off as something of an extremist, a man whose arguments seem distinctly anachronistic.[33] By contrast the older Maternus does not entirely disagree with Aper,[34] but if to this point he has appeared essentially uninterested in the political dimension of the debate, he now brings it to the fore.

Eloquentia, Maternus contends, died with the passing of *libertas* (27.3). Throughout the *Dialogus* Maternus subverts our expectations, for here too we expect regret yet find none. It becomes clear in the course of his concluding speech that Maternus harbors no nostalgia for the Republic. In his speech he famously redefines *libertas* (which, we recall from Chapter 1, had been closely associated if not synonymous with the Republic) as the term foolish people use to disguise what is really *licentia*:

"quid enim opus est longis in senatu sententiis cum optimi cito consentiant? quid multis apud populum contionibus cum de re publica non imperiti et multi deliberent sed sapientissimus et unus? quid voluntariis accusationibus cum tam raro et tam parce peccetur? quid invidiosis et excedentibus modum defensionibus cum clementia

---

[30] Brink (1989), 496. Cf. Luce (1993), 34 with n. 74; further on Aper, Goldberg (1999).

[31] This view of the fleeting and shifting value of *exempla* may have been first espoused, significantly, by Livy. Chaplin (2000), 107–8 and passim. The important difference is that Aper, living a generation or two after Livy, is now disinclined to reinvest those *exempla* with new meaning or any meaning at all.

[32] Brink (1989), 496. Cf. Brink (1993), 342 and passim.

[33] See Martin (1981), 65.   [34] Cf. Brink (1989), 497.

cognoscentis obviam periclitantibus eat? credite, optimi et in quantum opus est disertissimi viri, si aut vos prioribus saeculis aut illi
quos miramur his nati essent ac deus aliquis vitas ac [vestra] tempora
repente mutasset, nec vobis summa illa laus et gloria in eloquentia
neque illis modus et temperamentum defuisset. nunc, quoniam
nemo eodem tempore adsequi potest magnam famam et magnam
quietem, bono saeculi sui quisque citra obtrectationem alterius
utatur."

"For what need is there of long speeches in the Senate, when the best
men are quick to agree? And what need is there of ceaseless public
meetings, when it is not the ignorant rabble who makes decisions
about questions of state, but rather a single, exceedingly wise man?
What need is there for initiating indictments, when crimes are so rare
and inconsequential, or of hateful and unrestrained defenses, when
the clemency of the judge is available to those accused and at risk?
Rest assured, my distinguished and (insofar as is currently necessary)
eloquent friends, that if you had been born in the past, and the men we
admire been born in our own day, if some god had in fact abruptly
changed your lives and your age, the greatest fame and grandeur that
eloquence can confer would have been yours, and they too would not
have been without temperance and self-control. But at present, since
no one can simultaneously enjoy great renown and great tranquility,
let everybody make the best possible use of the blessings of their own
age without belittling someone else's." (*Dial.* 41.4–5)

It is not so much that *eloquentia* has declined; it is simply that the
political situation in Rome has stabilized to the point where orators
like Cicero are no longer needed. In a society where a single individual
makes the decisions, where *otium* and *quies* are the order of the day, not
discordia, men like Cicero have become relics. In what looks like a
blatant piece of revisionist history, Maternus alleges that it was not
talent that made Cicero great but circumstances, and he is not alone in
this speech in questioning the extent of Cicero's abilities. Maternus, it
turns out, agrees with Aper that the past is irrelevant to the present – at
least as far as oratory is concerned, the lifeblood of the Republic.

Not entirely irrelevant, however. Remember that the reason this gathering occurred in the first place was to scold Maternus for his *Cato*; and we
learn later in the text that he has plans for other historical dramas about

characters from the Republic (3.4). If in oratory those characters are dead and gone and should stay that way, Maternus is more than willing to bring them back from the dead – indeed, virtually to *become* them – in drama and in poetry. But not poor Cicero. In this text, at least, he is laid to rest once and for all. It would be interesting to have Maternus' explanation of why Cato takes pride of place over Cicero (why does he not enact Cicero's life?), but his is after all not a unique view (see Aper at 10.6). As a Stoic paradigm, Cato was by far the preferable candidate. This is the central problem of Maternus: if the political situation was so rosy, what need did they have for someone like Cato? This is a "problem" however, only if we believe that his invocation of Cato was made in the spirit of resistance and Republicanism. Clearly, it was not. Maternus, like Seneca, has reconfigured *libertas* not so much as a political or (better yet) public ideal, but as a personal one, a freedom that signals the Stoic ability to rise above *fortuna*. Survival, rather than resistance, explains why Maternus seeks to keep Cato alive. The distinctly Neronian anxiety evinced by Aper and Secundus is itself anachronistic, inappropriate under the enlightened Vespasian. Aper himself is out of touch, proof of his own proposition about the past.

The Dialogus *and the* Brutus

Maternus' *Cato* may conceal another ironic twist of memory and history. Cicero himself had written a *Cato* (solicited by none other than Brutus, who went on to pen his own *Cato*), a text so inflammatory that it moved Caesar to write an *Anti-Cato*.[35] The purpose of Cicero's text was manifestly revolutionary. Well over a century later, Maternus' *Cato* seems distinctly less threatening, a tale the medium for which (poetry) is more cause for discussion than the subject (the participants, that is, completely leave aside the question of Cato and focus on poetry). Yet Maternus' *Cato* establishes another, subtle link between this text and the author of the *Brutus*, a text composed shortly after the suicide of Cato. Let me return, therefore, by way of conclusion to the *Dialogus'* relationship to Cicero's *Brutus*.

As I have argued elsewhere, the *Brutus* drew attention to the plight of Roman oratory in the late Republic; it served as a warning issued on the eve of Caesar's dictatorship about the threat posed to Roman memory

---

[35] On these, Gelzer (1968), 301–4.

by the loss of *eloquentia*.[36] Cicero's fears about the fate of Roman oratory were partially realized; while oratory continued and flourished under the Principate, the presence of the emperor and the changes to the judicial system prompted (directly or indirectly) by him demonstrably affected the sort of speeches people might make in public. Maternus is quite right about that. The *Dialogus* constitutes a reaction to the situation the *Brutus* only imagined ... and feared.

The *Dialogus* responds to the *Brutus* in some purely formal ways. I have mentioned the deliberately Ciceronian style as well as the form. There are, moreover, additional subtle evocations: the play of personal memory, for instance, and the sense of anxiety overshadowing the discussion (in the *Brutus* over the aftermath of Thapsus, in the *Dialogus* about the reaction of "those in power" to Maternus' *Cato*). Messalla's image of a downtrodden *eloquentia*, exiled from "her realm" (*expulsam regno suo*), the washed-up mistress of all the liberal arts (*olim omnium artium domina*), cut up, dismembered, unadorned, dishonored, a symbol of innocence lost (*nunc circumcisa et amputata, sine apparatu sine honore, paene dixerim sine ingenuitate*, *Dial.*32.4), may well owe much to Cicero's powerful personification of *eloquentia*, whom he envisions at the end of the *Brutus* as a young woman removed from the Forum, walled up in the confines of his home in order to protect her from worthless suitors (*Brut.* 333).[37] Both texts are ultimately interested in oratory: the *Brutus* in the consequences of its loss, the *Dialogus* in its alleged "decline". But one is clearly a Republican text; the other, unambiguously imperial.

These connections, however, flag a broader interest on the part of Tacitus in evoking a text that linked the tradition and preservation of oratory with the survival of the Republic. If the *Brutus* argues that collective memory is impossible without oratory, and that the Republic cannot stand without memory, the *Dialogus* suggests instead that as times change, so do the needs of the community. Without fully denying the usefulness of remembering the past, the *Dialogus* signals a point in the early Principate when the Republic has indeed ceased to be the benchmark by which the Principate is to be measured. In a world in which *otium* and poetry are legitimate pastimes of the aristocracy (as

---

[36] Gowing (2000).

[37] For the personification of *eloquentia* in the *Brutus*, Stroup (2003). For other Ciceronian moves in this passage see Mayer ad loc.

they most definitely were not under the Republic), when service to the state no longer precludes the enjoyment of such pursuits, then what *is* the point of "remembering the Republic?" It is not therefore that oratory has "declined" or ceased altogether, but rather that the type of oratory practiced and its venues have changed with the times.

To my knowledge it has not been recognized that the *Dialogus* is very much in the imperial Roman tradition of appropriating established genres and texts for contemporary purposes. As Lucan's *Pharsalia* is heir to Vergil's *Aeneid*, which is in turn a descendant of the quintessential Republican epic, the *Annales* of Ennius; or as Horatian satire grows out of the Republican tradition established especially by Lucilius, and is subsequently transformed yet again by Persius in the Neronian period and Juvenal in the Flavian, so too does the *Dialogus* draw from but ultimately re-shape an important Republican text. Tacitus would achieve this in other ways as well; the *Annales* and the *Historiae* both draw inspiration from the historiographical traditions of the Republic, but they of course chronicle imperial rather than Republican history. It is not simply that the latter had already "been done," most notably by Livy, but rather the deliberate exclusion of Republican history was entirely in line with the tendency we shall observe in the Forum of Trajan that was being built at the time Tacitus wrote his historical works. By the Trajanic period, Rome had new traditions and new heroes to celebrate. The *Dialogus*, like the *Brutus*, marks the end of one phase of Roman history and the beginning of another.

This particular function – as markers of ends and beginnings – becomes apparent when one considers Rupert Haenni's persuasive argument, made in 1905, that the *Brutus* is in effect a funeral oration, a *laudatio funebris*.[38] The deceased, he suggested, is *eloquentia*; the laudator, Cicero; and Brutus, the representative in the audience of a new generation meant to ponder the memory of, and be moved to emulate, the deceased. As Cicero instructs him at the conclusion of the piece, Brutus' task is to revive and perpetuate *eloquentia* and with it his own memory (*Brut.* 331). The *Dialogus*, by contrast, does not easily lend itself to such an interpretation; it is instead something of an anti-*laudatio*. Whereas Brutus is made to gaze upon the face of the deceased as at a

---

[38] Discussed in greater detail in Gowing (2000), 58–9; see also Stroup (2003), 130–1, and in preparation.

funeral, Aper and his young companion turn their faces away from it; Brutus is specifically instructed to remember, Aper is reinforced in his wish to forget. Thus Maternus, in his concluding remarks, which parallel those of Cicero at the end of the *Brutus*, stresses neither the past nor even the future. Rather, he fixes attention squarely on the present: *bono saeculi sui quisque citra obtrectationem alterius utatur*, "let everybody make the best possible use of the blessings of their own age without belittling someone else's" (41.5).

In the *Dialogus*, Tacitus consigns Cicero and Ciceronian oratory, at least in terms of their *political* dimension, to the past with a finality that is missing in Velleius or even in Seneca. It is not that Tacitus *erases* all memory of Cicero, but he does suggest that the reasons for remembering and emulating him are no longer the same as they once were, robbing Cicero's memory (not his work) of any real political meaning or force. Velleius would have us believe that on December 7, 43 BC Cicero really did not suffer death; Tacitus, on the other hand, makes reference to that event in the *Dialogus* on two occasions but interestingly never as a "murder" (*Dial.* 17.3, 24.3). He is not interested in the manner of Cicero's death, but merely in its symbolic value as the precise moment when Republican *eloquentia* died – and gave rise to a new, imperial *eloquentia*. In contrast to Velleius, Tacitus attempts neither to conceal the fact that this event had profound political implications nor to evoke pity for Cicero. As the concluding sentence of Maternus' speech indicates, the Principate is now one thing, the Republic, at last, is something else, something entirely "other".

Pliny's *Panegyricus* and Trajan's new past

Our best example of imperial *eloquentia* is Pliny's *Panegyricus*, an oration delivered by the younger Pliny in AD 100 shortly after the accession of the emperor Trajan, although the text as we have it is a reworking of the actual speech.[39] A speech of praise for the new emperor, it is heavily laden with what to modern tastes appears excessive flattery – a speech that enjoys what F. R. D. Goodyear termed "universal contempt."[40]

---

[39] Pliny *Ep.* 3.18, with discussion by Morford (1992), 575–7. For discussions of the speech, Connolly (forthcoming); Bennett (1997), 63–6 and passim.

[40] Goodyear (1982), 164.

But the simple fact that we have few specimens of speeches from the early imperial period makes it of considerable interest. Indeed, the choice of medium (a speech) and its very publication evoke Republican practice and assert the vigor of a skill whose decline is lamented in the *Dialogus*.[41] Mark Morford (1992) noted that the *Panegyricus* makes great capital out of the theme of *libertas*, heralding Trajan as someone under whom the Republic has been restored – *libertas reddita* (58.3) – while at the same time schooling Trajan in the compatibility of *libertas* and the Principate.[42] Although it will turn out that *libertas reddita* does not *quite* mean "the Republic has been restored" (Pliny, too, will contribute to the redefining of imperial *libertas*), a significant portion of the speech is given over to comparisons between Republican practice (especially the consulship) and Trajan's Rome. Republican *exempla* provide material for comparison as well. At first glance this seems familiar, just the sort of use of (and reverence for) the past we have observed in other imperial authors. But in contrast to Seneca's *De clementia*, which is rather similar in purpose and in which, as we observed, the Republic figures very little, it would appear that in the *Panegyricus*, a text composed nearly fifty years later, the Republic has regained some ethical and political clout.

Libertas reddita

Indeed, throughout the speech one encounters explicit indications that the reign of Trajan represents an apparent return to the Republic (*libertas reddita*, 58.3).[43] But in what sense? For Pliny this means in essence restoring some measure of authority to the Senate: thus he imagines that looking at Trajan's Senate he sees the "Senate of old" (*illum antiquum senatum*, 61.1); and that Trajan has revived the traditional, Republican power of the consul (93 and passim). Trajan is credited with having created an atmosphere that recalls an idealized Roman Republic – a culture in which "that

---

[41] The Republican qualities of the speech – and its distinctly imperial nature – are fully explored by Connolly (forthcoming), chap. 7.

[42] The "restoration of freedom" (*libertas restituta*, *libertas publica*) had been declared with the death of Domitian and the accession of Nerva in AD 96 (cf., e.g., Pliny *Ep.* 9.13.4, *ILS* 274): see Boyle (2003), 58; Fearnley (2003), 624; Cizek (1983), 186–92.

[43] Cf. *Pan.* 66.2, 66.4, 78.3, 87.1.

same virtue" is once again "rewarded" just as it had been "in times of the liberty," during the Republic, in other words (*eadem quippe sub principe virtutibus praemia quae in libertate*, 44.6). This notion of "sameness" recurs shortly thereafter, as Pliny asserts that they live in the "same Republic" (*eadem res publica*) as "a Papirius or a Quinctius" (57.5).

In contrast to Velleius Paterculus and Valerius Maximus, however, Pliny does not argue for an uninterrupted Republic. On the contrary, he asserts that it "died" with the civil wars of Marius and Caesar (*exspirante...libertate*, 57.4), and simply "did not exist" in the intervening years (*erat autem omnino res publica?*, 66.4). When Pliny speaks early on of the *diversitas temporum* (2.3), therefore, he is remarking on the distinction between the reign of Domitian and that of Trajan, not between the Republic and Trajan. Indeed, the *imperial* past in this speech constitutes one standard by which Pliny seeks to evaluate Trajan. In short, there is now enough of a post-Republic history to remember, but this history is for the most part negative. Virtually every aspect of life in Rome, that is, is "better" under Trajan than under his predecessors – perhaps most happily, the opportunity now exists to speak one's mind.[44] It is worth noting, however, that while Pliny will often speak in disparaging terms about Domitian and other emperors, he rarely names them, and the persons and events he invokes are left deliberately vague.[45] In this he perhaps shares a concern for the reputation of well-known families similar to that expressed by his coeval Tacitus.[46]

---

[44] Pliny's observation that they should now put aside "all those expressions which fear forced out of us" (*abeant ac recedant voces illae quas metus exprimebat*, 2.2, cf. 66.4–5) recalls Lucan's famous characterization of the consequences of a lost Republic (5.385–6, discussed in Chap. 3). Cf. Tac. *Agr.* 2.

[45] Comparisons with previous emperors: (e.g.) 2.1, 24.5, 40.4, 41, 43.5, 45.1, 53.1–5, 57.1–2, 58, 63.6–8, 66.3, 70.5–7, 82.1, 88.1 and 7; with Domitian: 2.6, 18.1, 20.4, 48, 49.1–3, 52, 82 and passim. With the exception of Nerva, who is mentioned on several occasions, only at 11 does he *name* Trajan's predecessors (omitting, however, Gaius); Nero receives one additional, explicit mention at 53.4, as does Titus at 35.4. Trajan is addressed throughout as "Caesar Augustus," but it is nonetheless curious that only once (at 11.1) does Pliny refer by name to the first emperor.

[46] Cf. *Ann.* 14.14.3–4, a description of the games decreed by Nero in honor of Agrippina in AD 59, where Tacitus declines to provide the names of those who degraded themselves by participating; Dio, on the other hand, happily provides them (61.17.3, discussed in Chap. 3).

Trajan, a new and improved exemplum

When looking to define Trajan's good qualities, however, Pliny turns to standard (and some not-so-standard) Republican *exempla*. These he eagerly and repeatedly names, seemingly erasing the intervening decades in order to create a semblance of continuity between the Republic and Trajan's Rome. But there is considerable difference between Pliny's attitude toward his *exempla* and that of, say, Valerius Maximus. In Pliny's hands these *exempla* function not as representatives of standards toward which his fellow citizens should strive, but rather of standards Trajan has surpassed, a rhetorical move reminiscent of what we observed in both Horace and Ovid in Chapter 1 as well as in Martial earlier in this chapter. For example:

> hac mihi admiratione dignus imperator <vix> videretur, si inter Fabricios et Scipiones et Camillos talis esset; tunc enim illum imitationis ardor semperque melior aliquis accenderet. postquam vero studium armorum a manibus ad oculos, ad voluptatem a labore translatum est, postquam exercitationibus nostris non veteranorum aliquis cui decus muralis aut civica, sed Graeculus magister adsistit, quam magnum est unum ex omnibus patrio more patria virtute laetari, et sine aemulo [ac] sine exemplo secum certare, secum contendere ac, sicut imperet solus, solum ita esse qui debeat imperare!

> A general would scarcely strike me as worthy of this sort of admiration, if such a man were born in the time of the Fabricii, the Scipios, or the Camilli. For in their day, he would have had the passion for imitation and the presence of someone else's superior talent to spur him on. But since the zeal for war has passed from the hands to the eyes, from being real work to a source of pleasure, and since it is no longer one of our veterans decorated with the mural or civic crown who presides over our exercises, but some Greekling trainer, how splendid it is that there is one man who finds delight in the traditions and virtue of our forebears, who struggles and contends only with himself, with no rival, no *exemplum*, and who, since he alone rules, is the only one fit to rule. (*Pan*.13.4–5)

The message, in short, is that the men of the Republic may have been good, but Trajan is better, just as he is better than all previous emperors

(88.7). Trajan has displaced these icons as *exempla*, becoming himself the chief *exemplum* of the leading man in the state (cf., e.g., 44, 73.6, 75.4–5). Thus Trajan is not *like* one of these *exempla*, rather he *is* "one of them." As Pliny puts it, describing the somewhat improbable thoughts of Rome's subject people about Trajan, they see him as "one of the old-time Roman generals" (*vident enim Romanum ducum unum illis veteribus et priscis*, 12.1; cf. 76.9).

Yet for Pliny, the fact that Trajan is "one of them" is not sufficient. He is also the "best" of them. In arguing this point, he similarly looks to the Republic for appropriate titles for the new emperor. But the titles applied to the great men of the Republic – *Felix* (like Sulla), *Magnus* (like Pompey), *Frugi* (like the Pisones), *Sapiens* (like Laelius), *Pius* (like Metellus) – prove utterly inadequate. There can be only one title for a man of Trajan's character: *Optimus*, "The Best," for Trajan "surpasses all those who are best only in their individual, isolated qualities" (*optimis omnibus in sua cuiusque laude praestantior*, 88.6). Here, too, Trajan is seen to outstrip Republican *exempla*. Pliny is of course fully aware that this title associates him not with Republican heroes, but rather with Jupiter Optimus Maximus – a reminder that Pliny is addressing an emperor, and no mere Republican magistrate.[47]

Nonetheless, comparisons of Trajan with Republican *exempla* may still be used, chiefly to sustain the (apparent) notion that the emperor has restored the Republic. Consider, for instance, Pliny's comparison of Trajan with Camillus and Brutus:

> stant igitur effigies tuae, quales olim ob egregia in rem publicam merita privatis dicabantur; visuntur eadem e materia Caesaris statuae qua Brutorum qua Camillorum. nec discrepat causa: illi enim reges hostemque victorem moenibus depulerunt, hic regnum ipsum quaeque alia captivitas gignit, arcet ac summovet, sedemque obtinet principis ne sit domino locus.

> And so statues of you are erected, such as were once dedicated to private citizens for outstanding service to the Republic; statues of

---

[47] Although the speech opens by addressing the *patres conscripti* (a seemingly "Republican" move), Pliny moves rapidly on to address Trajan as *optimus princeps* (1.2; cf. 2.7) and to assert his divine connections (1.5–6, 5, and passim). On the latter as a leitmotif of the speech, Bartsch (1994), 163–4; cf. Henderson (2002), 149–51.

Caesar [i.e., Trajan] are to be seen, made of the same material as those of a Brutus or a Camillus. And for the same reason: for they drove off from our walls kings and the conquering enemy, while he forbids and removes monarchy itself and whatever else captivity breeds, and holds the position of emperor so that there be no place for a tyrant.

(55.6–7)

Perhaps there would have been an audible gasp, until the audience realized that he meant not Brutus the liberator, but the founder of the Republic.[48] But Pliny has cleverly aligned Trajan with the man associated with the demise of the "tyranny" into which the Roman monarchy had deteriorated (cf. 58.4) as well as with the man famed as a savior of the Republic. And implicitly, of course, he denies that the Principate itself constitutes a return to monarchy. It is something else. But is it the Republic?

Senatus princepsque Romanus

Pliny is trying to have his cake and eat it too. His rhetoric betrays him, however, for it is quite clear that the "restoration of *libertas*" does not equate to a restoration of the Republic. If it did – to state the obvious – there would be no emperor. Yet it is equally apparent that *without* the emperor Trajan (or an individual like him), the *res publica* would find itself totally at sea. It is *Trajan* who invests the Senate with authority, respects the consulship, restores military discipline, exercises fiscal responsibility. Thus while Trajan offers a *libertas* that may share some affinities with that enjoyed under the Republic, this new *libertas* not only accommodates but requires the presence of a single leader, of an emperor.[49] In essence, the *princeps* has now displaced the *populus* in the old Republican formula *SPQR*.

It is not difficult to illustrate the centrality and necessity of the *princeps* in the political system Pliny delineates. While *libertas* may be "restored," it is nevertheless possible only with obedience to the emperor (67.2); his willing subjects are ruled (*regimur*) by this emperor, although he has

---

[48] In Pliny's day, in fact, it was evidently not unheard of to find busts of the tyrannicides displayed in private homes (cf. *Ep.* 1.17). On the memory of the liberators in the imperial period, Rawson (1986); MacMullen (1966), 27–9 and passim.

[49] *Pace* Noè (1984), 144, who sees Pliny's Trajan as "il restauratore della *libertas* repubblicana." For Pliny's particular brand of *libertas*, Morford (1992), esp. 584–93.

restored some measure of authority to the laws as well (24.4); and *this* emperor is god-like (1.3, cf. 80 and passim), the chosen of the gods (5.2, 52.2, 79.4–5, 94, and passim), a man who has managed to make compatible the seemingly incompatible, the office of *princeps* and that of *consul*. This, Pliny adroitly argues, is under Trajan an acceptably "Republican" situation (*civile*, i.e., a state in which the citizen is as valued as the *princeps*), better than being consul alone (*non est minus civile et principem esse pariter et consulem quam tantum consulem*, "it is no less republican to be both consul and emperor than it is only to be consul," 78.3; cf. 59.6).[50] This blatant special pleading lays bare the extent to which this is assuredly *not* the Republic of the past. Moreover, Pliny seems entirely happy with the Principate as a system, provided one has the right *princeps* in place (cf. 53.1).

Memory plays an important role in making this system palatable, a fact of which Pliny seems acutely aware. In some respects, the *Panegyricus* is a fine illustration of the Roman drive to maintain a connection with the past I discussed in the first chapter. At the same time, it illustrates the importance the ruling power attached to memory. The "ruling power" envisioned in this speech, however, is not just Trajan, but Pliny and his fellow senators as well. In short, while the oration clearly seeks to insert Trajan into Roman memory (the chief function of the speech being to record Trajan's accomplishments), Pliny is equally interested in the degree to which the memory of the Senate is to be kept alive as well. What we witness in this text, however, is an emerging interest in the *recent*, post-Augustan as opposed to the distant, pre-Augustan past. Hand in hand with this, of course, goes the development of *exitus*-literature, which made *exempla* of imperial (rather than Republican) personalities.[51]

---

[50] Reminiscent of Tacitus' claim that Nerva had accomplished the seemingly impossible, the reconciliation of the Principate and liberty (*Agr.* 3.1). This reconciliation, Noè (1984), 142, argues, had been underway in historiography since the outset of the Principate but reaches its climax in the *Panegyricus*. See further Bartsch (1994), 183–4.

[51] Thus Herennius Senecio writes a biography of the elder Helvidius or Arulenus Rusticus, of Thrasea Paetus (Tac. *Agr.* 2.1, Suet. *Dom.* 10.3, Dio 67.13.2). Tacitus' *Agricola* gives some sense of the nature of the genre. See Freudenburg (2001), 215–34, a revealing discussion, centred on Juvenal, of how in Trajan's Rome the recent imperial past now becomes the chief preoccupation of writers such as Juvenal as well as Pliny and Tacitus.

First, Trajan. The memory of Trajan himself emerges as something of a leitmotif in the speech. In a move reminiscent of Cicero's *Caesarianae* (identified, not without reason, by Quintilian as model *deprecationes*, the form of oratory best suited for addressing an emperor, *Inst.* 7.4.17–18), Pliny shows an inordinate concern for how Trajan is to be remembered.[52] The reason is doubtless that for Pliny Trajan has become the *exemplum* of the "best" type of emperor, the paradigm for all future emperors (59.2; cf. *Ep.* 3.18.2–3). Trajan's memory, he maintains, resides in the strength of his deeds rather than in physical monuments that are subject to decay (*non trabibus aut saxis nomen tuum sed monimentis aeternae laudis inciditur*, 54.7, cf. 55.9–10).[53] As Pliny reminds him, an emperor need have no fear that he will be forgotten – whatever he may do, his memory will be eternal (*fama ... aeterna*). The question is whether his will be a good or a bad reputation (55.9).

Trajan's good deeds have earned him, as we observed above, the title of *Optimus*. Pliny compares this with the title of *Augustus* which, he rightly surmises, is such a distinctive title that it inevitably reminds people of the first emperor. *Optimus* will serve the same purpose for Trajan, ensuring in a word his memory: *haec Optimi adpellatio numquam memoriae hominum sine te recurret, quotiensque posteri nostri Optimum aliquem vocare cogentur, totiens recordabuntur quis meruerit vocari*, "this title Optimus will eternally be associated in memory with you, and however often our descendants are compelled to call someone Optimus, they will remember the man who deserved to be so called" (88.10).[54]

A mark of Pliny's senatorial perspective, however, is the hint that the memory of the Senate is just as important as that of the emperor. The Trajanic Senate itself, in Pliny's worldview, has itself achieved the status of an *exemplum* to future generations (cf. 53.5). One of Trajan's

---

[52] Not coincidentally, the *Panegyricus* has been shown to have particular affinities with one of the *Caesarianae*, the *Pro Marcello* (see Morford [1992], 578–9 with refs.). For Caesar's memory as a key theme of that speech, Gowing (2000), 59–61.

[53] And yet Pliny imagines that future generations will visit places associated with Trajan's campaigns and travels, the "trees and rocks" (*arbores ... saxa*) and "buildings" (*tectum*) which sheltered him (15.4).

[54] Cf. 20.6, where future generations will "remember" (*meminerint*) Trajan's fiscal responsibility.

acts which especially impresses Pliny is his "restoration" of the Roman nobility:

> tandem ergo nobilitas non obscuratur sed inlustratur a principe, tandem illos ingentium virorum nepotes, illos posteros libertatis nec terret Caesar nec pavet; quin immo festinatis honoribus amplificat atque auget, et maioribus suis reddit. si quid usquam stirpis antiquae, si quid residuae claritatis, hoc amplexatur ac refovet, et in usum rei publicae promit. sunt in honore hominum et in ore famae magna nomina <excitata> ex tenebris oblivionis indulgentia Caesaris, cuius haec intentio est ut nobiles et conservet et faciat.

> Finally, therefore, the nobility does not live in obscurity, but has been brought to the light by our emperor. Finally, Caesar neither terrifies – nor fears – those grandsons of great men, the heirs of freedom. On the contrary, he uplifts and increases them, returning them to their ancestors. If anywhere he observes any traces of old stock, of lasting fame, this he embraces, cares for, and returns to the service of the state. They are held in honor, their great names roused from the shades of oblivion through the grace of Caesar, who intends to preserve as well as create the nobility.   (69.5–6)

Here, too, we see a reversal of the destruction of the nobility perpetrated by Julius Caesar at Pharsalus (as Lucan sees it[55]) and perpetuated by Trajan's predecessors, most notably Domitian. Such a reversal, in Pliny's eyes, entails rescuing them from the oblivion to which those in power had consigned them. And yet one wonders exactly whom Pliny means. Looking out at the faces in the audience, he would scarcely have found more than a handful of men who could claim descent from the great Republican families or for whom this mattered; on one estimate, only some 2 percent of the Flavian Senate could trace their lineage back to the families of the Republic.[56] Most of them had died – or been killed off. A senator himself, Pliny is not so much describing the Rome of Trajan as prescribing what he hopes it will turn out to be.

Trajan contributes in other ways to preserving the memory of the Senate. Much to Pliny's satisfaction, under Trajan the *acta diurna*, the

---

[55] Cf. *Phars.* 7.580ff. with discussion in Chap. 3.
[56] Hammond (1957), 75, cited by Mellor (2003), 85; cf. Cizek (1983), 205–7.

daily record of the Senate's activities, have been expanded to include senatorial acclamations (*acclamationes*). As he observes, it had evidently been *imperial* practice to include in the *acta* only speeches made by the emperor. Pliny regards the shift in practice as a means of rescuing from forgetfulness (*ne qua interciperet oblivio*) these senatorial expressions of approval (or disapproval) of the emperor, yet another indication of the restoration of at least some regard for the opinion of this body (75.1–4; cf. 3.1).[57]

For Pliny this act of remembering has considerable historical significance. He imagines that from the *acta* future emperors will learn to distinguish flattery from sincere praise, the right path from the wrong (75.5–6). Memory, that is, informs correct behavior – but again, provided that the memory itself is correct. This proves to be yet another boon of the Trajanic period, the restoration of "history" to its proper place.[58] Trajan's Rome, it appears, enjoys a renewed appreciation of the deathless value of historical accounts. Rome, Pliny implies, had lost sight of this, but came to its senses via the cultural renewal effected by the new emperor: "serious poetry now honors you, and the endless glory of historical writing," *seria ergo te carmina honorque aeternus annalium ... colit* (54.2). The *Panegyricus*, with its ceaseless comparison of Trajan with past inferior emperors, is itself an illustration of this new-found freedom as well as of the value of historical memory. Pliny is quite explicit about the necessity of the emperor to be equipped with a good memory. In part this is his own personal memory or experience, specifically of the lot of senators under Domitian, a memory that allows him to understand better senatorial behavior under his own regime: *nec verendum est ne incautos putet si fidelitate temporum constanter utamur, quos meminit sub malo principe aliter vixisse*, "Have no fear that he should think us ill-advised who regularly profit from our current security, whom he remembers lived different lives under a bad emperor" (67.3; cf. 44.1). In part it is a transmitted memory, such as he experienced in visiting the places and battlefields once walked by the "great generals" (*ingentes duces*, 15.4). And in part it is self-awareness of his own nature, a memory

---

[57] On acclamations, Rowe (2002), 82–3.

[58] Trajan is similarly shown to have respect for the past through his restoration of dilapidated but venerable houses and buildings, though Pliny does not explicitly identify which buildings are meant – or their age (50).

of the fact that he is a man rather than a god (*nec minus hominem se quam hominibus praeesse meminit*, "and he remembers that he is himself a man no less than one who rules over men" (2.4; cf. 87.1).[59]

What needs to be stressed here is that while Pliny does adduce Republican *exempla*, and the speech itself bears a Republican veneer, the past in which he is most interested – the past that he *remembers* and asks to be remembered – is almost entirely post-Augustan. Thus Trajan's memory (as well as that of Pliny) has now been added to – and in some measure has displaced – the memory of Rome's Republican past. *That* past warrants remembering not for what it can teach or as a model for present and future behavior, but rather as a reminder that so long as the Principate is held by a man such as Trajan, Rome is better off than it was under the Republic. This is a thought to warm the heart of any emperor, but given the *Panegyricus'* blatant assertion of the Senate's prerogatives, it is difficult to imagine such a speech being well-received by many of Trajan's predecessors; in that respect, the speech suggests how the political atmosphere must have changed for the better (at least from a senator's perspective). In such an atmosphere, Pliny may talk of the *res publica* and *libertas reddita* with no fear that his remarks will be misconstrued as incitement to dissidence. Like Tacitus' Maternus, Pliny reflects the reality of a political system that is accepted for what it is, a Principate, not the Republic. In the *Panegyricus* we witness the appropriation of Rome's "new" past in the formulation of a political system finally coming into its own.

Memory in transit

Let me conclude with a fanciful speculation, to suggest how times have changed in the seventy or so years intervening between the reign of Tiberius and that of Trajan. Sitting in the audience, listening to the *Panegyricus*, was undoubtedly the historian Tacitus, a man with whom

[59] Pliny's gentle injunction to Trajan at this point resembles Seneca's wish that Nero not "forget himself" (*Clem.* 1.1.7, discussed in Chap. 3). The Senate similarly has a duty to remember: specifically, that the best way to praise an emperor is to criticize his predecessors (*meminerint ... sic maxime laudari incolumem imperatorem, si priores secus meriti reprehendantur*, 53.6). Cf. 8.5 for another instance of the Senate's need to remember the recent past.

Pliny desperately wanted to be friends. Few imperial writers identified more closely with the Republic and its traditions, and he must have listened with considerable amusement to Pliny's characterization of the new regime as *libertas reddita*. But if Morford is right, Tacitus might not have disagreed with the message, even if he disliked the medium. Tacitus was acutely aware of the moral and ethical force of the Republican past, and although he never wrote a history of the Republic, he incessantly alludes to it, especially in the *Annales*, which he began to write shortly after the publication of the *Panegyricus*. His comment on the trial of Cremutius Cordus in AD 25, quoted in the first chapter, neatly captures the essence of the point I am making here as well as the considerable gap between the view of the Republic in Tiberius' day and that of Trajan's Rome. Like Cremutius in his speech, Tacitus regards the chief function of history – however it is used and by whatever medium it is conveyed – as the preservation of memory; the case of Cremutius instructs us in the folly of any emperor, whether it be a Tiberius or a Trajan, who believes he can rob future generations of the memory that is their birthright. That remark could only be made, I would argue, in hindsight, in light of experiences under emperors like Tiberius, Nero, or Domitian. If the *Panegyricus* illustrates that the Republic still warranted a place in imperial rhetoric, Tacitus sees to it that such rhetoric still carries some bite. But Tacitean rhetoric, as powerful as it was, belonged to the past; the rhetoric of the future was to be put on display in the Forum of Trajan.

Remembering Rome

The city of Rome is a tapestry of memory, a landscape lush with buildings and monuments that bear witness to attempts over the centuries to remember as well as forget.[1] This is a crucial point to grasp when trying to appreciate the degree to which the Republic lingered in the Roman imagination. On a purely practical level it was impossible in the period under discussion to avoid reminders of pre-imperial Rome. It is a mark of the Roman veneration for the past and for tradition that old buildings and monuments were seldom deliberately destroyed to make way for the new. Rather, new buildings were squeezed in to sit cheek by jowl with their precursors, old ones regularly rebuilt or refurbished. Thus while it is true that beginning with Julius Caesar and, most dramatically, Augustus, the topography of Rome was transformed in some significant ways, in certain respects the city itself would have looked the same in AD 50 as it did in 50 BC. This was in part the point of the Augustan building program: while some new structures were built (*RG* 19), the name of the game was restoration (cf. the *refeci* of *RG* 20).

Armed with even a rudimentary knowledge of Rome's past, therefore, a person strolling through the city in the early imperial period encountered at every turn buildings and monuments associated with the men whose memory the *exempla* tradition perpetuated as well as with the

---

[1] On cities as memory landscapes, Terdiman (1993), 260–1 with n. 24; Young (1993), 7. On Rome in particular as a "repository of memory," above all Edwards (1996); cf. Fowler (2000), 203.

political traditions of the Roman Republic.[2] One thinks, for instance, of the Temple of Castor, one of the most prominent structures in the Roman Forum: vowed in 493 BC at the battle of Lake Regillus, it underwent constant refurbishing over the centuries, well into the imperial period. The temple was a familiar meeting place for the Republican Senate and regularly the site of *iudicia*.[3] The nearby Basilica Pauli (Aemilia) preserved in its name, as did many other buildings in the city, the memory of a respected Republican family. To keep the connection alive, under Tiberius in AD 22 L. Aemilius Paulus paid to restore the facility constructed by his Republican ancestor nearly three-quarters of a century earlier.[4] The Roman Forum itself, of course, was the most potent symbol of the Republic, and it would not have gone unnoticed that with each successive emperor it became less and less the focal point of political activity.[5] Elsewhere, elaborate tombs (and the ceremonies that would be regularly performed there) carried on the memory of Republican icons. Among the most famous was the Tomb of the Scipios, located just outside the city limits on the Appian Way, itself lined with Republican tombs and sepulchres. The tomb's prominent location would keep the memory of this famous Republican family very much in the minds of imperial Romans. Nor should one overlook the fact that Rome was littered with hundreds of inscriptions, statues, and reliefs memorializing the Republican past.[6] These were not simply Republican structures but rather (to use Nora's term), quintessential "sites of memory," *lieux de mémoire* – places associated with Republican events, activities, and individuals.

---

[2] For a helpful if impressionistic recreation of what walking through Augustan Rome might have been like, Favro (1996), 252–80. Edwards aptly notes (1996), 18, "The city was a storehouse of Roman memories, an archive which ordered them and made them accessible."

[3] Millar (1998), 70.

[4] Tac. *Ann.* 3.72; it had earlier been restored by Augustus, though interestingly in the name of Aemilius (Dio 54.24). See Bauer in Steinby (1993), 1.183–7; Nünnerich-Asmus (1994), 72–4.

[5] On the beginnings of this process (with Octavian), Zanker (1990), 79–85.

[6] Valerius Maximus (3.6.2), to cite one example, notes that a statue of L. Scipio Asiaticus (cos. 190 BC, who celebrated a triumph for his defeat of Antiochus) was still visible on the Capitoline in his day: people could "see" personalities from the Republic on public display. Cicero saw the same statue nearly a century before (*pro. Rab. Post.* 27).

While old, extant sites imparted a sense of continuity, even new structures might suggest that the political processes of the Republic were to be perpetuated. One thinks especially of the Saepta Julia, the voting enclosure in the Campus Martius. Begun by Julius Caesar in order to replace the earlier Ovile, it was completed by the triumvirs after his death and ultimately dedicated by Agrippa in the Augustan period in 26 BC – in the early years of the Principate, that is. Despite the gesture, however, Rome's citizens would have quickly abandoned the notion that this somehow signaled a restoration of Republican voting procedures as the area became in the early imperial period a site for gladiatorial combat, gymnastic contests, and even a market.[7] There were still other indications of a wish to maintain a connection with the Republican past: the practice of employing Republican portrait types, for instance, or reusing familiar Republican iconography.[8] It would perhaps be misleading to label such practices mere nostalgia – but did they signal a serious and continuing desire to bring back the Republic?

The Anaglypha Traiani, two historical reliefs of Trajanic or Hadrianic date, furnish one example of what such visual symbols of the Republic eventually came to mean. As Torelli has discussed, the two reliefs feature distinctly Republican "sites of memory": the *ficus Ruminalis* and the statue of Marsyas located in the Roman Forum. The former was the fig tree associated with the Lupercal, the spot where the she-wolf had suckled Romulus and Remus, once located at the foot of the Palatine but miraculously transferred to the Forum in the regal period, at what would become the Republican Comitium and on the *tribunal praetoris*; the latter, a Silenus figure whose statue showed him with chains broken in an apparent sign of liberation.[9] Both evoke Republican memory (as do the other structures represented on the reliefs), especially, in the case of Marsyas, of *libertas*. And yet the friezes themselves celebrate an act of magnanimity on the part of the emperor Trajan, the remission of taxes

---

[7] Richardson (1992), s. "Saepta Iulia."

[8] See Chap. 4, n. 12.

[9] For the *ficus Ruminalis*, Coarelli's article on the *ficus Navia* (the name given to the "transferred" *ficus Ruminalis* in honor of Attus Navius, the augur associated with the tree's relocation) in Steinby (1993–2000), 2.248–9; for the statue of Marsyas, Coarelli in Steinby (1993–2000), 4.364–5.

and distribution of an imperial donation (*congiarium*).[10] While Torelli is right to suggest that the use of such iconography promotes a sense of *continuitas imperii*, "the continuity of empire," the emphasis here is not on the continuity of the Republic as a political entity. This is instead simply another appropriation of the theme of *libertas* now viewed in terms of imperial *liberalitas* rather than of Republican liberty – a *libertas* vaunted, most relevantly for this particular relief (especially if it is of Trajanic date), in Pliny's *Panegyricus*. As Torelli puts it, while "the republican tradition is formally respected" it "appears to be entirely absorbed into the new formulas of imperial power and of the epiphany of the prince."[11] It should be stressed that this is the situation at the *end* of the period I have covered in this book; that such symbols resonated differently in the Augustan period than they did in the Trajanic is, I think, beyond doubt.

If early imperial culture could still make capital out of the Republic, the signs of change were nonetheless visible in the city. In his astute discussion of the late Republic's "constitutional topography," Fergus Millar observed how the changing urban landscape reflected a serious sea change in Rome's political habits. The Roman Forum, in particular, with its open spaces and central location, reminds us of the public and rather open nature of Roman Republican politics.[12] As I have suggested, it is no coincidence that the end of the Republic sees the beginning of the most ambitious building program the city had ever witnessed, a building program that would ultimately shift the political nucleus of the city away from the Forum itself, or at least dramatically broaden it; the construction of the Forum of Augustus was an important step in that process.[13] As he transformed the political landscape, so would Augustus transform the physical landscape of his city.

[10] Bennett (1997), 59–61.

[11] Torelli (1982), 131. Albertson's (1990), 815, characterization of Roman historical reliefs is apt: "a *memoria* of the past represented through the eyes of the present." On these reliefs, Torelli (1982), 89–190, esp. 90 (dating) and 99, 105–6, 131 (theme of *continuitas imperii* and Republican associations). See also Richardson (1992), 292–3, s. "Plutei Traiani"; Kleiner (1992), 248–50.

[12] Millar (1998), 19–20, 31, 38–9, 124–5, and passim. For the phrase "constitutional topography," 56, 158.

[13] Zanker (1968), 24.

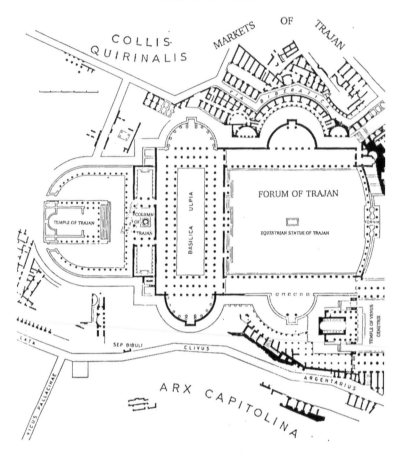

Fig. 1   Plan of the Imperial Fora

Augustus' move, of course, is anticipated over a decade prior to the inception of his principate by the Forum Iulium (the Forum of Caesar, (for which see Fig. 1). Substantially complete by 46 BC, this edifice inaugurated a new era in Roman building. Perhaps no structure better captures the essence of the change the city was experiencing. While the notion that buildings and monuments were one means for an individual to promote the reputation and standing of his family (and to secure their

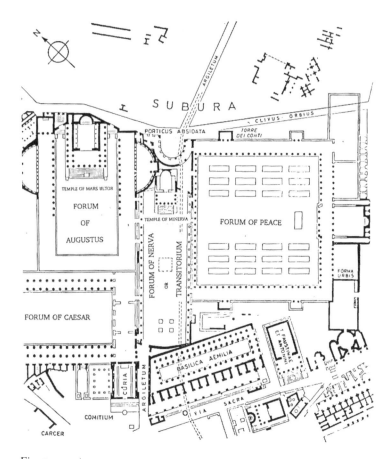

Fig. 1   cont.

memory) was hardly a novel idea, no one had gone to quite the same lengths as Julius Caesar to construct and ornament a space so obviously designed to promote himself and his lineage.[14] Dominated by the Temple

---

[14] Anderson (1984), 43 (date and purpose), 51. On the Republican practice of using buildings as an act of self-promotion, Edwards (1996), 21 with notes; Zanker (1990), 20–5. In design and purpose the Imperial Fora had much in common with their Republican predecessors: see La Rocca (2001), 185–6.

of Venus Genetrix, in front of which stood the famous statue of Caesar's horse (which, with its hooves in the form of human fingers, had been taken as a portent of Caesar's power), the Forum declared the divine origins of the Julian family, an early step in the development of the ruler cult that would eventually blossom in Rome and the Empire at large. The Forum's location, moreover, abutting but separate from the Roman Forum to the south, further declared its innovative nature as well as the elevated status of its creator. This was the structure from which Rome's first emperor took his cue for the eponymous forum he dedicated in 2 BC.

Memory on display in the Forum of Augustus

Despite its debt to that of Julius Caesar, the Forum of Augustus is considerably more sophisticated in intent and execution.[15] Focusing not merely on the new *princeps*' family and its place in Roman history, Augustus' Forum was an architectural and artistic declaration of the restored Republic. Certainly no Roman monument more ably showcases the seamless blending of past and present, public and private, domestic and foreign, Republican and imperial. It brought into public view the same sort of connections with the past that were being made in literature, most notably in Vergil's *Aeneid*, especially Books 6 and 8, and Livy's *History*.[16] But one did not necessarily need to read in order to get the point of the Forum.

As I suggested in Chapter 1, in some important respects the Forum of Augustus is best understood as a "house of memory," Carruthers' "architectural mnemonic."[17] Visually and structurally, it organizes the

---

[15] The bibliography on the Forum of Augustus is substantial: esp. Spannagel (1999), an exhaustive and detailed study of the whole complex; Anderson (1984), 65–100; Galinsky (1996), 197–213; Kockel in Steinby (1993–2000), 2.294–5; La Rocca (2001), 184–95; useful comparison of the differing functions of the Forum of Augustus and the Forum Iulium in Nünnerich-Asmus (1994), 55–64.

[16] See below with n. 32. For the relationship between Livy's *History* and the Forum, Luce (1990); Chaplin (2000), 168–96.

[17] See Chap. 1 with n. 54. Vitruvius in fact identifies the preservation of memory as one of the aims of the Augustan building program: *animadverti multa te aedificavisse et nunc aedificare, reliquo quoque tempore et publicorum et privatorum aedificiorum, pro amplitudine rerum gestarum ut posteris memoriae traderentur curam habiturum,* "I observe that you (i.e., Augustus) have built much and still are building; and that in the future, too, you will show a concern for both public and private buildings commensurate with the greatness of our history, so that they will

Roman past in much the same way as Quintilian (most fully, of ancient authors) recommended an orator should arrange in his mind the facts he needed to know, imagining a house with a series of rooms, with a place for everything and everything in its place.[18] Favro aptly observes the connection between this style of memory-training Romans received as a staple of their education and the way Rome was laid out; similarly, Edwards suggests that the city's buildings could work together in much the same way as the family masks worn at aristocratic funerals, another memory-prompting device.[19] Both observations have been made more narrowly of the Forum of Augustus (see below, with n. 34). But it is important to grasp that the Forum constituted one component of a much broader memory canvas; what these and other scholars have noted is that Rome's buildings, spaces, and visual imagery (e.g., statues and friezes) evoked particular associations with historical events and personalities – memories, in other words. The deep Roman ties to this spirit of place, and the ways those ties manifest themselves, especially in literature, have been amply investigated in recent years.[20] The Forum of Augustus has been understandably prominent in such discussions.

Especially important for my thesis is the gallery of heroes, the *summi viri*, the outstanding men of Rome's past (only from a post-Augustan perspective would one distinguish them specifically as *Republican* heroes). Entering the Forum through the main entrance, which faced or was actually joined to the north wall of the Forum Iulium,[21] the visitor was flanked on either side by a colonnade (Fig. 2). A series of rectangular niches was cut into the walls of each colonnade; the two walls eventually curved outward to form hemicycles, one on each side, also marked by niches. The bulk of the niches housed statues of well-known Republican characters accompanied by two inscriptions, an identifying *titulus* and an *elogium* briefly summarizing the honorand's accomplishments (Fig. 3). Image and text here work together to present a fairly fixed

be consigned to memory for the benefit of our descendants" (Vitr. 1, *praef.* 3). Favro (1996), 247.

[18] Quint. *Inst.* 11.2.17–22. See the refs. cited in Chap. 1, n. 50.

[19] Favro (1996), 5–7; Edwards (1996), 43. Cf. Flower (2004b), 338.

[20] E.g., Edwards (1996); Vasaly (1993), esp. 15–39; Jaeger (1997), 1–29; Gregory (1994).

[21] See La Rocca (2001), 178–9.

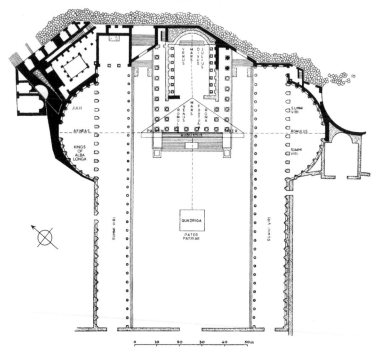

Fig. 2   Ground plan of the Forum of Augustus, with sculptural program

memory of a very select group of men; both media, sculpture and inscription, by their very nature suggest a sense of permanence and continuity.[22] The use of *statues*, in particular, was one especially common means of making present and keeping alive the character represented; the effect is rather like the use of *enargeia* I discussed in connection with Velleius, Valerius Maximus, and Seneca.[23]

---

[22] Cf. Val. Max. 5.8.3, discussed in Chap. 2. Compare Asinius Pollio's practice of putting busts of writers in his library in order to associate faces with text. As David (1998b), 16, concludes, this juxtaposition of image and text is a very Roman way of "fixing" memory. On the Roman experience of reading an inscription – and the sense of permanence inscriptions impart – Susini (1988), esp. 119.

[23] On the Roman use of statues to "bring to life individuals who were no longer alive," Gregory (1994), 87. This is why the comparison of the Forum with an aristocratic funeral is so compelling (above and below with n. 34).

Fig. 3   Reconstruction of a statue of a *summus vir*, with *titulus* and *elogium*, in the gallery of the Forum of Augustus

The precise number of statues of *summi viri* displayed here is unknown, though it was at least twenty-six.[24] We know many of their

[24] Anderson (1984), 83.

identities: for example, A. Postumius Regillensis, the dictator whose famous victory against the Latins in 496 at Lake Regillus prompted the building of the Temple of Saturn; Camillus, the Roman icon who defeated the Gauls in 390; Appius Claudius Caecus, the censor of 312 BC known for the construction of the Via Appia; Tiberius Gracchus, who celebrated in 178 BC a triumph over the Celtiberians and was the father of the tribune of 133 BC; Marius and Sulla, the former an ancestor of Julius Caesar, the latter Marius' most bitter opponent and, prior to Caesar, Rome's most famous dictator.[25]

The *elogium* of Marius provides a telling example of the way these texts manipulate memory:[26]

> C. Marius C. f. cos. VII, pr., tr. pl., q., <u>augur, tr. mil. Extra</u> sortem bellum cum <u>Iugurtha rege Numid</u>. cos. gessit. Eum cepit et <u>trium-phans in</u> secundo consulatu <u>ante currum suum</u> duci iussit. Tertium <u>consul apsens creatus</u> est. IIII cos. Teuto<u>norum exercitum</u> delevit. V cos. <u>Cimbros fugavit, ex | ieis e</u>t Teutonis iterum triump<u>havit. Rem p. turbatam</u> seditionibus tr. pl. | et praetor., <u>quei arma</u>ti Capitolium occupaverunt, VI <u>cos. vin</u>dicavit. | Post LXX annum patria per arma civilia expulsus armis restitutus | VII cos. factus est. De manubiis | Cimbris et Teuton. aedem Honori | et Virtuti victor fecit. Veste | triumphali calceis patriciis [*in senatum venit*] . . .

> Gaius Marius, son of Gaius, was consul seven times, praetor, tribune of the plebs, quaestor, augur, and military tribune. Chosen without drawing lots, as consul he waged war with Jugurtha, king of the Numidians. He captured him, and commanded that he be led in front of his chariot during the triumph he celebrated in his second consulship. He was elected consul for a third time *in absentia*. In his fourth consulship he destroyed the army of the Teutones. As consul for a fifth time, he routed the Cimbri, celebrating a second triumph for both this victory and that over the Teutones. In his sixth consulship he freed the Republic

---

[25] For discussion of the identities of those represented here, with references, Anderson (1984), 80–8; cf. Sage (1979), 193. The Forum's *elogia* are collected in Degrassi (1937), 1–36. For analysis, Zanker (1968), 14–17, and Zanker (1990), 210–15; Spannagel (1999), 256–358.

[26] I quote the text as reconstructed in *ILS* 59; cf. Degrassi (1937), 22–4 (*Inscr. Ital.* 17). For the history of the inscription, Spannagel (1999), 318–20 with n. 391.

when it was wracked by sedition sown by the tribunes of the plebs and the praetors, who had seized the Capitoline under arms. At over seventy years of age he was restored by arms to the homeland from which he had been driven out by arms, and elected consul a seventh time. With the spoils won from his victories over the Cimbri and Teutones he built a temple to Honor and Virtue. In triumphal garb, and with the shoes of high office, he came into the Senate ....

This contains the fairly standard elements of a straightforward career inscription and *res gestae*, from which one does not typically expect much emotional content. This is not to say that it cannot elicit an emotional response: some viewers may well have experienced a sense of national pride and admiration as they read this summary of Marius' achievement. But they would have to know their history well in order to supply from their own memory the low points of Marius' career (and it should be stressed that each "read" of these images and texts will depend very much on the viewer's own knowledge and experience): the guile with which he secured his fourth consulship in 103 BC, a reputation for faithlessness, or the exceptional cruelty of his conduct during the civil war of 87–86 BC.[27] As Beard describes it, this *elogium* is "expertly reticent," a text that effects "the transformation of Marius from butcher of the civil war to hero of the republic."[28] Much the same may be said of Augustus' own *Res gestae*, which are similarly silent about the more unsavory aspects of the emperor's rise to power.[29]

While military success seems to have been one of the criteria by which the selection was made, as the *elogia* of Marius and others suggest, Sage is justified in stressing that the chief criterion was simply a significant contribution to the rise or expansion of Rome – in Suetonius' words, *qui imperium populi Romani ex minimo maximum reddidissent*, "those who

---

[27] Fourth consulship: Plut. *Mar.* 14.7–8, Liv. *Per.* 67; faithlessness: Liv. *Per.* 69 (*homo vari et mutabilis ingenii consiliique semper secundum fortunam*), Cic. *Rab. Perd.* 10.28; civil war: (e.g.) Liv. *Per.* 79–80. The sources are collected in Greenidge and Clay (1960²).

[28] Beard (1998), 88. This is an excellent case study of an imperial cursus inscription and the ways in which it exhibits a tension between imperial and Republican modes of self-expression.

[29] Tac. *Ann.* 1.9–10 is the best place to appreciate the conflicting interpretations of the emperor's triumviral career.

had raised from least to the greatest the empire of the Roman people" (*Aug.* 31.5).[30] Anderson persuasively expands on this, speculating that the men represented would also be understood to share, by virtue of the offices they held and their accomplishments, some connection with the new emperor.[31] Augustus' own presence in the Forum merely positioned him as another in a long line of illustrious *Republican* magistrates, taking his rightful place in this Republican memory palace.

Some clue as to the purpose of such a move is to be found in the apparent parallels scholars have found between the Forum's gallery and various passages in Augustan literature: Ovid's survey of Republican *exempla* who were worthy of the title "Augustus" in *Fasti* 1.590–608 (cited in Chap. 1), for example, and, as mentioned above, Vergil's parade of famous Romans in *Aeneid* 6.725–886. These include, to cite just a few of the overlaps, the Scipios, L. Aemilius Paulus, T. Manlius Torquatus, the Fabii, and others.[32] The period gives rise, in other words, to a canonical list of acceptable Republican *exempla*, a list that would set the standards by which the emperor himself wished to be judged.[33] As a final reminder of the importance the emperor attached to the men represented in this space, images of his ancestors and relatives – including Pompey the Great – were similarly displayed at Augustus' funeral. Appropriately, the function of the Forum's gallery has often been compared to that of the *imagines* displayed at a funeral or in the atria of aristocratic homes.[34] The influence of the Forum's gallery has also been detected in the *History* of Velleius Paterculus, yet another indication of the continuing sway of the Republic (and the Augustan version of it) in the Tiberian period.[35]

[30] Sage (1979), 194.

[31] Anderson (1984), 83–5; cf. Spannagel (1999), 332–44.

[32] Anderson (1984), 85–7; Millar (1993), 7; Spannagel (1999), 259–62. Barchiesi (2002) explores a similar connection between the Forum's Temple of Mars Ultor and Augustan poetry.

[33] Zanker (1990), 214. Chaplin's (2000), 173–96, discussion of the Forum's *elogia* and Augustan *exempla* is informative.

[34] Augustus' funeral: Dio 56.34, with Swan's (2004) extensive commentary ad loc. See Zanker (1968), 27; Zanker (1990), 213–14; Favro (1992), 253; Flower (1996), 224–36; Spannagel (1999), 259, 263–6.

[35] Rowe (2002), 63–4; Schmitzer (2000), 291–2.

And yet one thing is certain: many well-known Republicans are left out. Just as the *elogium* of Marius omits details, so too does the Forum of Augustus omit reference to other, less desirable icons of Republican history. It is admittedly not surprising that this Augustan showplace would deny a place in memory, at least in this context, to men such as Cato Uticensis, Cicero, Brutus, or Cassius. On a Julian view, these are not men whom one could claim, in all fairness, to have contributed to the "rise of Rome." As we have seen, their memory was clearly a source of discomfort to some, and their absence in the Forum should be viewed as a deliberately memory-effacing move, a means of replacing one narrative of Roman history with another. In Augustus' version of Republican history, as displayed in this space, these men did not warrant remembering. Yet nonetheless they *were* the men whom many would most closely identify with the Republic and the spirit of Republicanism. In Tacitus' *Dialogus* Maternus has recited before the emperor an anxiety-producing tragedy about Cato, not Camillus.

The aim of the gallery, however, was to put the new emperor and his family into visual play with those Republican characters with whom he wished to be most closely associated, not those from whom he wished to distance himself. Thus the sight-lines enjoyed by the visitor to the Forum made connections between the *summi viri* and the equestrian statue of the emperor in the center, and in addition, as one approached the point where the two hemicycles toward the end and on either side of the Forum revealed themselves, with Aeneas and Anchises flanked by members of the *gens Iulia* in the central niche of the left hemicycle, and Romulus and more *summi viri* in that on the right as one faces the temple (Fig. 2). Raising the eyes to the pedimental sculpture adorning the Temple of Mars at the Forum's northern end, the visitor glimpsed Mars flanked by Fortuna and Venus, Romulus and Roma seated nearby.[36] The whole complex worked in concert to memorialize the divine ancestry of the new *princeps* and place him squarely in the memory of the viewer together with the other makers of the Republic, not with those whom the new regime claimed had sought to disrupt it.

---

[36] Zanker (1990), 201–2 (statues in *exedrae*). On Mars see also n. 40.

The Forum of Trajan and the new past

Nearly one hundred years later, the emperor Trajan undertook the construction of his own forum. Although new excavations in the Forum of Trajan may well alter our views of the entrances, it seems certain that one would have been able to walk from the Forum of Augustus into the adjacent Forum of Trajan.[37] Such a physical connection symbolized, in a way Romans would particularly appreciate, a sense of continuity. And yet to stroll in the Forum of Trajan in AD 112, the year of its dedication, was to witness a very different past, a past in which the icons of the Republic were replaced with the new icons of the Principate. The two structures invoke and perpetuate memories of two different periods in Roman history, now separated in time just as they are separated in space. Not, to be sure, entirely severed, but certainly separated.[38]

A reasonably knowledgeable visitor walking from the Augustan building to the new forum could scarcely have missed the profound differences between the two which, in their decorative program and even in their very dimensions, convey the extent to which the memory of the Republican past had faded away, supplanted by both the memory of and hope for Empire. Whereas in Augustus' Forum our visitor would see the gallery of Republican heroes (the perspective now being post-Augustan), a structure that celebrated the past and venerated the divine will that had guided it, Trajan's Forum exalted the recent conquests and the power of the man who was in control. We do not know with certainty whether or not this Forum included any statues of famous Republicans. It seems highly unlikely, given what we *do* know of the Forum's sculptural program. In light of the magnitude of what surrounded them, it scarcely mattered. Trajan's Forum was chiefly a celebration of Trajan:

---

[37] For recent work on the complex of the Imperial Fora, and how these spaces were linked together, see La Rocca (2001) and fig. 4, for a revision of the Gismondi plan (I use J. E. Packer's revision of the Gismondi plan in my Fig. 1) that incorporates new excavations and hypotheses.

[38] As Packer (1997), 272, has summarized the effect, "the magnificent monuments of Trajan's Forum – and the great events they commemorated – were to be understood not as a revolutionary break with the revered past but only as the newly achieved perfection of preexisting artistic – and by implication, political – forms." See further Bennett (1997), 153–8.

like Pliny's *Panegyricus*, it made nods to the past, but only in the service of venerating the man who constructed it. The focal point of Augustus' Forum was the great temple to Mars, dwarfing a quadriga with Augustus in front, flanked by the niches with their *summi viri*. Trajan's Forum and Basilica, by contrast, were not organized around a temple; overseeing if not dominating the space was the famous towering column supporting a gilt bronze statue of Trajan.[39] When you raised your eyes, you saw not Mars, but the emperor.[40] The column's relief, commemorating the emperor's Dacian campaigns of AD 101–2 and 105–6, positioned the emperor at the center of recent history rather than past.

As a measure of the extent to which one structure works with the other (and thus establishes continuity), it is instructive to observe the ways in which Trajan's Forum responds to that of Augustus. As Packer and others have noted, the former regularly quotes the latter.[41] Hölscher draws attention to the ways in which the ornamental program of the Forum of Trajan transforms the message of the Forum of Augustus even when alluding to it. He remarks, for instance, that the Caryatids surmounting the attics above the colonnades in the Forum of Augustus find a parallel in the statues of captive Dacians in that of Trajan: both symbolize servitude (the Augustan architect Vitruvius explains why Caryatids constituted a *servitutis exemplum*, 1.1.5), but one requires a rather sophisticated viewer conversant with such abstractions, whereas the other offers the concrete in place of the abstract, real over mythic conquest. By the

---

[39] Packer (2003) has argued that the Temple of Divus Traianus, located to the north of the Basilica Ulpia and generally believed to have been a Hadrianic afterthought (e.g., Richardson [1992], s. "Forum Traiani", pp. 177–8) was probably under construction at the time of the Forum's dedication in AD 112. On the significance of the temple to the designs of both the Forum of Augustus and the Forum Iulium, Zanker (1968), 6.

[40] The Forum of Trajan featured multiple images of Trajan: Packer (1997), 282–3, and (1994), 181–2. As Zanker (1968), 22, points out, Mars in the Forum of Augustus was very much *identified* with Augustus, but the fact remains that it is Mars and *not* the emperor we see; further on Mars, Barchiesi (2002).

[41] E.g., the hemicycles of Trajan's Forum recall those of Augustus'; the *imagines clipeatae* featured on the façade of the central arch of the former and elsewhere recall those found on the attics of the latter's colonnades. Packer (1997), 260 with n. 7, 270–1, 276–9; see also Anderson (1984), 141–77.

same token, Hölscher explains that the *summi viri* of the Forum of Augustus – through whom Augustus declared his reverence and respect for the old Roman nobility (or at least some of them) – are answered in Trajan's Forum with statues of early emperors and their relatives, including women (in sharp contrast to the Forum next door). They similarly occupied niches concealed behind colonnades and hemicycles constructed in clear imitation of those in the adjacent Forum of Augustus; among those we may identify from the surviving heads are Livia, Agrippina the Younger, and the emperors Vespasian and Nerva.[42] But again, as did the historical relief on Trajan's column, *these* statues served as memorials to recent (and not exclusively military) personalities, not to those of the distant past.[43]

Young's views on the effects of monuments can shed some light on the contrasting effects of these two Fora. In a discussion of Holocaust memorials, he alleges that monuments often serve to "relieve viewers of their memory burden." The drive to memorialize traumatic events, in other words, coexists with the "opposite and equal desire to forget."[44] Individually, the *summi viri* of the Forum of Augustus were hardly associated with a national trauma; but to those contemplating their memory from the perspective of the Augustan Principate and for a time, at least, even later, the institution those men represent, the Republic, *was* associated with just such a trauma, precipitated by civil war, assassination, executions, proscriptions, and confiscations. For some viewers, *this* would be the memory evoked by the sight of so many illustrious men, the builders of a Republic that no longer existed. The Forum of Augustus therefore may have achieved a paradoxical effect, an effect that could be truly felt only by those who had experienced or remembered the Republic: built to commemorate and celebrate the Republic, in its capacity as a site of memory it must also have become associated with the *loss* of and mourning for the Republic. Again, Young's observation on a monument's

---

[42] Hölscher (1984), 10–11; cf. Zanker (1968), 13 (on the Caryatids and Dacians); Packer (1997), 105 n. 38 (who believes, *contra* Zanker, that these heads belong to the *imagines clipeatae* on the attic of the colonnades). Further on the Forum's sculptural program, Kleiner (1992), 212–24.

[43] Anderson (1984), 160–1.

[44] Young (1993), 5.

capacity to achieve such paradoxical ends is instructive: "memorials created in the image of a state's ideals actually turn around to recast national ideals in the memorial's image."[45] In place of the Republic stood the institution celebrated in the Forum constructed next door a century later.

But this precise paradox does not apply to the Forum of Trajan. Physically and visually overpowering, the Forum of Trajan displaced its predecessors in magnificence and importance; it memorializes, to be sure, but a very different set of events and personalities from those found in the Forum of Augustus. Considered together, the two Fora typify the "agonistic" relationship Fowler observes "between old and new," one example of which he tellingly locates in Propertius 3.11 as the poet describes the eclipsing of Rome's former monuments by the newly built temple of Leucadian Apollo.[46] A century later, the Forum of Trajan similarly eclipses the Forum of Augustus.

One well-known piece of evidence for the overpowering and displacing nature of the Forum of Trajan is the experience of the emperor Constantius II recorded by the fourth-century historian Ammianus Marcellinus (16.10.13–17). Visiting Rome for the first time in AD 357, the emperor is said to have been amazed at the wondrous buildings and structures that greeted him. Yet with few exceptions (the Temple of Jupiter on the Capitoline, the Roman Forum and the Theater of Pompey), the monuments Ammianus specifically identifies as having impressed him are all imperial: the baths, the Hadrianic Pantheon

---

[45] Young (1993), 120. This paradox may be further appreciated by considering Freud's views on the nature of mourning as described in *Mourning and Melancholia*. Roth (1995), 196 summarizes those views: "The lost object is 'saved' through introjection, the past is retained but at great cost, because the past becomes that which enables the present to be seen as something that is never good enough, always missing that which is essential." If one imagines that the Roman Republic constitutes a "lost object" (as it came to be regarded by some), and that the Forum of Augustus in some sense "saves" or preserves its memory, Freud's thinking about memory and loss (especially as articulated in *Mourning and Melancholia*) is as applicable to a society as it is to an individual. Freud (1924), 153, himself anticipates this: "Mourning is regularly the reaction to the loss of a loved person, or to the loss of some abstraction which has taken the place of one, such as fatherland, liberty, an ideal, and so on."

[46] Fowler (2000), 203–5.

and Temple of Roma, the Flavian Colosseum, Stadium, Odeum, and Forum of Peace, and the Forum of Trajan. The last astonishes him:

> Verum cum ad Traiani forum venisset, singularem sub omni caelo structuram, ut opinamur, etiam numinum adsensione mirabilem, haerebat attonitus per giganteos contextus circumferens mentem nec relatu effabiles nec rursus mortalibus appetendos. omni itaque spe huiusmodi quidquam conandi depulsa Traiani equum solum locatum in atrii medio, qui ipsum principem vehit, imitari se velle dicebat et posse.

> But when he came to the Forum of Trajan, the most unique building under all of heaven (in our opinion), a marvel even by common consent of the gods, he stood astounded, taking in the gigantic complex, a sight that can neither be described nor attempted again by mortals. And with all hopes dashed of ever trying anything of this sort, he remarked that he would and could imitate only the equestrian statue in the middle of the atrium, which bore the emperor himself.
> (Amm. Marc. 16.10.15)

Entirely erased from the landscape memorialized in the narrative of this moment is the Forum of Augustus – the building that Pliny the Elder, writing in the early Flavian period roughly two centuries earlier, had identified as "the most beautiful building in the world," *pulcherrimum operum, quae umquam vidit orbis* (*NH* 36.15.102).[47]

What this moment underscores is that the Principate fed on change. It was inevitable, that is, that the Forum of Augustus should ultimately be eclipsed by a grander structure, just as the message of one is eclipsed by that of the other. Change, or rather change successfully negotiated, is the one constant of an enduring Empire.[48] This is at odds, however, with the Roman insistence on the continuity and constancy of Rome itself – the *absence* of change, in other words. This insistence is manifest, I have suggested, in the very nature of Roman attitudes towards memory. In imperial propaganda this emerges in the notion of *aeternitas imperii*, the "eternity of the Roman rule."[49] Thus, as we have seen, Roman emperors

---

[47] Edwards (1996), 97–8, discusses the Ammianus passage.

[48] Edwards and Woolf (2003), 8–9.

[49] Edwards (1996), 86–8. Cf. the *imperium sine fine* of Verg. *A.* 1.279. The notion is paralleled in the Roman view of tombs as *domus aeternae* (see Chap. 1, n. 35). Despite their efforts to differentiate the Roman Empire from their modernized

typically celebrate restoration and renewal rather than change. Well after any semblance of the Republic survived, for instance, we find the emperor Septimius Severus proclaiming in AD 203 the erection of his arch *ob rem publicam restitutam*, "to commemorate the restoration of the republic" (*CIL* 6.1033) – no one of course would have misread this as "the Republic," but the continued use of the term was one more way to stress some semblance of continuity: the *Respublica* might be gone, but the *res publica* remained.

This urge to promote the *aeternitas imperii* is fully apparent in the Forum of Augustus, and yet as I have suggested, through the memory-erasing achieved by the exclusion of certain icons of the Republic, it simultaneously signals the emergence of a new, distinctly imperial identity – one that actually dissociates itself from certain aspects of the Republican past. Despite the many connections it seeks to make with the Republic, we should not overlook the degree to which it showcased the greatness of the empire, the *maiestas imperii*. Indeed, while venerating the past, in its use of exotic materials and ornamentation it expressed the supremacy and stability of Rome in the Mediterranean world.[50] It is, in short, very much an *imperial* structure, though one that effaces the distance and difference between the Augustan era and the Republic. Tiberius inherited the ideology symbolized in this structure; each successive emperor adopted and altered it. The Forum of Trajan symbolizes the logical conclusion of that process, the point at which the memories of the Republic are overtaken by a new and altogether different past.[51]

"Res est publica Caesar" (Ovid, Tr. 4.4.15)

Writing from the banks of the Black Sea, with only his memories of Rome to console him, the full weight of these words – *res est publica*

conception of "Empire," Hardt and Negri's characterization applies well to the Principate (2001), 11: "Empire exhausts historical time, suspends history, and summons the past and future within its own ethical order. In other words, Empire presents its order as permanent, eternal, and necessary."

[50] Zanker (1968), 12. On the Forum's role in redefining the nature of imperium, see Richardson (1991), 9.

[51] Cf. Hölscher's (1984), 11–12, summary of the differences between the two Fora and what they represent.

Caesar, "the state *is* Caesar" – was entirely apparent to Ovid.[52] At this particular point in time, in the age of Augustus, and in contrast to Septimius Severus' empty use of the term *res publica* over two centuries later, one might reasonably render this "the Republic *is* Caesar." Either way, Ovid's point remains the same: the rule of the Senate has given way to the rule of the emperor, the *princeps*.[53] Ovid perhaps alludes to Cicero's assertion that where there is a tyrant, there can be no *res publica* (*ergo ubi tyrannus est . . . dicendum est plane nullam esse rem publicam*, *Rep.* 3.43), a hypothesis now proven in Ovid's experience to be true. And yet, not quite *fully* true. It is easy in hindsight, that is, to understand that after Actium there would be no going back, no matter what the emperor might want you to believe. Yet in the event, someone living in the Augustan and even Tiberian period might well have believed that the Principate was, as the triumvirate had been conceived (and proven) to be, merely a sort of interregnum, that the Republic and its ideals would ultimately survive. Whatever the truth of the matter, the idea of the Republic faded neither quietly nor quickly.

But to repeat a point made in the first chapter, what clearly distinguishes the early imperial period from the Republic, at least in its heyday, is the presence of the *princeps*. The emergence of a single, nearly all-powerful individual in the Roman state was accompanied, as all momentous political changes are, by the struggle to control memory. Given the degree to which Romans viewed memory as an essential means of connecting with the past, and thereby of preserving their sense of self and identity, no one who wished to be a successful *princeps* could afford to ignore the past. And yet the past could be dangerous. Machiavelli, one of the more astute observers of the ancient Roman political scene, puts it thus: "in republics there is more vitality, greater hatred, and more desire for vengeance, which will never permit them to allow the memory of their former liberty to rest; so that the safest way is to destroy them or to reside there."[54]

---

[52] For the sentiment, Luck (1977), ad loc.

[53] Lactantius summarizes the difference most succinctly: the Republic features the rule of *leges*, "laws," the Principate, the *regimen singularis imperii*, the "rule of a single authority" (*Div. Inst.* 7.15). See Sion-Jenkis (2000), 26.

[54] "Ma nelle repubbliche è maggiore vita, maggiore odio, più desiderio di vendetta; né li lascia, né può lasciare riposare la memoria della antiqua libertà: tale che la più sicura via è spegnerle o abitarvi" (*Il Principe*, chap. 5).

The nature of a republic, that is, militates against the tendencies of a monarchy, a Principate; Machiavelli's point echoes the sentiments of Cicero in the passage from the *De re publica* quoted above (*Rep.* 3.43). Yet the early emperors achieved something Machiavelli did not envision, a sort of reconciliation of the two choices: a destruction, albeit a gradual destruction, of the Republic, while giving the appearance of still "residing" there. That balancing act eventually became too difficult if not unnecessary. With time, the ideology of the Republic was simply discarded.

Romans were fully aware of the risks posed to memory by time, for time brings change – and forgetfulness. Livy knew this (8.10.11–13); so did Seneca the Elder (*Con.* 1. *praef.* 2–3) and Cicero (*Rep.* 6.23–4). Change is seldom easy, especially when it is not clear that the change is for the better. The loss of the Republic was of course associated with the loss of *libertas*. In many instances, as we have seen, the memory of the Republic was invoked in the name of *libertas*, as a means of reminding Romans what they had lost. But eventually, after Nero or Domitian, *libertas* could be seen as something that had been *gained*. Clever emperors were very adept at adapting Republican memories to suit their own purposes.

What happens over the course of the first century of the Principate, then, is the process of individuation of one political – and cultural – system from another.[55] The role of the imperial Senate was clearly not precisely analogous to that of the Republican; at the same time, literature and art acquired new dimensions. Nothing of what we know of Republican drama looks much like the distinctly imperial tragedy of Seneca; nor does what survives of Ennius strike the same tone as Lucan; few would mistake Catullus for an imperial writer, or Martial for a Republican poet; and structures such as the Forum of Trajan served very different purposes from that of, say, the Basilica Pauli (Aemilia). As I have suggested, this individuation is precisely what Maternus envisions in the concluding sentence of his speech in the *Dialogus*, where the Republic is one thing, and the Principate is another. This is, of course, a far cry from Velleius, who in the early throes of the Julio-Claudian dynasty still wants his readers to believe that the Republic really does exist.

[55] See Woolf (1993), esp. 176–85.

By the time of Seneca and Lucan, the Neronian period, Romans had moved on. Seneca clearly harbors no nostalgia for the Republic as a political entity, and a diminishing attachment to its ethical traditions; Lucan, on the other hand, seems angry not at the loss of the Republic (if he would even have conceived of it in those terms) but rather at the excesses of overwhelming power and the human suffering it entails. His memories are not fond ones, but they are summoned not so much in the service of the past but of the future. Tacitus is the author who ultimately addresses and resolves the problem of the Republic. At the conclusion of the first chapter, I posed the question: why did Tacitus not write a history of the Republic? Certainly, as many have noted, the influence of the Republic is evident at many levels in Tacitus' writings. One could simply claim that "it had been done" – by Livy, most notably. Livy's version of Republican history, however, was designed to support the idea that the Augustan Principate was the *culmination* of Roman history; as I suggested in Chapter 2, this is what perhaps lies behind Velleius' temporal perspective, writing a history *a temporibus nostris* rather than *ab urbe condita*. Tacitus, on the other hand, was faced with an altogether different past. For him remembering the first century of the Principate was as pressing a need as Livy's to remember the Republic. His are histories for the realities of the Trajanic period, not the Augustan. Tacitus knew there was no going back; but he would see to it that in going forward, Rome learned the lessons of the past – an *imperial* past that had its beginnings in AD 14. For him, there could be no doubt that the *res publica* was indeed *Caesar*.

Principate and Republic

There is also no doubt that the memory of the Republic provided the foundation on which the Empire was laid. Just as an individual's identity is inevitably the product of past experience and thus memory, the Principate initially took its form and political identity from the institutions of the past. Precisely the same may be said of the physical city, whose present appearance bears the marks of its past. Memory, in other words, manifests itself in all manner of ways. In this book I have been especially concerned to show ways in which the memory of the Republic impressed itself on imperial literature as well as on the physical landscape; I have also stressed that this phenomenon is very much a function of the central place of memory in Roman culture.[56] It is apt, therefore, that Freud should have chosen the city of Rome for the famous analogy he draws in the course of discussing the nature of memory and forgetting:

> Since we overcame the error of supposing that the forgetting we are familiar with signified a destruction of the memory-trace – that is, its annihilation – we have been inclined to take the opposite view, that in mental life nothing which has once been formed can perish – that everything is somehow preserved and that in suitable circumstances (when, for instance, regression goes back far enough) it can once more be brought to light. Let us try to grasp what this assumption involves by taking an analogy from another field. We will choose as an example the history of the Eternal City ....

Following a brief survey of the history of Rome, Freud imagines what a reasonably knowledgeable modern-day visitor to the city might learn of Rome's past:

> Of the buildings which once occupied this ancient area he will find nothing, or only scanty remains, for they exist no longer. The best information about Rome in the republican era would only enable him at the most to point out the sites where the temples and public buildings of that period stood. Their place is now taken by ruins, but not by ruins of themselves but of later restorations made after fires or destruction. It is hardly necessary to remark that all these remains of ancient Rome are found dovetailed into the jumble of a great metropolis which has grown up in the last few centuries since the Renaissance. There is certainly not a little that is ancient still buried in

---

[56] In this respect I hope to have contributed to the thesis put forward in Habinek and Schiesaro (1997), that the Roman Revolution cannot be fully understood apart from the Roman Cultural Revolution. Cf. in particular Wallace-Hadrill's (1997), 6, articulation of the situation in his contribution to that volume: "the political and social revolutions of the first century BCE ... involved a parallel revolution in ways of knowing. ... Just as the political changes implicit in Augustus' transformation of the republic can be seen in a different light when put, as by Syme, in the context of changes of the social composition of the ruling class, so both these transformations emerge in a different light when set in the context of changes in the cultural arena." My project pushes that observation into the imperial period.

the soil of the city or beneath its modern buildings. This is the manner in which the past is preserved in historical sites like Rome.

Freud then compares this archaeological palimpsest to human memory, albeit an extraordinary memory, one that stretches back as far in time as the city itself. The chief difference, he notes, is that in the mind the various layers of the past are able to co-exist with one another, each able to be seen with equal clarity. Thus "[o]n the Piazza of the Pantheon we should find not only the Pantheon of to-day, as it was bequeathed to us by Hadrian, but, on the same site, the original edifice erected by Agrippa."[57]

What Freud's analogy – and the flaws he uncovers – neatly demonstrate is that *monumenta*, and the ruins they eventually become, have a limited capacity to preserve memory. Time and decay overtake them, and if they manage to survive at all, they may become invested or associated with still other memories and meanings. Viewed – or read (we should emphasize that for Romans the word *monumentum* denotes physical structures as well as texts[58]) – by someone whose memory does not encompass the events or people they commemorate or who has repressed in memory those events, the ruins will have little – or perhaps more accurately, a *different* – meaning. The moment at which a culture's or society's memorials cease to have any obvious meaning for its members constitutes a significant stage in the deterioration or even loss of memory. This was just the sort of situation Romans feared, and against which they vigorously guarded. Whatever its motives, the rebuilding and refurbishing of older buildings effected by Augustus was clearly a memory-saving move. Ultimately, however, as the preservation of the past they represented became less and less important, those buildings were for the most part allowed to fall into ruin or used for some other purpose. As we saw, Lucan concretizes something quite similar to this in his narrative of Caesar's visit to Troy.

The Empire's foundation in memory, as is true of all foundations, became obscured by the buildings it underlays. Freud's analogy is especially fitting. Peel away the layers of Rome, and you will glimpse the Republic. It is additionally useful to think about the texts examined in

---

[57] Freud (1961), 16–17. Fine discussion of this passage by Edwards (1996), 27–8.
[58] Fowler (2000), 197–8, citing Kraus. Cf. Miles (1995), 17.

this book in light of Freud's analogy and the two Fora discussed here. The works of Valerius Maximus and Velleius Paterculus, products of the immediate post-Augustan period, have much in common with the Forum of Augustus (see above, with n. 35): repositories of memory, they assert the continuity of the *res publica*, not quite acknowledging an explicit break between Republic and Principate yet clearly written under the aegis of the new *princeps*. A couple of decades later, under Nero, Lucan finds fresh use for a narrative of what is now unambiguously regarded as the Republic's demise and brings to the fore the tension implicit in the Forum of Augustus, a tension palpable only to those who could claim to possess some memory of the Republic. The *Pharsalia*, that is, returns to Roman memory the characters and events the Forum had excluded, making that tension felt once again. Seneca, whose *Epistulae* at least represent a desire to move past the Republic and recognize a new aristocratic ideology, in some sense seeks to defuse the tension apparent in Lucan's epic, as we saw especially in the way he depoliticizes Cato. With the end of the Julian-Claudian dynasty and the ascension of the Flavian, we hear less and less about the restoration of the old Republic. Pliny's *Panegyricus* embodies best the new imperial ideology, a textual parallel to the Forum of Trajan that was under construction in AD 100 when Pliny delivered the speech. He adduces Republican *exempla* in much the same way as the Forum of Trajan alludes to the Forum of Augustus' gallery of Republican heroes: Trajan embodies yet surpasses the virtues signified by those *exempla*, just as his Forum builds on, yet ultimately transforms the message of its predecessor. Tacitus' *Dialogus*, on the other hand, in its examination of Republican versus imperial oratory, captures the contrasts made manifest in these two monuments.

As with Freud's Rome, lurking just below the surface of these texts one glimpses the memory of the Republic at work. Indeed, as the Republic imparts meaning to the Forum of Augustus, so too does it provide an important impetus for the texts examined here. In the absence of the Republic and its literary and political traditions (and, I might add, to those unfamiliar with them), they would look very different. Like the imperial buildings that came to overlay Republican structures, these texts build upon precedents: Valerius Maximus on writers such as Cornelius Nepos; Velleius on Livy and ultimately the Republican historiographical tradition; Lucan on Vergil and ultimately Ennius; Seneca,

Pliny, and Tacitus – all with very different results – on Cicero, most obviously. As the Principate progresses from the Tiberian through the Trajanic period, a new energy develops, an energy arising from the Principate's own history and experience which infuses texts such as the *Dialogus* and the *Panegyricus* and invigorates the structure that instantiates the values of the latter, the Forum of Trajan.

While these texts and buildings would find new uses and meaning over time, the memory of the Republic hardly disappears altogether. We still find Cicero in the letters of Fronto; Republican *exempla* litter Aulus Gellius and even Apuleius; historians such as Granius Licinianus still rewrite Republican history. Still later, Republican *exempla* become a staple of the *Panegyrici Latini*, Symmachus (345–402), Claudian, Ammianus Marcellinus, to cite the more notable examples.[59] And of course, in imperial Greek historians such as Appian and Cassius Dio (not to mention Plutarch), Republican history finds fresh expression and purpose. Just as the physical ruins of the Republic linger and persist – indeed, are even preserved – so too does the Republic linger in the imperial imagination and thus in memory. If, as I have suggested, recording and remembering are not separate enterprises, then the urge to memorialize the Republic in some fashion cannot be said to disappear.

But the edge is gone. Little of post-Trajanic art and literature may be said to find its impetus in the Republican past to the same degree or, most importantly, with the same emotion and intensity as the texts discussed in this book; nor would any subsequent Roman building or monument ever equal – or attempt to equal – the appeal to the Republican past visible in the Forum of Augustus. When Tacitus rhetorically wonders, in his narrative of the death of Augustus and accession of Tiberius, *quotus quisque reliquus, qui rem publicam vidisset?* "how many were left who had seen the Republic?" (*Ann.* 1.3.7–4.1) he is by implication asking who remembered it. Although the anticipated answer is obviously "very few," his own writings show that response to be wrong. And yet his own refusal to write – and thereby memorialize – the history of the Republic constitutes a move away from the Republic, an acknowledgment that the Principate has come into its own as a

---

[59] On the use of Republican *exempla* in late antiquity, above all Felmy (1999).

political and cultural entity. This is precisely the point Maternus unapologetically makes. Gazing back at the Julio-Claudian period from the
reign of Trajan, Tacitus harbors no doubts: the Principate of Augustus
marked the demise of the Republic and set in motion the metamorphosis
of its memory.

Bibliography

Ahl, F. (1976) *Lucan: An Introduction*. Ithaca

Albertson, F. C. (1990) "The Basilica Aemilia Frieze: Religion and Politics in Late Republican Rome," *Latomus* 49: 801–15

Alcock, S. (1994a) "Landscapes of Memory and the Authority of Pausanias," in *Pausanias Historien*. Fondation Hardt Entretiens XLI, 241–67. Geneva

   (1994b) "Nero at Play? The Emperor's Grecian Odyssey," in J. Elsner and J. Masters (eds.), *Reflections of Nero: Culture, History and Representation*, 98–111. Chapel Hill

Anderson, J. C. (1984) *The Historical Topography of the Imperial Fora*. Brussels

Assmann, J. (1997) *Moses the Egyptian: The Memory of Egypt in Western Monotheism*. Cambridge, MA

Austin, R. G. (1960) *Cicero. Pro M. Caelio Oratio*. 3rd edn. Oxford

Baar, M. (1990) *Das Bild des Kaisers Tiberius bei Tacitus, Sueton und Cassius Dio*. Stuttgart.

Bailey, C. (1947) *Titi Lucreti Cari De Rerum Natura Libri Sex*. 3 vols. Oxford

Barchiesi, A. (2002) "Martial Arts. Mars Ultor in the Forum Augustum: A Verbal Monument with a Vengeance," in G. Herbert-Brown (ed.), *Ovid's Fasti: Historical Readings at its Bimillenium*, 1–22. Oxford

Barnes, T. D. (1986) "The Significance of Tacitus' *Dialogus de Oratoribus*," *HSCP* 90: 225–44

Bayley, J. (1966) *Tolstoy and the Novel*. London

Baroin, C. (1998) "La maison romaine comme image et lieu de mémoire," in C. Auvray-Assayas (ed.), *Images Romaines*, 177–91. Paris

Bartsch, S. (1994) *Actors in the Audience: Theatricality and Doublespeak from Nero to Hadrian*. Cambridge, MA

   (1997) *Ideology in Cold Blood: A Reading of Lucan's Civil War*. Cambridge, MA

Beard, M. (1998) "Vita Inscripta," in *La Biographie antique*. Fondation Hardt Entretiens XLIV, 83–114. Geneva

Bennett, J. (1997) *Trajan, Optimus Princeps: A Life and Times*. London and New York

Bettini, M. (1991) *Anthropology and Roman Culture*. trans. J. van Sickle. Baltimore

Blight, D. (2001) *Race and Reunion: The Civil War in American Memory.* Cambridge, MA

Bloomer, M. (1992) *Valerius Maximus and the Rhetoric of the New Nobility.* Chapel Hill

Blum, H. (1969) *Die antike Mnemotechnik.* Hildesheim

Bodel, J. (1997) "Monumental Villas and Villa Monuments," *JRA* 10: 5–35

Boyle, A. J. (2003) "Introduction: Reading Flavian Rome," in Boyle and Dominik (eds.), 1–67

Boyle, A. J., and Dominik, W. J. (2003) (eds.) *Flavian Rome: Culture, Image, Text.* Leiden and Boston

Brink, C. O. (1989) "Quintilian's *De causis corruptae eloquentiae* and Tacitus' *Dialogus de Oratoribus*," *CQ* 39: 472–503

(1993) "History in the 'Dialogus de oratoribus' and Tacitus the Historian," *Hermes* 121.3: 335–49

Briscoe, J. (1998) (ed.) *Valerii Maximi facta et dicta memorabilia.* 2 vols. Stuttgart and Leipzig

Brunt, P. A. (1975) "Stoicism and the Principate," *PBSR* 43: 7–35

Brunt, P. A. and Moore, J. M. (1967) (eds.) *Res Gestae Divi Augusti.* Oxford

Burke, P. (1989) "History as Social Memory," in T. Butler (ed.), *Memory: History, Culture and the Mind,* 97–113. Blackwell

Carruthers, M. (1990) *The Book of Memory: A Study of Memory in Medieval Culture.* Cambridge

Castagna, E. (1991) "Storia e storiografia nel pensiero di Seneca," in A. Setaioli (ed.), *Seneca e la cultura,* 91–117. Naples

Champlin, E. (2003) *Nero.* Cambridge, MA

Chaplin, J. D. (2000) *Livy's Exemplary History.* Oxford

Chassignet, M. (1998) "La deuxième guerre punique dans l'historiographie romaine," in David (ed.), 55–72

Citroni, M. (2003) (ed.) *Memoria e identitá. La cultura romana costruisce la sua immagine.* Florence

Cizek, E. (1983) *L'Époque de Trajan: Circonstances politiques et problèmes idéologiques.* trans. C. Frantescu. Paris

Connerton, P. (1989) *How Societies Remember.* Cambridge

Connolly, J. (forthcoming) *Citizens and Subjects: The Uses of Rhetoric in Ancient Rome.*

Connors, C. (1998) *Petronius the Poet.* Cambridge

Conte, G. B. (1966) "Il proemio della *Pharsalia*," *Maia* 18: 42–53

(1985) *Memoria dei poeti e sistema letterario.* Turin

(1994) *Latin Literature: A History,* trans. J. B. Solodow. Baltimore

Coudry, M. (1998) 'La deuxième guerre punique chez Valère Maxime', in David (ed.), 45–53

Cumont, F. (1949) *Lux Perpetua.* Paris

D'Ambra, E. (1993) *Private Lives, Imperial Virtues.* Princeton

D'Arms, J. (1970) *Romans on the Bay of Naples.* Harvard

David, J. -M. (1998a) "Les enjeux de l'exemplarité à la fin de la République et au début du principat," in David (ed.), 9–17

(1998b) "Valère Maxime et l'histoire de la République Romaine," in David (ed.), 120–130

David, J. -M. (1998) (ed.) *Valeurs et Mémoire à Rome. Valère Maxime ou la vertu recomposée.* Paris

Davis, N. Z. and Starn, R. (1989) "Introduction," *Representations*, 26: 1–6

Degrassi, A. (1937) *Inscriptiones Italiae.* Vol. 13.3. Rome

Deroux, C. (1986) (ed.) *Studies in Latin Literature and Roman History IV.* Collection Latomus 196. Brussels

Dunbabin, K. (2004) *The Roman Banquet: Images of Conviviality.* Cambridge

Dyson, S. L. and Prior, R. L. (1995) "Horace, Martial, and Rome: Two Poetic Outsiders Read the Ancient City," *Arethusa* 28.2/3: 245–63

Eder, W. (1990) "Augustus and the Power of Tradition: The Augustan Principate as Binding Link between Republic and Empire," in K. A. Raaflaub and M. Toher (1990) (eds.) 71–122

Edwards, C. (1996) *Writing Rome.* Cambridge

Edwards, C. and Woolf, G. (2003) "Cosmopolis: Rome as World City," in C. Edwards and G. Woolf (eds.), *Rome the Cosmopolis*, 1–20. Cambridge

Ehrenberg, V. and Jones, A. H. M. (1955) *Documents Illustrating the Reigns of Augustus and Tiberius.* 2nd edn. Oxford

Fantham, E. (1985) "Caesar and the Mutiny: Lucan's Reshaping of the Historical Tradition in *De Bello Civili* 5.237–373," *CP* 80: 119–29

(1992) *Lucan: De Bello Civili Book II.* Cambridge

Farrell, J. (1997) "The Phenomenology of Memory in Roman Culture," *CJ* 92.4: 373–83

Favro, D. (1996) *The Urban Image of Augustan Rome.* Cambridge

Fearnley, H. (2003) "Reading the Imperial Revolution: Martial, *Epigrams* 10," in Boyle and Dominik (eds.), 613–35.

Feeney, D. (1991) *The Gods in Epic: Poets and Critics of the Classical Tradition.* Oxford

(1998) *Literature and Religion at Rome.* Cambridge

Feldherr, A. (2000) "*Non inter nota sepulcra*: Catullus 101 and Roman Funerary Ritual," *CA* 19.2: 209–31

Felmy, A. (1999) *Die Römische Republik im Geschichtsbild der Spätantike.* Diss. Freiburg i.Br.

Fentress, J. and Wickham, C. (1992) *Social Memory.* Blackwell

Flower, H. (1996) *Ancestor Masks and Aristocratic Power in Roman Culture.* Oxford

(1998) "Rethinking Damnatio Memoriae: The Case of Cn. Calpurnius Piso in A.D. 20," *CA* 17: 155–86

(2004a) "Introduction," in H. I. Flower (ed.), *The Cambridge Companion to the Roman Republic*, 1–11. Cambridge

(2004b) "Spectacle and Political Culture in the Roman Republic," in H. I. Flower (ed.), *The Cambridge Companion to the Roman Republic*, 322–43. Cambridge

Fowler, D. (2000) "The Ruin of Time: Monuments and Survival at Rome," in *Roman Constructions*, 193–217. Oxford

Freud, S. (1924) "Mourning and Melancholia," trans. J. Riviere, *Sigmund Freud: Collected Papers.* Vol. 4, 152–70. New York

(1961) *Civilization and its Discontents*, trans. J. Strachey. New York.

Freudenburg, K. (2001) *Satires of Rome: Threatening Poses from Lucilius to Juvenal.* Cambridge

Freyburger, M. -L. (1998) "Valère Maxime et les guerres civiles," in David (ed.), 111–17

Galinsky, K. (1996) *Augustan Culture.* Princeton

Gallia, A. B. (2003) *Remembering the Roman Republic, A.D. 68–117.* Diss. Pennsylvania (n.v.)

Gedi, N. and Elam, Y. (1996) "Collective Memory – What is it?," *History and Memory* 8.1: 30–50

Gelzer, M. (1968) *Caesar: Politician and Statesman*, trans. P. Needham. Cambridge, MA

George, D. B. (1991) "Lucan's Cato and Stoic Attitudes to the Republic," *CA* 10.2: 237–58

Gillespie, D. (1992) *The Mind's We: Contextualism in Cognitive Psychology.* Illinois

Gillis, J. R. (1994) "Memory and Identity: The History of a Relationship," in J. R. Gillis (ed.), *Commemorations: The Politics of National Identity*, 3–24. Princeton

Giovannini, A. and Berchem, D. van (1986) (eds.) *Opposition et Résistances à l'Empire d'Auguste à Trajan.* Vandœuvres-Genève

Goldberg, S. (1999) "Appreciating Aper: The Defence of Modernity in Tacitus' *Dialogus de oratoribus*", *CQ* 49.1: 224–37

Goodyear, F. R. D. (1982) "History and biography," in E. J. Kenney and W. V. Clausen (eds.), *The Cambridge History of Classical Literature.* Vol. 2, Pt. 4 "The Early Principate," 143–70

(1984) "Tiberius and Gaius: Their Influence and Views on Literature," *ANRW* II.32.1: 603–10

Gowing, A. (2000) "Memory and Silence in Cicero"s *Brutus*," *Eranos* 98: 39–64

Greenidge, A. H. J. and Clay, A. M. (1960) *Sources for Roman History 133–70 BC.* 2nd edn. Rev. E. W. Gray. Oxford

Gregory, A. (1994) "Responses to Portraits and the Political Uses of Images in Rome," *JRA* 7: 80–99

Griffin, M. (1968) "Seneca on Cato the Younger: *Epistle* 14.12–13," *CQ* 18 n.s.: 373–5

(1974) "Imago vitae suae," in C. D. N. Costa (ed.), *Seneca*, 1–38. Routledge

(1976) *Seneca: A Philosopher in Politics.* Oxford

(1984) *Nero: The End of a Dynasty.* New Haven

(2000) "Seneca and Pliny," in C. Rowe and M. Schofield (eds.), *The Cambridge History of Greek and Roman Political Thought*, 532–58. Cambridge

Gudeman, A. (1894) *P. Cornelii Taciti Dialogus de Oratoribus.* Boston

Gurval, R. (1995) *Actium and Augustus.* Ann Arbor

Habinek, T. and Schiesaro, A. (1997) (eds.) *The Roman Cultural Revolution.* Cambridge

Haenni, R. (1905) *Die litterarische kritik in Ciceros Brutus.* Sarnen

Halbwachs, M. (1941) *La topographie légendaire des évangiles en terre sainte: Etude de mémoire collective.* Paris

(1992) *On Collective Memory*, trans. L. A. Coser. Chicago

Hales, S. (2003) *The Roman House and Social Identity.* Cambridge

Hammond, M. (1957) "Composition of the Senate AD 68–235," *JRS* 47: 74–81

Hampl, P. (1985) "Memory and Imagination," in McConkey (1985) (ed.) 201–11

Hardie, P. (1993) *The Epic Successors of Virgil*. Cambridge

(1994) (ed.) *Virgil Aeneid Book IX*. Cambridge

Hardt, M. and Negri, A. (2001) *Empire*. Cambridge, MA

Hedrick, C. W. (2000) *History and Silence: Purge and Rehabilitation of Memory in Late Antiquity*. Austin

Hellegouarc'h, J. (1984) "État present des travaux sur l'Histoire Romaine de Velleius Paterculus," *ANRW* II.32.1: 404–36

Henderson, J. (1998) "Lucan: The Word at War," in *Fighting for Rome: Poets and Caesars, History and Civil War*, 165–211. Cambridge

(2001) *Telling Tales on Caesar*. Oxford

(2002) *Pliny's Statue: The Letters, Self-Portraiture and Classical Art*. Exeter

(2004) *Morals and Villas in Seneca's Letters: Places to Dwell*. Cambridge.

Hobsbawm, E. (1997) *On History*. New York

Hölkeskamp, K. -J. (2000) "The Roman Republic: Government of the People, by the People, for the People?" Review of Millar (1998). *SCI* 19: 203–33

(2004) *Rekonstruktionen einer Republik*. Munich

Hölscher, T. (1984) *Staatsdenkmal und Publikum: Vom Untergang der Republik bis zur Festigung des Kaisertums in Rom*. Konstanz

Holtorf, C. (2001) *Monumental Past*. Diss. Wales 1998. published electronically: *http://hdl.handle.net/1807/245*

Hutton, P. (1993) *History as an Art of Memory*. Hanover and London

Jacquemin, A. (1998) "Valère Maxime et Velleius Paterculus," in David (ed.), 147–56

Jaeger, M. (1997) *Livy's Written Rome*. Ann Arbor

Johnson, W. R. (1987) *Momentary Monsters. Lucan and his Heroes*. Ithaca and London

Judge, E. A. (1974) "'Res Publica Restituta': A Modern Illusion?," in J. A. S. Evans (ed.), *Polis and Imperium: Studies in Honour of Edward Togo Salmon*, 279–311. Toronto

Kenan, O. (2003) *Between Memory and History: The Evolution of Israeli Historiography of the Holocaust, 1945–1961*. New York

Kleiner, D. E. E. (1992) *Roman Sculpture*. New Haven

Koestermann, R. (1930) "Der Taciteische *Dialogus* und Ciceros Schrift *De re publica*," *Hermes* 65: 396–421

Koortbojian, M. (1996) "*In commemorationem mortuorum*: Text and Image along the 'streets of tombs,'" in J. Elsner (ed.), *Art and Text in Roman Culture*, 210–33. Cambridge

Koutroubas, D. E. (1987) "ο Κικερων στο Διαλογο περι ρητορων του Τακιτου," in *3. Panellenio Symposio Latinikon Spoudon*, 125–47. Thessalonika

Kraus, C. S. (1997) "Livy," in C. S. Kraus and A. J. Woodman (eds.), *Latin Historians*, 51–81, Greece & Rome New Surveys in the Classics 27. Oxford

Kuntze, C. (1985) *Zur Darstellung des Kaisers Tiberius und seiner Zeit bei Velleius Paterculus*. Frankfurt-am-Main

LaCapra, D. (1998) *History and Memory after Auschwitz*. Ithaca

Laistner, H. (1947) *The Greater Roman Historians*. Berkeley and Los Angeles

La Rocca, E. (2001) "La nuova immagine dei fori Imperiali: Appunti in margine agli scavi," *RömMitt* 108: 171–213

Le Goff, J. (1992) *History and Memory*, trans. S. Rendall and E. Claman. New York

Leigh, M. (1997) *Lucan: Spectacle and Engagement*. New York

Levick, B. (1976) *Tiberius the Politician*. London

Lind, L. R. (1986) "The Idea of the Republic and the Foundations of Roman Political Liberty," in Deroux (ed.) 44–108

Lindsay, H. (1998) "Eating with the Dead: The Roman Funerary Banquet," in I. Nielsen and H. Sigismund Nielsen (eds.), *Meals in a Social Context: Aspects of the Communal Meal in the Hellenistic and Roman World*, 66–80. Aarhus

Lintott, A. W. (1971) "Lucan and the History of the Civil War," *CQ* 21.2: 488–505

Litchfield, H. W. (1914) "National Exempla Virtutis in Roman Literature," *HSCP* 25: 1–71

Loraux, N. (1997) *La cité divisée: L'oubli dans la mémoire d'Athènes*. Paris

Lowenthal, D. (1985) *The Past is a Foreign Country*. Cambridge

Luce, T. J. (1990) "Livy, Augustus, and the Forum Augustum," in Raaflaub and Toher (eds.) 123–38

   (1993) "Reading and Response in the *Dialogus*," in T. J. Luce and A. J. Woodman (eds.), *Tacitus and the Tacitean Tradition*, 11–38. Princeton

Luck, G. (1977) *P. Ovidius Naso. Tristia*. Vol. 2. Heidelberg

Mackie, N. (1986) "*Res publica restituta*. A Roman Myth," in Deroux (ed.) 302–40

MacMullen, R. (1966) *Enemies of the Roman Order*. Cambridge, MA

Martin, R. (1981) *Tacitus*. Berkeley

Martindale, C. (1984) "The Politician Lucan," *G & R* 31: 64–79

   (1993) *Redeeming the Text*. Cambridge

Maso, S. (1999) *Lo sguardo della verità*. Padova

Mayer, R. (1978) "On Lucan and Nero," *BICS* 25: 85–8

   (1991) "Roman Historical Exempla in Seneca," in *Sénèque et la prose latine*. Fondation Hardt Entretiens XXXVI, 141–76. Geneva

Mayer, R. (2001) (ed.) *Tacitus. Dialogus de Oratoribus*. Cambridge

McConkey, J. (1996) (ed.) *The Anatomy of Memory: An Anthology*. Oxford

McKay, A. G. (1972) *Naples and Coastal Campania: Ancient Campania*. Vol. 1. Hamilton, Ontario

Meadows, A. and Williams, J. (2001) "Moneta and the Monuments: Coinage and Politics in Republican Rome," *JRS* 91: 27–49

Meier, C. (1997) *Res publica amissa*. 3rd edn. Wiesbaden

Mellor, R. (2003) "The New Aristocracy of Power," in Boyle and Dominik (eds.), 69–101

Michel, A. (1960) *Rhétorique et philosophie chez Cicéron*. Paris

   (1962) *Le "Dialogus des Orateurs" de Tacite et la philosophie de Cicéron*. Paris

Miles, G. (1995) *Livy: Reconstructing Early Rome*. Ithaca

Millar, F. (1977) *The Emperor in the Roman World*. London

   (1993) "Ovid and the *Domus Augusta*: Rome seen from Tomoi," *JRS* 83: 1–17

   (1998) *The Crowd in Rome in the Late Republic*. Michigan

Moles, J. (1998) "Cry Freedom: Tacitus *Annals* 4.32–35," *Histos* 2: 1–54 (*http://www.dur.ac.uk/Classics/histos/1998/moles.html*)

Morford, M. (1992) "*Iubes Esse Liberos*: Pliny's *Panegyricus* and Liberty," *AJP* 113: 575–93

Morrison, T. (1984) "Memory, Creation, and Writing," in McConkey (ed.), 213–25

Most, G. (2003) "Memoria e oblio nell'Eneide," in Citroni (ed.), 185–212

Motto, A. L. (1970) *Guide to the Thought of Lucius Annaeus Seneca, in the Extant Prose Works*. Amsterdam

Narducci, E. (1979) *La provvidenza crudele: Lucano e la distruzione dei miti augustei*. Pisa

   (2001) "Catone in Lucano," *Athenaeum* 89.1: 171–86

Narducci, E. (2003) (ed.) *Aspetti della fortuna di Cicerone*. Florence

Nisbet, R. G. M. and Hubbard, M. (1970) *A Commentary on Horace: Odes Book 1*. Oxford

Noè, E. (1984) *Storiografia imperiale pretacitana: Linee di svolgimento*. Florence

Nora, P. (1984) *Les Lieux de Mémoire*. Vol. 1. Paris

Nünnerich-Asmus, A. (1994) *Basilika und Portikus*. Köln

Oexle, O. G. (1995) "Memoria als Kultur," in O. G. Oexle (ed.), *Memoria als Kultur*, 9–78. Göttingen

Packer, J. E. (1994) "Trajan's Forum Again: The Column and the Temple of Trajan in the Master Plan Attributed to Apollodorus(?)," *JRA* 7: 163–82

   (1997) *The Forum of Trajan in Rome*. 2 vols. Berkeley

   (2001) *The Forum of Trajan: A Study of the Monuments in Brief*. Berkeley

   (2003) "Templum Divi Traiani Parthici et Plotinae," *JRA* 16: 109–36

Peter, H. (1967) *Historicorum Romanorum Reliquiae*. 2 vols. Stuttgart

Pierini, R. Degl'Innocenti (2003) "Cicerone nella prima età imperiale: Luci ed ombre su un martire della repubblica," in Narducci (ed.), 3–54

Purcell, N. (1987) "Tomb and Suburb," in H. von Hesberg and P. Zanker (eds.), *Römischer Gräberstraßen*, 25–41. Munich

Quint, D. (1993) *Epic and Empire: Politics and Generic Form from Virgil to Milton*. Princeton

Raaflaub, K. A. (1986) "Grundzüge, Ziele und Ideen der Opposition gegen die Kaiser im I. Jh. n.Chr.," in Giovannini and van Berchem (eds.), 1–55

Raaflaub, K. A. and Toher, M. (1990) (eds.) *Between Republic and Empire: Interpretations of Augustus and His Principate*. Berkeley

Rawson, E. (1986) "Cassius and Brutus: The Memory of the Liberators," in I. S. Moxon, J. D. Smart, and A. J. Woodman (eds.), *Past Perspectives*, 101–19. Cambridge

Richardson, J. S. (1991) "*Imperium Romanum*: Empire and the Language of Power," *JRS* 81: 1–9

Richardson, L., Jr. (1992) *A New Topographical Dictionary of Ancient Rome*. Baltimore

Roller, M. (1997) "*Color*-Blindness: Cicero's Death, Declamation, and the Production of History," *CP* 92.2: 109–30

   (2001a) *Constructing Autocracy: Aristocrats and Emperors in Julio-Claudian Rome*. Princeton

(2001b) Review of Chaplin (2000), *BMCR* 2001.7.3

Rossi, A. (2001) "Remapping the Past: Caesar's Tale of Troy (Lucan *BC* 9.964–999)," *Phoenix* 55: 313–26

Roth, M. (1994) "We Are What We Remember (and Forget)," *Tikkun* 9.6: 41–2, 91
(1995) *The Ironist's Cage: Memory, Trauma, and the Construction of History*. New York

Rowe, G. (2002) *Princes and Political Cultures: The New Tiberian Senatorial Decrees*. Ann Arbor

Rudich, V. (1997) *Dissidence and Literature under Nero: The Price of Rhetoricization*. Routledge

Sage, M. M. (1979) "The *Elogia* of the Augustan Forum and the *de viris illustribus*," *Historia* 28: 192–210

Schmitzer, U. (2000) *Velleius Paterculus und das Interesse an der Geschichte im Zeitalter des Tiberius*. Heidelberg

Scullard, H. H. (1981) *Festivals and Ceremonies of the Roman Republic*. Ithaca

Setaioli, A. (2003) "Seneca e Cicerone," in Narducci (ed.), 55–77

Shackleton-Bailey, D. R. (2000) (ed. and trans.) *Memorable Doings and Sayings: Valerius Maximus*. Cambridge, MA

Shrimpton, G. (1997) *History and Memory in Ancient Greece*. Montreal

Shumka, L. (2000) *Designing Women: Studies in the Representation of Femininity in Roman Society*. Diss. Victoria

Sinclair, P.(1994) "Political Declensions in Latin Grammar and Oratory 55 BCE–CE 39," *Ramus* 23: 92–109

Sion-Jenkis, K. (2000) *Von der Republik zum Prinzipat: Ursachen für den Verfassungswechsel in Rom im historischen Denken der Antike*. Stuttgart

Skidmore, C. (1996) *Practical Ethics for Roman Gentlemen: The Work of Valerius Maximus*. Exeter

Small, J. Penny (1997) *Wax Tablets of the Mind: Cognitive Studies of Memory and Literacy in Classical Antiquity*. Routledge

Small, J. Penny and Tatum, J. (1995) 'Memory and the Study of Classical Antiquity', *Helios* 22.2: 149–77

Smallwood, E. M. (1984) *Documents Illustrating the Principates of Gaius Claudius and Nero*. Bristol

Spannagel, M. (1999) *Exemplaria Principis: Untersuchungen zu Entstehung und Ausstattung des Augustusforums*. Heidelberg

Steinby, E. M. (1993–2000) (ed.) *Lexicon Topographicum Urbis Romae*. 6 vols. Rome

Strothmann, M. (2000) *Augustus – Vater der res publica*. Stuttgart

Stroup, S. (2003) "*Adulta Virgo*: The Personification of Textual Eloquence in Cicero's *Brutus*," *MD* 50: 115–40
(in preparation) *A Society of Patrons: Cicero, Catullus, and the Body of the Text*

Sturken, M. (1997) *Tangled Memories: The Vietnam War, the Aids Epidemic, and the Politics of Remembering*. Berkeley

Sullivan, J. P. (1985) *Literature and Politics in the Age of Nero*. Ithaca and London

Susini, G. (1988) "Spelling out Along the Road: Anthropology of the Ancient Road, or rather, the Roman Reader," *Alma Mater Studiorum* 1.1: 117–24

Swan, P. M. (2004) *The Augustan Succession: An Historical Commentary on Cassius Dio's Roman History 55–56 (9 BC–AD 14)*. Oxford

Syme, R. (1939) *The Roman Revolution*. Oxford

(1958) *Tacitus*. 2 vols. Oxford

Terdiman, R. (1993) *Present Past: Modernity and the Memory Crisis*. Ithaca and London

Timpe, D. (1986) "Geschichtsschreibung und Opposition," in Giovannini and van Berchem (eds.), 65–95

Tipping, B. D. A. (1999) *Exemplary Roman Heroism in Silius Italicus' Punica*. D.Phil. Oxford

(forthcoming) "*Haec tum Roma fuit*: Past, Present, and Closure in Silius Italicus' *Punica*," in proceedings of *Classical Constructions: A Symposium in Memory of Don Fowler*, co-ordinated by S. J. Heyworth, Wadham College, Oxford.

Torelli, M. (1982) *Typology and Structure of Roman Historical Reliefs*. Ann Arbor

Treggiari, S. (1999) "The Upper-class House as a Symbol and Focus of Emotion in Cicero," *JRA* 12: 33–56

Ungern-Sternberg, J. von (1986) "The Formation of the 'Annalistic Tradition': The Example of the Decemvirate," in K. A. Raaflaub (ed.), *Social Struggles in Archaic Rome*, 77–104. Berkeley

Varner, E. R. (2001) "Portraits, Plots, and Politics; Damnatio Memoriae and the Images of Imperial Women," *MAAR* 46: 41–93

Vasaly, A. (1993) *Representations. Images of the World in Ciceronian Oratory*. Berkeley

Vernant, J.-P. (1965) *Mythe et pensée chez les Grecs: Études de psychologie historique*. Paris

Viansino, G. (1979) "Studia Annaeana II," *Vichiana* 8: 168–96

Vittinghoff, F. (1936) *Der Staatsfeind in der römischen Kaiserzeit: Untersuchungen zur "Damnatio Memoriae"*. Berlin

Walbank, F. W. (1957) *A Historical Commentary on Polybius*. Vol. 1. Oxford

Wallace-Hadrill, A. (1987) "Time for Augustus: Ovid, Augustus and the *Fasti*," in M. Whitby, P. Hardie, and M. Whitby (eds.), *Homo Viator*, 221–30. Bristol

(1997) "Mutatio Morum: The Idea of a Cultural Revolution," in Habinek and Schiesaro (eds.), 3–22

Wardle, D. (1997) "'The Sainted Julius': Valerius Maximus and the Dictator," *CP* 92.4: 323–45

Watts, W. S. (1998) *Vellei Paterculi Historiarum ad M. Vinicium Consulem Libri Duo*. Stuttgart and Leipzig

Weinrich, H. (2000) *Lethe. Kunst und Kritik des Vergessens*. 3rd edn. Munich

White, H. (1987) *The Content of the Form: Narrative Discourse and Historical Representation*. Baltimore and London

Williams, G. (1978) *Change and Decline: Roman Literature in the Early Empire*. Berkeley

Winterbottom, M. (1982) "Cicero and the Silver Age," in *Eloquence et rhétorique chez Cicéron*, 237–66. Geneva

Wirszubski, C. (1968) *Libertas as a Political Idea at Rome During the Late Republic and Early Principate*. Cambridge

Wolpert, A. (2002) *Remembering Defeat: Civil War and Civic Memory in Ancient Athens*. Baltimore

Woodman, A. J. (1969) "Sallustian Influence on Velleius Paterculus," in J. Bibauw (ed.), *Hommages à Marcel Renard*, vol. 1, 785–99. Collection Latomus 101. Brussels

(1977) *Velleius Paterculus: The Tiberian Narrative (2.94–131)*. Cambridge

(1983) *Velleius Paterculus: The Caesarian and Augustan Narrative (2.41–93)*. Cambridge

(1988) *Rhetoric in Classical Historiography*. Portland

Woolf, G. (1993) "Roman Peace," in J. Rich and G. Shipley (eds.), *War and Society in the Roman World*, 171–94. London and New York

Wright, A. (2001) "The Death of Cicero. Forming a Tradition: The Contamination of History." *Historia* 50.4: 436–52

Yates, F. A. (1966) *The Art of Memory*. Chicago

Yoneyama, L. (1999) *Hiroshima Traces: Time, Space, and the Dialectics of Memory*. Berkeley

Young, J. (1993) *The Texture of Memory: Holocaust Memorials and Meaning in Europe, Israel, and America*. New Haven

Zanker, P. (1968) *Forum Augustum*. Tübingen

(1979) "Prinzipat und Herrscherbild," *Gymnasium* 86: 353–68

(1990) *The Power of Images in the Age of Augustus*, trans. A. Shapiro. Ann Arbor

Zetzel, J. E. G. (1994) "Looking Backward: Past and Present in the Late Roman Republic," *Pegasus* 37: 20–32

Zissos, A. (2003) "Spectacle and Elite in the *Argonautica* of Valerius Flaccus," in Boyle and Dominik (eds.), 659–84

Index of passages discussed

General Index